Jane Addams in the Classroom

Jane Addams in the Classroom

Edited by

DAVID SCHAAFSMA

University of Illinois Press

URBANA, CHICAGO, AND SPRINGFIELD

Library of Congress Cataloging-in-Publication Data
Jane Addams in the classroom / edited by David Schaafsma.
  pages   cm
Includes bibliographical references and index.
ISBN 978-0-252-03866-2 (cloth : acid-free paper)
ISBN 978-0-252-08025-8 (pbk. : acid-free paper)
ISBN 978-0-252-09660-0 (ebook)
1. Addams, Jane, 1860–1935. 2. Social reformers—United States.
3. Education—Philosophy. 4. Progressive education—United States—
Philosophy—History. 5. Addams, Jane, 1860–1935. On education.
I. Schaafsma, David, 1953- editor.
LB875.A332J36   2014
306.43'2—dc23   2014014546

To the memory of my parents, Arnold and Ruth Schaafsma, who taught me well, and to the present and future of my children, Sam, Ben, Harry, Henry, and Lyra, and children everywhere: We who teach must all find the best ways to teach them well.

Contents

Acknowledgments

I would like to thank the staff of the Hull-House Museum, especially two former directors, Peg Strobel and Lisa Lee, who have both been very generous in inviting us to hold seminars, classes, and conference workshops in the Hull-House Dining Hall. As a group of authors, we've been invited there to participate in events too numerous to mention here. I thank the American Educational Research Associaetion (AERA) for twice inviting us to create special sessions on Jane Addams at the Hull-House when they were holding their annual conferences in Chicago. I also thank two former Hull-House education directors, Rima Lunin Schultz and Lisa Junkin Lopez, the latter the current associate director.

I'd like to thank the University of Illinois at Chicago's Center for Study of Learning Instruction and Teacher Development, including its former director Susan Goldman, for a grant toward the support of various campus Addams activities, including several UIC conferences, for supporting on several occasions travel to conferences for presentations on our work, and for bringing into our conversations such Addams luminaries as Charlene Haddock Seigfried, Katherine Joslin, and Louise Knight. The contributions that such important Addams scholars have made to this project can only partially be measured by an accounting of citations, of course. This book would not exist were it not for their guidance, encouragement, and inspiration through their work and talks with us.

I would like to thank the College of Literature, Science, and the Arts and the Department of English for sabbatical support to allow me to work on this manuscript, and specifically former Dean Stanley Fish and those who have been UIC's English heads in the past several years, including Donald Marshall, Lennard Davis, Walter Benn Michaels, and Mark Canuel.

I would like to include in my thanks all those who did not end up writing pieces for this volume, but who were part of the talk and the presentations and inevitably helped us shape our writing, including especially Sue Weinstein and Tony Tendero.

All the students of the doctoral class on Jane Addams I taught at the Hull-House were instrumental in shaping my thinking on matters relevant to this book. Many of them have essays in the present volume, as you'll soon be delighted to read.

We are grateful to the staff of Special Collections at UIC's Richard J. Daley Library, especially with respect to the Jane Addams archives there (including the Jane Addams Personal Library Collection and the Hull-House Centennial Program Collection).

To the editorial staff at the University of Illinois Press, much, much thanks, especially to Laurie Matheson, Dawn Durante, and Jennifer Clark. To our incredibly helpful reviewers, Sarah Robbins and Katherine Joslin: your support and advice made this a much better manuscript than it had a right to be. To our copy editor, Matt Mitchell, thanks for making this a much better manuscript.

This book took a very long time coming to fruition. Most of us who were working on it gave up on it at one point or another, but I want to thank two friends and authors in this collection who never gave up and never allowed me to give up, helping me see the importance of this contribution to Addams scholarship and the scholarship of teaching and learning: Beth Steffen and Todd DeStigter.

To my mentors and friends Patti Stock and Ruth Vinz for their guidance and support: love.

To my children Sam, Ben, Harry, Henry, and Lyra, all of whom were born after I had initially agreed to do this book: love.

And finally, to my wife Tara, without whose sacrifices and support I would never in a million years have completed this manuscript (she even helped with the index!): much, much love.

Introduction

In Search for a Form: Jane Addams, Hull-House, and Connecting Learning and Life

DAVID SCHAAFSMA AND
TODD DESTIGTER

The reopening of the Hull-House dining room took place, fittingly, on a sunny day in May 2008. Historically speaking, the event was an unlikely one. Originally built in 1907 atop a boiler room, the dining hall—also known as the coffee house—had been slated for demolition in 1963 to make room for the downtown campus of the University of Illinois at Chicago. Due to the efforts of earnest preservationists, however, the building was instead pivoted ninety degrees, hauled several dozen feet across the grounds, and restored to approximate its original decor. Of the thirteen buildings that once made up the Hull-House compound, the dining room is, with the original residence, the only structure left standing, as the vision of Jane Addams has yielded to the imperatives of higher education.

Invitations to the reopening had been extended across the city via flyers, emails, and word of mouth, and the dining hall, which in recent years had been used mostly to host university administrative functions and academic conferences, was at last accessible to the public for this first in a weekly series of luncheons that promised—according to a brochure distributed to guests—"healthy soup" along with "thoughtful conversation" about food-related issues. This central topic of food—the ways it is grown, transported, sold, and consumed—was to be the focal point of discussions linking a broad range of social, economic, and political concerns. Thus, the dining room was being reintroduced as a way to renew what the brochure described as the Hull-House residents' legacy of carving out "public spaces where people of all classes and ethnicities can interact" with the aim of creative problem solving.

This spirit of public interaction was embodied in the scores of university faculty and students, community organizers, local business owners, and others who gathered around the long wooden tables. A couple in their fifties had driven from central Indiana to visit their daughter, a Chicago resident who had seen the lunch advertised online and decided to attend because, in her words, "I've always wanted to visit Hull-House." Across the table a young mother, originally from Germany, took a small loaf of bread from the basket in front of her, broke off a few pieces, and handed them to a child beside her in a booster seat. To the mother's left, a spry woman with short grey hair set her bicycle helmet on the table and shared stories about the North Side neighborhood where she had lived for nearly sixty years.

Despite the diversity in age and background of the lunch guests, Lisa Lee, the director of Hull-House, highlighted the group's unity when she concluded her welcoming remarks by saying, "Everyone eats"—a statement with serious implications in both its declarative and imperative modes. To say "everyone eats" declares that people, no matter their varied histories and circumstances, ultimately share certain fundamental needs and interests. But "everyone eats" is also an imperative, an admonition that might otherwise be phrased, "Together, we must do everything we can to ensure that no one goes hungry." Understood in this way, "everyone eats" is an affirmation that people have the right and responsibility to envision and effect a better life for themselves and others. More, it is a call to action informed by the recognition that people's aims and actions have material consequences, a sentiment articulated by Addams herself in a quotation featured on the cover of the lunch brochure: "It is part of the new philanthropy to recognize that the social question is largely a question of the stomach." Put yet another way, "everyone eats" implies that the reopening of the dining room was meant to encourage a specific kind of collective intellectual work—that which refuses to admit any separation between the scholarly and the social, the academic and the ethical. That Hull-House and the dining hall still cling to the edge of a large university campus serves as a reminder that despite the persistent tendency to isolate education from the rest of the world, limit its scope, and ignore the contexts that make it meaningful and relevant, teaching and learning at their best are never separated from concerns about how people live, how and why they work, and what they eat.

This book is the result of its authors' attempts to pursue such an expansive and ambitious vision of education, one that connects schooling to real issues in students' lives and communities. In a sense, what became this book began several years ago when Todd came to Dave with a biography of Addams (2002a) by Jean Bethke Elshtain, after having heard her talk on campus. Inspired by Elshtain's book, we formed a Jane Addams reading group made up of Chicago-area friends who were eager to engage in conversations about how Addams's life and work illustrate and advance some of our priorities as teachers. Over the next several years, we received a collaborative research-and-development project grant, organized on-campus symposia that included some of the nation's leading Addams scholars, and presented papers based on our collective interest in the work of Jane Addams and Hull-House at national conferences. Several chapters in this collection began as conference presentations, and other contributions are versions of what were originally master's theses that emerged from a course Dave taught on Addams at Hull-House.

As we met regularly to discuss work we were reading and its connections to our scholarship, community projects, and teaching, the group expanded and contracted over time. Although we began with mostly Chicago-area and midwestern teachers and English educators, as we presented at conferences, we began to attract a wider group of people, including scholars from across the country and teacher educators from disciplines other than English. In this fashion, we felt we were being true to Addams's principle of listening to and working with an ever-expanding array of friends.

Elshtain (2002a) writes that Addams's life "was a search for a form, a way to give shape to her enthusiasms" (43), and in many ways, we have looked to Addams's legacy to help shape the "form" of our own teaching practices and a form as well for our need to talk about ways to make education relevant to community and student needs. However, unlike a form as described by Plato—an eternal, metaphysical "essence"—Addams (1893/2002a) made clear her view that "the social spirit discharges itself in many forms, and no one form is adequate to its total expression" (17). Similarly, through our reading and talking, Dave's course focusing on Addams, several conference presentations, and now this collection of essays, our aim has been to explore Addams's life and writings for lessons as to how we as teachers might render our experience and interests useful to ourselves and our students in the ever-changing contexts of our schools and communities. We see the legacy of Addams for education not only in the things that she says directly about schooling; her value to us as educators lies also in the example she set through her actions at Hull-House and in the disposition that inclined and enabled her to enter into new modes of fellowship and action with other people.

As we shall see in the teachers' stories in this book, though Addams's educational legacy can be measured in many ways, no lesson she affords is more crucial than this: While she began her work determined to improve poor people by bringing to them the high culture she embodied, she learned over time the importance of establishing responsive and mutually influential relationships with those whom she presumed to serve. Indeed, early in her career, Addams wrote that "[a settlement] aims . . . to lead whatever of social life its neighborhood may afford, . . . to bring to bear upon it the results of cultivation and training" (1893/2002a, 25). This charitable impulse is, we think, analogous to the good intentions of many teachers as we enter the profession intending to share with young people what we understand to be the benefits of education. For English teachers specifically, such benefits include the pleasure and personal enrichment of reading and writing, as well as the professional and political benefits that literacy affords us as workers and citizens. We want, in short, to impart to our students those ways with words that we have learned to be both pleasing and profitable.

Addams learned throughout her career, however, that her work could not merely involve conferring to people the refined culture, skills, and sensibilities that she had accrued through her privileged upbringing and education. Rather, as Addams put it, she discovered that her best efforts required that she be not "good to people" but "with them" (1912/2002a, 173). In other words, as Bridget O'Rourke and Beth Steffen explain later in this volume, Addams evolved to see reciprocity as necessary to inform and implement the emerging forms of progressive thought and action that she called "social adjustment" (1902/2002b, 68). For educators, Addams's willingness to respond to changing circumstances by revising her fundamental conceptions of her work suggests that good teaching is not a one-way transfer of information from those who have it to those who don't, but a dialogic exchange of understandings and priorities. Furthermore, Addams teaches us that educators must pay attention and adapt not only to our students but also to the broader sociopolitical contexts in which learning takes place—what Addams's associate, the union organizer Abraham Bisno, called "the meat of human life" (qtd. in Knight 2005, 234). Thus, the story of Addams's own evolution as a settlement worker and activist serves as a "form" we educators might well look to as a model for our own growth as teachers.

The central idea of this book is that Jane Addams, through her work at Hull-House in Chicago dating from the early 1890s well into the twentieth century, has relevance for today's classrooms. Though she did teach classes in her tenure in the settlement-house movement, she more importantly modeled ways of working with people that teachers from kindergarten to college can emulate in working with their students and communities. This volume focuses on principles she developed in and through her work organizing for social change with the Halsted Street community around issues of health care, educational reform, and fair wages—principles she enacted in the work itself, and in speech and writing. In this era in which teachers see the field of education as primarily driven by test scores, this volume of essays will provide inspiration for another way, a return to learning connected with the personal and social needs of students and communities.

Our interest from the beginning of this project was rooted in Addams's—and her Hull-House colleagues'—commitment to *listening to* and *learning from* the people living in the neighborhood in which Hull-House was located. This resonates with our own deeply felt conviction that one cannot work toward democracy *for* others, but only *with* others. We have also been interested in the ways that Addams—in both form and content—draws on experience, memory, and story in her research and activism. Each of the contributors to this collection works in education at the secondary and/or university level and is committed to a vision of democracy for and through education. While new editions of Addams's writing have been published recently, along with a number of new—and new editions of—critical biographies, our collection is important in its connecting of Addams's work to contemporary classrooms in ways we cautiously imagine she would have appreciated. While Ellen Condliffe Lagemann's introductory essay for her collection of Addams's writings on education (1994) remains seminal in the area, it is one of the few essays on the subject, so we are happy to make a space for teachers, teacher educators, and scholars to lend their voices to the conversation. Each of the authors in this collection takes seriously Addams's work as one model for storytelling about social issues, so the essays, to honor her narrative impulse, share stories of democratic practice.

This volume thereby balances theoretical and practical considerations. Four essays are written by Addams scholars who explore the ways that she drew on experience, history, and story in her narrative theorizing for practice. These essays set the stage for six essays written by teacher scholars who share stories of classroom practice, making links between the principles Addams espoused and the exciting things that happen in their classrooms. As we see it, readers of this volume will be inspired to read Addams as an antidote to the despair they are feeling about schooling in these times, and also to develop the courage to enact some of her principles in their own classrooms. Katherine Joslin (2010) helps us see Addams as a fellow-traveler in our work: "We read Jane Addams because, for all the years that separate us from her, she still seems one of us. The truth is that her issues, the vexing social and political questions of her day, remain unresolved, for the most part, a hundred years later" (31).

By continuing to explore possible answers to these unresolved questions, we hope that our work may be understood as instances of teaching dispositions that are responsive to students and communities in a similar way to how Addams learned to be responsive to issues of her day and the people with whom she worked. Elshtain has noted that "Addams shared with George Eliot [one of Addams's favorite authors] the belief that—as Eliot writes at the conclusion of *Middlemarch*—the 'growing good of the world is partly dependent on unhistoric acts'" (2002a, 31). Though Addams is a rightfully renowned historical figure, the things she did in and around Hull-House were, in many instances, "unhistoric": seeing that garbage was collected, visiting the sick and infirm, serving tea, and listening to the lonely and frightened. These small acts are, we think, analogous to the daily work of teachers as we plan lessons, find ways to encourage and challenge our students based on their diverse abilities and needs, and do what modest things we can to increase the likelihood that young people will have the chance to develop their unique potential and participate in creating the lives they choose. Such acts may be "unhistoric," but we hope, as did Addams, that they will contribute to a world in which everyone eats.

Works Cited

Addams, Jane (1893/2002a). "The Subjective Necessity for Social Settlements." In *The Jane Addams Reader.* Ed. Jean Bethke Elshtain. New York: Basic Books. 14–28.

——— (1902/2002b). "Filial Relations." In *Democracy and Social Ethics.* Urbana: University of Illinois Press. 35–47.

——— (1912/2002a). "A Modern Lear." In *The Jane Addams Reader.* Ed. Jean Bethke Elshtain. New York: Basic Books. 163–76.

Elshtain, Jean Bethke, ed. (2002a). *The Jane Addams Reader.* New York: Basic Books.

———. (2002b). *Jane Addams and the Dream of American Democracy.* New York: Basic Books.

Joslin, Katherine (2010). "Re-reading Jane Addams in the Twenty-First Century." In *Feminist Interpretations of Jane Addams.* Ed. Maurice Hamington. University Park: Pennsylvania State University Press. 31–53.

Knight, Louise W. (2005). *Citizen: Jane Addams and the Struggle for Democracy.* Chicago: University of Chicago Press.

Lagemann, Ellen Condliffe (1994). Introduction to *On Education,* by Jane Addams. Ed. Ellen Condliffe Lagemann. New Brunswick, N.J.: Transaction. 1–42.

1 In Good Company

Jane Addams's Democratic Experimentalism

TODD DESTIGTER

About two hours northwest of Chicago, ten miles south of the Wisconsin border, a sign beside a two-lane blacktop at the outskirts of an Illinois town, population 715, greets visitors with these words: "Cedarville, birthplace of Jane Addams, 1860–1935, Humanitarian, feminist, social worker, educator, author, publicist, founder of Hull-House pioneer settlement center, Chicago, 1889. President, Women's International League for Peace and Freedom, Nobel Peace Prize, 1931." Though the sign is a fitting tribute to Cedarville's most famous resident, it also serves as an abbreviated curriculum vitae attesting to Addams's broad repertoire of activities and her long list of associations as these grew over time and in often unexpected ways. In what follows, I'll explore some of the ways in which Addams's ever-expanding network of relationships led her to develop an evolving and complex conception of democracy that drew upon and contributed to the experimentalist impulses of American pragmatism. For contemporary teachers, to understand democracy as Addams did—as continually reconstructed on a shifting foundation of human interconnectedness and social conditions—represents what I think is a desirable alternative to much of the thinking in our current educational climate, in which democratic ideals like freedom, equality, and opportunity are too often defined according to the imperatives of individualism, the logic of the marketplace, and the certainty of standardized conceptions of knowledge.

More than Friends

Although Jane Addams and Ellen Gates Starr founded Hull-House in the company of a few other settlement residents whose privileged backgrounds were similar to their own, over the course of her career Addams steadily expanded her professional interests and increased the number and types of people whom she recognized as essential to her work. This revision of what was initially a parochial project of benevolence occurred because Addams eventually figured out that the priorities and abilities of the people she hoped to serve were indispensable in defining the problems that her settlement work should address, in determining possible solutions to these problems, and in taking action to ameliorate them.

Addams learned of this need to join others in addressing a wide range of social issues early in her career as a settlement worker. As she reflects in *Twenty Years at Hull-House* (1910/1990), "One of the first lessons we learned at Hull-House was that private beneficence is totally inadequate to deal with the vast numbers of the city's disinherited" (180). To explain how this inadequacy might be overcome, Addams introduces a conceit that recurs in many of her writings: namely, that of the "family" and the "social" claim. As Erin Vail explains later in this book, Addams (1902/2002b) describes the "family claim" as that which weighed upon young women of her time to direct their energies—indeed, to devote their lives—to the needs and interests of their households (36). However, while holding fast to the family claim in her relationships with her own relatives and several Hull-House residents, Addams understood that people could not address the family claim without also accepting the "wider inheritance" of responsibility and activism that she called the "social claim." In Addams's view, honoring the family claim depends upon heeding the social claim because one cannot address the specific needs of a family without also creating favorable conditions for doing so within the broader social environments in which families live and work. Drawing upon her experience as a settlement worker, Addams illustrates the inseparability of the family and social claims in her 1915 pamphlet, "Why Women Should Vote":

> In a crowded city quarter, if the street is not cleaned up by the city authorities—no amount of private sweeping will keep the tenement free from grime; if the garbage is not properly collected and destroyed, a tenement house mother may see her children sicken and die of diseases from which she alone is powerless to shield them. . . . In short, if a woman would keep on with her old business of caring for her house and rearing her children, she will have to have some conscience in regard to public affairs lying quite outside of her immediate household. (qtd. in Elshtain 2002a, 166–67)

Addams's view of the reciprocity of the family and social claims was not limited, however, to issues related to women in domestic settings. Rather, the logic that led her to disregard false distinctions between the family and social claims prompted Addams to pursue a broad strategy of activism. To ensure that the citizens of her neighborhood had proper political represen-tation, for instance, she and other Hull-House residents documented and crusaded against corruption in the Chicago city council. To promote the rights of workers afflicted by what she called "grief on the industrial side" (1899/2002, 63), she was instructed and persuaded by her friend Florence Kelley to become an advocate of organized labor. To alleviate the suffering of addicts, she lobbied to close liquor stores and opium houses. To provide guidance and opportunities to bored and wayward young people, she initi-ated the establishment of the nation's first juvenile justice system and helped create a network of recreational city parks. She ran for alderman, served on the Chicago School Board, became a prominent voice in national politics, and eventually led international efforts to promote justice and peace.

In this process of expanding the range and type of her own and her Hull-House colleagues' ambitions, however, Addams learned that she had to include in her efforts an ever-widening circle of people. Indeed, her upbringing in Ce-darville, her studies at the nearby Rockford Female Seminary, and her "grand tour" of England and the Continent proved to be inadequate preparation for settlement work on the mean streets of Chicago. To do such work effectively— to operate at the intersection of the family and social claims—Addams grew to rely increasingly on the local knowledge and skills to be found in the Hull-House-area community rather than to try to fix it from the outside. As Addams put it a few years after the settlement opened, "The residents at Hull-House find in themselves a constantly increasing tendency to consult their neighbors on the advisability of each new undertaking" (1893/2002b, 41).

Addams's dependence on her neighbors did not end, however, once they had clarified for her what she ought to do. Rather, she looked to community members not only as sources of the Hull-House agenda but also as resources essential to pursuing it. Recounting the host of people involved in the day-to-day work of Hull-House, she writes, "We constantly rely more and more on neighborhood assistance" (1893/2002b, 41). Significantly, Addams makes a point of mentioning that this "neighborhood assistance" came not only from individuals but also from previously existing groups and institutions. In the context of describing the settlement's reliance on its community, Addams notes that on the wall next to the Hull-House telephone hung a list for easy reference that included the Cook County Hospital, the Visiting Nurses' Association, the Maxwell Street police station, the Chicago Health Department, and City Hall. Moreover, Addams writes that from the "very nature of our existence and purpose," she and her fellow settlement workers "have been on very good terms with" the Hebrew Relief and Aid Society, the Children's Aid, the Humane Society, and "the various church and national relief associations" (1893/2002b,

40). Far from being merely a gracious nod of appreciation, Addams's extended acknowledgment of the people and organizations who contributed to the settlement's activities underscores how crucial it was that Hull-House had adopted a culture of partnering with individuals and institutions in order to define and accomplish its goals.

By emphasizing the importance of such partnerships, Addams anticipated the work of contemporary sociologists who study the ways in which people attempt to join together to define and pursue what they perceive to be their common interests. Paul Lichterman (2005), for instance, has shown that civic groups are most successful in building "social capital"—social networks that empower civil society—when they develop what he calls "customs" of self-reflexivity and communication that encourage reflective talk about their aims and concrete relationships in the wider social world. Such customs, Lichterman contends, increase the likelihood that a group will be able to "spiral outward" and create "enduring, civic bridges across a variety of social differences" (15–17). In Lichterman's view, Addams's writings corroborate his findings in that her accounts of settlement life promote modes of communication and reflection that he found to be essential for civic life, and he cites Addams as among the best examples we have of someone who was able to create the kind of informed relationships necessary to address at once the family and social claims.

For teachers who aspire to have their work be consequential beyond the walls of their classrooms, Addams's conceptualization of the family and social claims provides useful insights regarding the proper nature and scope of education. Her description of the family claim, for instance, can enrich educators' understanding of how frequently and powerfully many students feel the pull of this claim as they work long hours to support themselves and their families, care for younger siblings or aging parents, and generally take on responsibilities that most people postpone until adulthood. Additionally, however, Addams's insights about the family claim can be useful to educators in a less literal sense. I'm referring to the likelihood that most readers of this book can recall times when the family claim has exerted itself within their classrooms. For insofar as teachers are able to cultivate strong personal bonds with and among their students, we might with some justification think of our students as family, and in so doing posit as our highest priority their individual and immediate well-being.

As we have seen, however, Addams's experience holds important lessons for teachers about how the family claim cannot be seriously attended to if we disassociate it from the social claim. Keeping such lessons in mind, we teachers might well emphasize the connections between school and society, broaden our forms of association, and expand our understandings of what our goals should be and how best to accomplish them. Addams herself encouraged this kind of conceptual connection between schooling and the "form" of her settlement work. Writing specifically of the need to revise education for women in the emerging industrial society of her day, Addams lamented that such training "has been singularly individualistic" and "has fostered ambitions almost exclusively in the direction of intellectual accumulation" (1902/2002b, 42). What was needed, Addams argued, was education that would instead foster an "enlarged interest in life and the social movements around us" and thereby explicitly connect a student "with human interests outside of her family and her own immediate social circle." Such an education, Addams insists, is the best hope of cultivating in young people the knowledge, skills, and "motive power" to address both the family and social claims (1902/2002b, 43).

If what Addams is describing here sounds familiar, it is not only because her description of "individualistic" education directed toward "intellectual accumulation" goes a long way toward describing current school "reform" efforts but also because a long and distinguished line of educators has queued up behind her to make the same essential argument about what education should ideally do. John Dewey's claim that the purposes of education should "grow and take shape through the process of social intelligence" (1938/1963, 72); Paolo Freire's advocacy of education as "praxis: reflection and action upon the world in order to transform it" (1972/2002, 36); Henry A. Giroux's desire for a "critical pedagogy" that will "put equality, liberty, and human life at the center of notions of democracy and citizenship" (1988, 28); Maxine Greene's conception of education as a "dialectical" process characterized by "projects of action . . . conducted by and for those willing to take responsibility for themselves and for each other" (1988, 22); bell hooks's struggle to "transgress" education "that merely strives to reinforce domination" (1994, 4); Marilyn Cochran-Smith's contention that "teacher education needs to be conceptualized as both a learning problem and a political problem aimed at social justice" (2004, 1–2)—all of these writers echo Addams's central point when she writes specifically about education: namely, that for schoolwork to be socially and politically relevant, educators must look for opportunities to follow the Hull-House example of venturing out into the world, bridging the gaps that separate us from sites where important work needs to be done, and establishing reciprocal relationships with people on whom we must rely if such work is to be productive.

Thus, as I believe Addams's example suggests, perhaps a beginning point for teachers rests in our committing to the necessity of conversation as we seek to broaden our understandings of our work. As Addams wrote in reference to her own learning process, such conversations will likely be "perplexing" and accompanied by "pangs and misgivings" (1899/2002, 75) in that they will have to include some fundamental questions that we might be reluctant to ask—questions like: Why, ultimately, do we want our students to be better readers and writers? To what extent do our literature and composition courses increase students' abilities to work with others in ways that are consequential beyond our classrooms? What's the sense in preparing student readers and writers to be "college- and career-ready" when college will leave them with decades of debt and most careers available these days don't come with a living wage or health care? What good does it do for young people to gain a critical awareness of various forms of injustice if they don't have the opportunity to do anything about it?

I raise these questions not to be dismissive of the work we teachers typically do, but to suggest that asking such questions opens the door to new possibilities regarding what our teaching might involve and what it might accomplish. Such possibilities will remain unimagined, however, unless we follow Addams in venturing beyond our familiar settings and circle of acquaintances to enrich our understandings of what we should do and why. As Addams learned, such ventures in no way guarantee success, and they are ambitious in that they acknowledge that our work must at times be more expansive and complicated than we initially assume it will be. Still, as Addams also came to know, when we do not reach far and outwardly enough, when we do not care deeply enough about the perspectives and priorities of others, the solutions we propose to a society's emerging dilemmas are too often simplistic and, ultimately, ineffective.

The overlapping, interactive, and mutually influential relationship between schools and society requires that we see schools not as hermetically sealed sites of decontextualized teaching and learning, but as operating dialectically with and within broader sociocultural circumstances. And if we continually strive to understand the specific ways in which our schoolwork might attend to both the family and social claims, we increase the likelihood that we will be able to shape—rather than merely to accept—these circumstances. As professionally isolating as teaching often is, and as difficult as it may seem to have a cumulative and lasting impact on the world outside of schools, this notion that teaching and learning is, at its best, a process of thinking and acting in the company of ever-more-inclusive groups of people is worthy of our efforts as educators.

Streetwise Democracy

By the time Hull-House opened its doors on Chicago's South Halsted Street in 1889, the United States was well along the path of profound social and economic transformation. As the nation moved from a largely rural, agricultural economy to one based on urban industrialization, few places revealed the effects of these changes more than did the Hull-House neighborhood, where the mostly immigrant residents struggled to make a living in the city's burgeoning stockyards, factories, and sweatshops. The list of specific projects Addams initiated to improve the lives of her neighbors is impressively long and varied. Hull-House hosted classes in literature; it was the meeting site of clubs for adolescents and members of labor unions. In the dining hall, meals were served at bargain prices to minister to those whose hunger exceeded their wages.

But while Addams's efforts were diverse and responsive to the immediate priorities of her community, these measures were not haphazard; rather, they were all specific instances of her larger project of promoting democracy in contexts where its definitions and alleged manifestations were rapidly changing. Most fundamentally, Addams held that to foster democracy was to promote social conditions in which all people could take part in identifying problems that affected their lives, devising and implementing solutions to those problems, and then sharing equitably in the consequences of their activities. As Addams herself put it, she wanted to promote efforts to "socialize democracy," by which she meant that she wanted to "make the entire social organism democratic, to extend democracy beyond its political expression" (1893/2002a, 15). More than three decades before John Dewey famously described "the idea of democracy" as constituted by "the clear consciousness of communal life, in all its implications" (1927/1988, 328), Addams urged her fellow citizens to understand democracy not only as a function of national and local politics (nominating political candidates, voting, etc.) but as "our ideal in social intercourse" (1893/2002a, 15). Within this general definition, Addams's apparently disparate efforts should be understood as her ongoing attempt to foster new forms of deliberative and participatory democracy that were adequate to the challenges of the age. Moreover, the associations and initiatives she pursued in her attempts to address the social claim compelled her to continually revise her understandings of how the promises of democracy might be realized. Thus, Addams's conception of democracy was "streetwise" in the sense that it was an evolving amalgam of theories and definitions of democracy that she adjusted in response to the emerging problems she encountered in her work.

We of the "Jane Addams reading group" who have contributed to this book share the notion that Addams's complex and evolving understanding of democracy as an ideal of social intercourse (1902/2002a, 7) is among the "forms" that we might emulate in our work as educators. That is to say, we do not presume to define "democracy" with any precision or permanence, nor do we pretend to know what democracy looks like across contexts. Rather, following Addams, while we hope that we might play a modest role in promoting democratic institutions and actions, we have explored as teachers what it might mean to do so in our particular schools and communities. This relationship that we recognize between education and democracy, including the notion that democracy requires an educated citizenry, has its antecedents at least as far back as the early years of the Republic, when Thomas Jefferson (1820) wrote, "I know no safe depositary of the ultimate powers of the society but the people themselves; and if we think them not enlightened enough to exercise their control with a wholesome discretion, the remedy is not to take it from them, but to inform their discretion by education." Though Jefferson's views were famously realized in his early legislative advocacy of public schooling and his founding of the University of Virginia, the most influential twentieth-century advocate of education in support of democracy was Addams's friend and intellectual colleague John Dewey, who argued that "since a democratic society repudiates the principle of external authority, it must find a substitute in voluntary disposition and interest; these can be created only by education" (1916/1988, 93). To Dewey, one of the crucial tasks of educators is to make obvious to students the connections between school and society and to cultivate in young people an awareness of what he called their "common interests," along with the competence and desire to act in pursuit of those interests. In this way, Dewey promoted democracy not only as a form of government but as a "mode of associated living" in which each person participates "in an interest so that each has to refer his own action to that of others, and to consider the action of others to give point and direction to his own" (1916/1988, 93). These ideas are powerful among progressive educators like Lanette Grate (in this volume) who aspire to have their work contribute to social justice. For such teachers, Addams's understandings of and efforts to promote democracy are instructive in that what she modestly understood as her "unhistoric acts" (Elshtain 2002a, 31) are all aimed at equipping individuals with the ability, inclination, and opportunity to participate intelligently and productively in a self-governing society.

However, to include democracy as among the aims of education may seem unworkable, even quaint, given the ample historical evidence that people will co-opt the ideals of democracy to serve their own, often predatory interests. Wariness of democracy has a long history, of course, including Plato's preference for a small ruling class of "philosophers" to lead his republic, James Madison's *Federalist Papers,* and the U.S. Constitution's representative organization and separation of powers. Moreover, the rise of industrial capitalism in late nineteenth- and early twentieth-century America led to additional forms of skepticism about democracy, skepticism that Addams knew well. Addams's contemporary Walter Lippmann, for instance, argued in *The Phantom Public* (1925/1993) that, contrary to the Jeffersonian ideal of an enlightened citizenry participating directly in public affairs, an informed and politically competent public is a myth—a "phantom." To Lippmann, because of the necessary limits on a person's expertise and the time he or she can devote to public affairs, an individual "lives in a world which he [or she] cannot see, does not understand, and is unable to direct" (4). In Lippmann's view, average citizens should accept their role as "spectators of action" who can (and should) participate in politics only by periodically supporting "one of the interests directly involved" in public policy and those individuals who have the expertise and opportunity to conduct it (93).

A similar suspicion of democracy in Addams's time came from Arthur Bentley, who was born in Freeport, Illinois, only a few miles from Addams's birthplace, Cedarville, nineteen years before the founding of Hull-House. In *The Process of Government* (1908/1949), which Nicolas Lemann (2008) notes was "long considered the most important study of politics and society ever produced in America" (1), Bentley argues that while ideal democracy is impossible, its most feasible approximation lies in sustained conflict among interest groups. To Bentley, all forms in which power is exercised in a society—whether these forms be, for instance, the dissemination of propaganda, bribery, suffrage, or the work of federal, state, and local governments—are "techniques" used by groups operating in opposition to each other. Bentley does not dispute the utility of cherished ideals like "democracy" and the will of "the people," but he describes such ideals as a "matter of speech alone, . . . a slogan or rallying cry for some particular groups at special stages of their activity," while "the real facts" of political activity can be found "in the groups as we analyze them, and there only" (455).

In addition to the writings of political theorists like Lippmann and Bentley, the context in which Addams was developing her views of the limits and possibilities of democracy included the dramatic sociopolitical changes brought on by industrialization, as people moved in large numbers from rural farms to urban manufacturing centers in search of work. In these sites, the traditional ties of family and community yielded to notions of democracy shaped largely by classical liberalism's faith in the efficacy of market capitalism and its emphasis on the rights and responsibilities of individuals. Complementing the new economy of the late nineteenth and early twentieth centuries, this zeitgeist of liberalism justified long hours in factories and sweatshops, unsafe and unsanitary working conditions, child labor, and the absence of job security—all of which were protected from progressive legislation by Supreme Court decisions that relied on liberal readings of the constitutional guarantee of the sanctity of private property and contracts. As William Forbath (1991) has shown, the cumulative effect of these rulings was particularly onerous for organized labor, as workers were forced to adjust not only their strategies for action but also their long-term aims (xi). Specifically, Forbath demonstrates that labor's goals drifted away from socialist ideals like joint ownership of the means of production and an understanding of "value" as being determined not only by demand but also by human labor. Instead, labor was compelled to moderate its aspirations and accept "voluntarist" notions of interaction between capital and labor as consensual agreement in the form of collective bargaining. Similarly, Leon Fink (1987) contends that due largely to Supreme Court rulings, workers "detached themselves from economic theories that explicitly justified the use of collective action to control or govern the marketplace. Instead, workers placed their faith in a looser tradition of individual 'rights' that linked their interests and freedom of maneuver to those of the citizenry at large" (909). In other words, the court's decisions, at once reflecting and strengthening liberal ideals of the free market, forced workers to restrict their efforts to addressing site-specific grievances rather than to bringing about broader, class-based social reform. Thus, even among the working class, the dominant material, ideological, and political forces of Addams's time were combining to foster a narrow conception of democracy not as equitable participation or collective well-being but as the liberty to pursue one's individual interest.

   This liberal mode of democracy has been resurrected in recent times in the form of "neoliberalism," which, as David Harvey has explained, "took the political ideals of human dignity and individual freedom as . . . the central values of civilization" and relied on the belief that such individual freedoms are best secured by the state's maintaining the freedom of the marketplace (2005, 5–6). However, Harvey points out that, in fact, the ascendancy of liberalism in its "neo" form has been "a *political* project to re-establish the conditions for capital accumulation and restore the power of economic elites" (19). Further, Wendy Brown has argued that neoliberalism is not confined to the realm of economics but extends into all forms of human relationships, creating an "ethic" emerging as "governmentality—a mode of governance encompassing but not limited to the state, and one which produces subjects, forms of citizenship and behavior, and a new organization of the social" (2003, 2). Thus, the ethic that emerges from liberalism—whether of the classical sort ascendant in Addams's day or of the current "neo" version—is one that limits democracy to protecting and promoting what Isaiah Berlin (1970) has called a "negative" freedom *from* others to accumulate property and power (117).

Therefore, as we contemporary educators consider how our teaching might support democracy, we do so in a sociopolitical climate that is in some ways similar to the one in which Addams lived and worked. (Neo)liberalism reveals itself, for instance, in the recent wave of school privatization, in the popular notion that schools must be held accountable to high standards as measured by standardized tests, and in the belief that schools whose students score below certain norms can justifiably and productively be punished by censure, withdrawal of already scarce resources, or even dissolution. This is how, supposedly, we ensure that "no child [will be] left behind" and that all schools can "race to the top" by achieving mastery of common core standards. These alleged reforms betray a dominant assumption that to speak of "democratic education" is to define "democracy" according to the liberal antecedents I've noted above—ones that posit democracy as a justification to do as we please, to promote our own rather than the general welfare, and to consume without regard for material or moral consequence.

Addams, however, doubted that individual aspiration alone would promote social well-being. Instead, she based her work on an understanding of democracy characterized by a positive freedom to work *with* others to develop individuals' unique potentials and to enlist these potentials in the collective work of improving the lives of all people. "It is doubtful," Addams wrote, "if personal ambition, whatever may have been its commercial results, has ever been of any value as a motive power for social reform. But whatever it may have done in the past, it is certainly too archaic to accomplish anything now. Our thoughts, at least for this generation, cannot be too much directed from mutual relationships and responsibilities" (1912/2002, 175). Addams thus refused to submit to a restrictively individualistic creed of democracy, opting instead for what she called a "newer conception" of democracy based on "an acceptance of social obligations involving in each new instance a new line of conduct" (1902/2002a, 9). Addams's understanding of democracy thus combined an unwavering belief in the value of each person with an appreciation for the need to adapt people's aims and actions to meet the challenges of new and often unforeseeable circumstances. Put another way, Addams's ideas about democracy were, quite literally, "streetwise" in that she developed them over time and in response to her work on Halsted Street.

In addition to Addams's emphasis on being attuned and responsive to changing social conditions, among the reasons her definition of democracy continued to evolve is that it held in uneasy tension two apparently conflicting paradigms:

On the one hand, Addams understood democracy as a moral framework that emphasizes human solidarity and common interest. On the other hand, she recognized that in the contentious arena of state and labor politics, democracy would not be advanced in the absence of a class-based struggle for power. In describing this first aspect of democracy as a "social ethic," Addams emphasized a communitarian impulse that she believed must be cultivated in individuals because they are inevitably connected in countless ways: "We are learning that a standard of social ethics is not attained by traveling a sequestered byway, but by mixing on the thronged and common road where all must turn out for one another, and at least see the size of one another's burdens. To follow the path of social morality results perforce in the temper if not the practice of the democratic spirit, for it implies that diversified human experience and resultant sympathy which are the foundation and guarantee of Democracy" (1902/2002a, 7).

To Addams, then, what she elsewhere described as "the zeal and affection with which [a person] regards his fellows" (1910/1990, 73) provides both the knowledge and the motive to advance the "social progress" that character-izes a democratic society (1893/2002a, 73). But in addition to providing such sociopolitical benefits, Addams also believed that an attentiveness to others is the only adequate response to a deeply felt need to foster the better aspects of our humanity. "Nothing so deadens the sympathies and shrivels the power of enjoyment," she wrote, "as the persistent keeping away from the great op-portunities for helpfulness and a continual ignoring of the starvation struggle which makes up half the race" (1893/2002a, 69). Addams was not so vexed by the fate of the nation or the world as to be untroubled by the lesser plights of people who showed up at the Hull-House doorstep. On the contrary, she held that the two are inseparable.

The "zeal and affection" with which Addams regarded her Hull-House neighbors was evident in her demeanor when interacting with them and in her famously tireless work ethic. Unwilling to relinquish face-to-face contact with those who came through the Hull-House doors, Addams was known to suspend her heavy administrative duties and come down from her upstairs office to help cook and serve food in the dining room, greet visitors, and guide tours of the settlement complex. Though her responsibilities and the demands on her time grew with her fame as a public figure, that Addams never lost this commitment to fellowship with her neighbors comes through clearly in her peculiar story of the "Devil Baby," originally published in her 1916 book *The Long Road of Women's Memory*. According to Addams's account, a rumor began to circulate in the Halsted Street area that a neighbor had given birth to a so-called Devil Baby, the result—depending on the version one happened to hear—of some sort of horrific sin committed by the baby's father, and that the monstrous infant was being sequestered at Hull-House. The settlement was inundated for weeks by visitors demanding to see the Devil Baby, and the rumor persisted despite the staff's efforts to dispel it. Significantly, although Addams admits that she eventually grew impatient with the "contagion of emotion" that fueled the rumor, her response to the mostly elderly, immigrant women who came to Hull-House clinging to a belief in the veracity of the story was not to dismiss them as ignorant and annoying. Rather, as Addams put it, "Whenever I heard the high eager voices of old women, I was irresistibly interested and left anything I might be doing in order to listen to them" (1916/2002a, 384). Over time, by listening and seeking to understand, Addams learned the usefulness of the Devil Baby story to the women who believed and retold it. She realized, for instance, that the story "put into [the women's] hands the sort of material with which they were accustomed to deal" (1916/2002a, 385), that it allowed them to draw upon their memories to offer "a fleeting glimpse of wisdom" in what to them was an unfamiliar place, and that it affirmed the hope for justice upon the blasphemous father (1916/2002b, 402).

In sum, by honoring her neighbors' curiosity and concerns, Addams learned that this story was of profound importance in the women's struggle to make sense of a world very different from the ones they had left behind in their home countries and to rediscover the value of the knowledge held in their memories. To modern readers, the Devil Baby story may seem even more fanciful or absurd than it initially did to Addams. Nonetheless, her carefully attuned responsiveness—her rising from behind a desk covered with Hull-House accounting sheets, for instance, or suspending work on drafts of articles she was under deadline to write, in order to sit down with her guests and listen to them—is a gesture that many educators continually emulate in their own ways. Perhaps this gesture takes the form of talking with a distressed student after school, writing encouraging words in the margins of a paper, revising an assignment to accommodate a young person's learning style, or calling attention in class to a student's interests or successes. As Addams insisted throughout her career, such measures of fellowship and sympathy are indispensable to creating and sustaining the kinds of relationships that lead to democratic collective action and social progress.

Addams's belief that democracy depends upon generous and attentive human relationships endured not because she was naïvely dismissive of people's potential for corruption and contestation but because, according to her broader sociopolitical philosophy, human conflict is essentially a mistake. Dewey, in a letter to his wife, Alice, recounts how Addams explained this conviction to him during one of his many visits to Hull-House. Apparently, during his conversation with Addams, Dewey had clung to his Hegelian academic roots and contended that ongoing conflict—thesis and antithesis—is the engine of social growth, with progress emerging in the dialectical process of humans' acting to create history. Dewey recalls, however, that Addams sought to disabuse him of such ideas, and he summarizes what he calls her "astonishing" counter-argument in this way:

> Antagonism is not only useless and harmful, but entirely unnecessary. Antagonism never lies at the heart of objective differences, which will always grow into unity when left alone, but arises when a person mixes into reality his own personal reactions. . . . What is more, historically, only evil has come from antagonisms. . . . The antagonism of institutions is always unreal. It may be simply due to the personal attitude and individual reactions, and then, instead of adding to the recognition of unified meaning, it delays and distorts it. (qtd. in Martin (2002), 165–66)

Dewey confessed to Alice that he "had never had anything take hold of [him] so" as had Addams's view that antagonism is a perversion of the proper and natural state of individuals and institutions brought on by people's short-sighted egos and emotions (Dewey 1894/1999, qtd. in Menand 2001 313). And although Dewey was initially skeptical, the next day he admitted to Alice that he was convinced by Addams's reasoning. As Menand has explained, Dewey saw "that the resistance the world puts up to our actions and desires is not the same as a genuine opposition of interests" (313). Indeed, as Dewey's correspondence reveals, tacking against the prevailing intellectual winds of her time and establishing a leitmotif that Dewey would wind through his writings on social and political philosophy for decades, Addams refused to reduce democracy to a carefully balanced contest of people's ambitions. Instead, she insisted, democracy is fostered when people realize that their interests are, in the end, common ones.

Although Addams never abandoned her progressivist faith in human fellowship and cooperation, her politics nonetheless had a steelier side in that it evolved as a corrective to enthusiasms about the potential of goodwill alone to improve the human condition. For Addams learned over the years that if her democratic vision were to be advanced, she and others would have to wrest power from those who abused it. In 1895, for instance, six years after she and Starr had established Hull-House, the mission statement of the settlement was revised to announce that its aims were "to provide a center for a higher civic and social life; to initiate and maintain education and philanthropic enterprises; and to investigate and improve the conditions in the industrial districts of Chicago" (Hull-House Association minutes, March 28, 1895, qtd. in Knight 2005, 336). This progressively ambitious list of the Hull-House goals is evidence of Addams's evolving understanding that she and her colleagues were called to move beyond offering hospitality from a relatively safe and potentially patronizing position of benevolence. Rather, by asserting that their mission included investigating and improving "conditions in the industrial districts of Chicago," the settlement workers had begun to see themselves as activists charged with fostering democracy in the public sphere. Moreover, as Addams explains in *Democracy and Social Ethics,* through her experiences at Hull-House she had been "brought to a conception of Democracy not merely as a sentiment which desires the well-being of all men, but that which affords a rule of living well as a test of faith" (1902/2002a, 7). By positing "living well" as the final measure of democracy, Addams again confirms that the communitarian inclinations that underlay her understandings of democracy had to be complemented by her engagement in a public struggle for the equitable distribution of decision-making power.

This lesson that democracy, if it is to be more than a noble purpose, requires ambition and conflict in the pursuit of justice is one that Addams learned by inserting herself into the political machinations of Chicago's Nineteenth Ward, where Hull-House was located. There she saw her efforts to have mounds of garbage removed from the streets and alleys of her neighborhood temporarily blocked by a corrupt alderman; there she learned of sweatshop owners' conspiring to fix wages so low that their workers could not adequately feed their families; there she saw striking workers beaten by federal troops, idle and hopeless youth slip into lives of delinquency and addiction, and women—in her words—"chained down" because they were disenfranchised, abandoned, and poor. Indeed, in the city that Carl Sandburg (1914/1980) described as the "Stormy, husky, brawling / City of the Big Shoulders," the city where "under the faces of woman and children / [are] seen the marks of wanton hunger," Addams came to understand that her vision of democracy depended upon extending power to some people while taking it away from others.

That Addams could at once insist that antagonism is unnecessary and demonstrate through her actions that it was an indispensable part of her social ethic may confound those who would hope to assign an intellectual consistency to her words and work. Nonetheless, for we teachers who presume to think of ourselves and our students as citizens, Addams's democratic paradox—her juxtaposition of community and conflict—is inevitably our own. We who would teach for democracy know the importance of establishing learning communities where a plurality of voices is valued and where students can explore unfamiliar ideas and change their minds in a safe and supportive environment. We also know, however, that if we are, as Deborah Stern (1994) has put it, to "teach English so it matters," our classroom reading and writing cannot ignore broader public struggles for human dignity and opportunity. This is why, I think, that teachers so often do things like honor Atticus Finch for defending Tom Robinson in *To Kill a Mockingbird*, challenge students to affirm that the vast and appalling inhumanity described in *Night* must "never again" be repeated, and urge young people to cry out and act against the sexual violence described in *Speak*. Such teaching and learning acknowledges that democracy can be created and manifested in a host of apparently competing ways: It can come in a moment of listening to the story of an elderly woman over tea and from behind barricades. It can appear in the form of a fair wage and safe working environment and in the organized struggle that makes these conditions possible. It can be advanced by clearing streets of disease-ridden trash and by establishing a well-equipped and productive classroom.

Although hers was an evolving and unsettled understanding of democracy, Addams remained firm in her commitment to the fundamentally democratic notion that all people should have the ability and opportunity to develop their unique potentials and use these in concert with others to build and live a life that they choose. "We must learn to trust our democracy," she wrote, "giant-like and threatening as it may appear in its uncouth strength and untried applications" (1895/2002, 47). If Addams is right—and I think that she still is—about democracy's "uncouth strength" and "untried applications," it is fitting that teachers follow her example and continually rethink how their work might reflect and promote democratic ideals. We would do well, in other words, to establish professional aims not only of mastering our content knowledge and employing effective teaching methods but also of habitually disturbing ourselves by asking questions like these: What does it mean to teach for democracy? Are some pedagogical practices or materials more democratic than others? What, specifically, does democracy look like in schools that are so heavily invested in the status quo? How might schools misappropriate and misuse rhetorics of democracy? What assets and options are available to teachers, and what structural and ideological challenges do they face as they attempt to foster democratic ideals in an educational culture such as ours—a culture in which democracy seems to be narrowly defined or dismissed as facile and unworkable?

If we teachers unsettle ourselves with such questions, we will learn that working for democracy—whether it be at a settlement house or in a classroom—is a confusing, serendipitous, and often uncertain business. For my part, however, Addams's approaches to solving the problems she encountered were not so much mercurial as flexible and appropriately responsive to facts on the ground as she tried to determine how best to foster democracy in particular places and at specific times. As I have been suggesting, Addams's efforts have their corollaries in classrooms and among the students we see daily, and I believe that in sites such as these, our understandings of how to teach for democracy will have to be revised according to the "streetwise" knowledge we gain from participating in a changing world.

Addams, Experimentalism, and American Pragmatism

One day, after Addams had already been working in and around Hull-House for several years, she embarked on what she thought would be a routine call to an ailing neighbor but instead ended up assisting in the delivery of the young woman's baby. Reflecting on that experience, Addams wrote to a friend that she was continually astonished by how her and her colleagues' work involved what she described as "this doing things we don't know how to do" (1935, 52–53; qtd. in Elshtain 2002a, 92–93).

Of all the instructive and inspiring stories Addams composed about her work, this one perhaps best captures the evolving and exploratory nature of her understandings of her efforts as a settlement worker and activist. As we have seen, Addams continually broadened the associations she cultivated as she sought to honor the family and social claims, and this exposure to new ideas and priorities prompted her to adopt a complex and evolving understanding of democracy. Constantly challenged with new problems and perspectives, repeatedly renegotiating the meaning and manifestations of democracy, Addams required a philosophical framework that could accommodate her changing understandings of what she should do and why. She satisfied this requirement by drawing from and contributing to what at the time was an emergent intellectual movement that came to be known as American pragmatism, which was characterized by a spirit of experimentalism that, in my view, is as useful to current teachers as it was to Addams.

From Addams's own written reflections and the work of her biographers, it is clear that her adopting pragmatism represents a significant shift in her thinking. As Louise W. Knight explains, in the years preceding her decision to establish Hull-House, Addams's impulses to cultivate her gifts and interests to alleviate human suffering were guided by values she had learned primarily from her father, John Addams, who was Cedarville's most prominent business owner, a holder of statewide office, and a stalwart leader in the local Presbyterian church. These values included moral fortitude, a firm grounding in inviolable principles, and a solitary heroism expressed in the works of Ralph Waldo Emerson and in the example of her father's friend Abraham Lincoln.

Informed by her settlement experiences, however, Addams learned that her efforts required more humility, self-critique, and adaptability than were afforded by the principles she inherited from her father. Put another way, Addams discovered that she had to "unlearn" what she thought she knew about bringing the benefits of her education and social status to the downtrodden and dispossessed. Addams found guidance in this process in Leo Tolstoy's *My Religion,* a book that she said "changed [her] life" (qtd. in Knight 2005, 145). As Knight explains, Tolstoy's own emergence from feelings of failure to work in solidarity with the poor encouraged Addams to let go of an ideal of unwavering moral heroism and instead accept the notion that, as Addams put it, "if the new social order ever came, it would come by gathering to itself all . . . pathetic human endeavor" (1910/1990, 261; qtd. in Knight 2005, 145). Addams thus turned away from striving for a predetermined, idealized form of perfection and instead embraced her vocation as a neverending and imperfect search for provisional solutions to emerging problems.

In making this shift from idealizing perfection to acknowledging the sufficiency of imperfection, from following fundamental principles to exploring the utility of fallible guidelines, Addams was adopting pragmatism as it was being conceptualized and articulated in the late nineteenth and early twentieth centuries, primarily by Charles Sanders Pierce, William James, and John Dewey. As these writers explained, pragmatism evades succinct definition in that it's not a "philosophy" in the sense of being a static set of beliefs about immutable and universal "Truths." Rather, as James describes it, pragmatism is better thought of as a method of raising questions, inquiring into possible answers to those questions, and then acting on what these inquiries reveal in order to improve society (21).

In other words, in contrast to the Western philosophical tradition's supposition that Truth is abstract and absolute, that it is waiting to be discovered as corresponding to or underwritten by some kind of extra-human reality, pragmatism posits an antifoundationalist notion of "truths" as fallible human constructs that earn their status as "truth-apt" by the consequences of believing in them. Put another way, pragmatists hold an "instrumental" theory of truth, which is to say that "true" ideas or theories are those that help people solve problems and achieve desired consequences. Or, as James puts it, "Pragmatism unstiffens all our theories, limbers them up and sets each one to work" (1907/1995, 21).

Decades later, Richard Rorty wrote that to adopt this pragmatist framework, to accept "the *contingency* of starting points, is to accept our inheritance from, and our conversation with, our fellow humans beings as our only source of guidance." Rorty continues, articulating not only pragmatism's provisional notions of truth but also its attendant communitarian inclinations, inclinations that Addams acted upon throughout her career:

> To attempt to evade this contingency [of starting points] is to hope to become a properly programmed machine. If we give up this hope, we may lose what Nietzsche called "metaphysical comfort," but we may gain a renewed sense of community. Our identification with our community—our society, our political tradition, our intellectual heritage—is heightened when we see this community as *ours* rather than *nature's, shaped* rather than *found,* one among many which [people] have made. In the end, pragmatists tell us, what matters is our loyalty to other human beings clinging together against the dark, not our hope of getting things right. (1982, 166)

Given this emphasis on collective inquiry guided by experience and the material consequences of ideas, pragmatists prefer to retool philosophy by seeking truths in informed, agile, and competent responses to the troubles of their time. For her part, while Addams acknowledged what she called the "virtues" of preceding generations, she insisted that "a task is laid upon each generation to enlarge" the application of such virtues, "to ennoble their conception, and, above all, to apply and adapt them to the particular problems presented to it for solution" (1912/2002, 171). Thus, the questions pragmatists ask arise from real, concrete problems affecting the way people live, and the answers they propose are directed back toward ameliorating those problems by acting in ways that are never exactly the same.

As a consequence, despite all its communitarian and democratic impulses, pragmatism is a deeply unsettling method in that it precludes the comfort of certainty. Instead, it demands the relentless asking of what we might have missed, how we might be wrong, in what ways we might have to change our minds and our behavior. Nonetheless, it is precisely in this way that uncertainty ceases to be an impediment to progress and instead emerges as a requirement for it. For while uncertainty harbors the danger of aimless confusion and even despondency, uncertainty as a disposition encourages openness to new ideas and adaptability in attempts to effect solutions to emerging and unforeseeable problems.

Addams's lifelong work powerfully demonstrates this kind of productive uncertainty, for her grounded experimentalism was necessary to provide provisional answers to the kinds of questions she was compelled to ask when she ventured beyond the Hull-House grounds and the rigid moral framework of her early years. In writings that span the decades of her career, Addams argues that restive inquiry is essential to avoid the stagnation, and eventual death, of the kind of democratic society she envisioned. She knew, in other words, that

while people who aspire to mitigate injustice, suffering, and grief must draw
from the lessons of their individual and collective histories, they must also keep
their plans forward-looking and be constantly on the lookout for new ways to
identify and meet the novel challenges that arise in a changing world.

Through her work in what were then the slums and industrial districts of
Chicago's South Side, Addams modeled such inquiry-driven experimentalism
when she refused to shrink from what she called "the grief of things as they
are" (1910/1990, 17) but chose instead to embark on "this doing things we
don't know how to do." Central to these efforts, Addams emphasizes, is this
spirit of experimentation that pragmatism affords. Speaking of settlements
like Hull-House, she asserted that "the one thing to be dreaded . . . is that
it loses its flexibility, its power of quick adaptation, its readiness to change
its methods as its environment may demand" (1893/2002a, 26). Thus, she
who intended to be a teacher learned to be a student of her community and
its residents. She who went to Chicago with a plan to feed and instruct the
people of a particular neighborhood ended up enmeshed in city politics,
lobbying national governments, and winning a Nobel Peace Prize. She did
all this in conversation with others, through the careful assessment of social
conditions, and often, I am convinced, to her utter astonishment.

Although when Addams wrote of "this doing things we don't know how
to do" she was talking of the unpredictability of settlement life, her example
acts as an invitation for educators to apply her experimentalist impulse to the
methods they employ in their classrooms and to the kinds of relationships
they establish with students, colleagues, and community members. That is
to say, to the extent that teachers can manage to emulate Addams's curiosity,
imagination, and adaptability, we will likely also grow in our understanding
of teaching as one essential aspect of what must be more broadly conceived
as efforts to improve people's lives. This would be an understanding of teaching that begins not with the questions, What is this world like, and how can
I impart that knowledge to people? but What might this world possibly be,
and what can we do to improve it?

Because Addams's work was prompted in all but the first few years of
her career by these latter questions, teachers would do well to note that her
measures of success could not always be pinned down as specific goals. To
be sure, Addams wanted people to have adequate food, shelter, education,
and employment, along with a host of other things that her standards of
morality required. However, in words that reflect Addams's priorities and
that I think she would have embraced had they been written in her lifetime,
Rorty cautions against conceptions of "moral progress" as movement toward
fixed measures of justice or as behavior that more closely approximates a

metaphysical code. Rather, Rorty describes moral progress as "a matter of wider and wider sympathy," of "taking more people's needs into account than you did previously" and thereby "being able to respond to the needs of ever more inclusive groups of people." In Rorty's view, progress "happens" to the extent that members of a society get better at imagining and effecting ways in which "the existing order of things" might be replaced by one that affords a greater number of people a choice in how they will live (1999, 82–83). As Addams discovered, advancing moral progress as Rorty later defined it is slow, painstaking work, and those teachers who attempt to promote such progress in their classrooms will discover that the lessons of Addams's life are not clear and fixed directives of how to behave or what policies or pedagogical practices to implement. Rather, these lessons are models of disposition and process—stories and guidelines, at best, for how to get out into the communities one presumes to serve, to listen to and learn from others, and to actually do the work that you discover needs to be done.

If we educators enter into this process that Addams herself embraced, we may, with her, learn that such efforts are a never-ending task and that our own work can sometimes seem to be—as a critic once described Addams's efforts—a "speck in an ocean of misery, suffering, and poverty" (qtd. in Elshtain 2002a, 188). Nonetheless, especially in this time when it is easy to be discouraged into silence by the current state of education, striving to find more inclusive and useful ways of talking about teaching and learning is among the best hopes we have for making sure that education fosters democracy for all and not only a few. And although it may seem overly optimistic and even presumptuous, we who have contributed to this book are encouraged by Addams's assertion that "the tentative and actual attempts at adjustment" to a "newer conception of democracy" are "largely coming through those who are simpler and less analytical" (1902/2002a, 9). To be sure, the essays in this volume are clearly analytical, written by teachers who engage in serious reflection on what they and their students do. However, these teachers are, above all, practitioners for whom their intellectual work begins and ends in their classrooms. We are, in this sense, the "simpler" ones who learn, as Addams argues we must, from experience, in conversation with others, and indulging the spirits of democracy and experimentalism that are the hallmark of Addams's life work.

WWJD? (What Would Jane Do?)

I would never have found the Jane Addams Trail if I hadn't stopped at a mini-market gas station to ask directions. Beside me at the checkout counter stood a thin kid, about fifteen years old, with a mop of brown hair and a black rock-and-roll t-shirt, waiting to pay for his bottle of Mountain Dew. "Yeah, I been there," he said with sleep in his voice. "It's not far." Early that sweltering July morning, I had set out from Chicago with my bicycle in the trunk of my car and a folder of Mapquest directions on the seat beside me. After confirming my plans with a stop at the county visitors' center, I had no doubt that I knew exactly where I was going. Then I got lost and needed the Mountain Dew kid to show me the way.

Twenty minutes later, I was pedaling happily along a comfortably wide, hard-packed gravel surface. Shaded by a canopy of trees, the trail winds past thick groves of brush, beyond which lie rolling cornfields, swamps, weathered barns, and modestly distinguished farmhouses. After thirteen miles, I reached the Wisconsin state line, turned around, and headed back on paved county roads that took me into Cedarville.

When I finished my lunch of a sandwich and Coke at a low-ceilinged bar called the Cedar Inn, I got back on my bike and headed out through the heat in search of Addams's childhood home. Though I was pretty sure I had correctly followed the map given to me by the folks at the visitors' center, the street was strangely quiet. Few cars passed by, children's toys sat out on the sidewalks, and nothing indicated that this was the former neighborhood of a Nobel Laureate. After riding up and down the street a couple of times, I spotted a woman in shorts and a sun hat who was picking up branches that had fallen from the large trees in her front yard during a recent thunderstorm. I stopped, apologized for my appearance, and asked if she could tell me where Jane Addams used to live. She smiled and pointed to the house behind her at the top of the sloping lawn. "This is it right here," she said. "I'd be happy to show you around." The two-story brick house was fairly large but not ostentatious, painted white with dark shutters. Around back was a garden that the woman told me had been there in Addams's day, and about fifty yards away Cedar Creek, where Addams used to play with her brother William, ran along the edge of the property. The place was beautiful—peaceful and fragrant. I thought of the old photos I'd seen of the Chicago stockyards and crowded tenement houses, people staring vacantly at the camera. I also recalled Addams's descriptions of the smells of fetid garbage and human waste that lay like a canvass over the Hull-House neighborhood. Why, I wondered to myself, would she leave here for that?

The woman then directed me to the Cedarville Cemetery not far down the road, just around a curve and over the creek, where a small metal sign pointed the way to the "Jane Addams Burial Site." I laid my bike on the grass and walked toward a stone obelisk about fifteen feet high that I assumed to be what I was looking for. But again I was wrong. Instead, Jane's headstone lay at my feet, just before the level ground drops steeply into a heavily-wooded ravine. I estimated the stone's dimensions to be no more than about eighteen by thirty inches, and it rose from the grass to a height just above my ankle. On it was etched these words: "Jane Addams of Hull House and The Women's International League for Peace and Freedom." I knelt and ran my fingers over the letters. Scattered on the headstone were thirty-four pennies—a nod, I guessed, to the admiration for Lincoln that Jane had inherited from her father.

As much as I was enjoying the moment of reverent solitude, I couldn't help wondering why I was out there all by myself. I should have been surrounded by admirers and activists. Where were the banners, the kiosks selling Jane Addams posters, statuettes, and video tributes? Where were the busloads of progressive pilgrims? By all rights, I should have had to buy a ticket and nudge my way through a crowd to get a glimpse of the final resting place of such an historic figure. At the very least, a few people should have been paying tribute by hanging around like they do for Jim Morrison. Still, the more I thought about it, the more it made sense that I was out there alone, for anyone who cares enough about Jane Addams to visit her gravesite doesn't likely have time to linger in homage for long. There's just too much to be done. Back in Chicago, I knew, were neighborhoods struggling with poverty and violence, streets where thousands of homeless people eat and sleep, and high schools where only about half of the students graduate. I rested for a while in the shade, took some pictures, got on my bike, and headed for home and work. I think that's what Jane would have done.

Works Cited

Addams, Jane (1893/2002a). "The Subjective Necessity for Social Settlements." In *The Jane Addams Reader*. Ed. Jean Bethke Elshtain. New York: Basic Books. 14–28.

——— (1893/2002b). "The Objective Value of a Social Settlement." In *The Jane Addams Reader*. Ed. Jean Bethke Elshtain. New York: Basic Books. 29–45.

——— (1895/2002). "The Settlement as a Factor in the Labor Movement." In *The Jane Addams Reader*. Ed. Jean Bethke Elshtain. New York: Basic Books. 46–61.

——— (1898). "Social Settlements." In *Proceedings of the National Conference of Charities and Corrections, Twenty-fourth Annual Conference, July 7–14, 1897.* Boston: N.p., 1898. 338–46.

——— (1899/2002). "The Subtle Problems of Charity." In *The Jane Addams Reader*. Ed. Jean Bethke Elshtain. New York: Basic Books. 62–75.

——— (1902/2002a). Introduction to *Democracy and Social Ethics*. Urbana: University of Illinois Press. 5–9.

——— (1902/2002b). "Filial Relations." In *Democracy and Social Ethics*. Urbana: University of Illinois Press. 35–47.

——— (1909/1972). *The Spirit of Youth and the City Streets*. Urbana: University of Illinois Press.

—— (1910/1990). *Twenty Years at Hull-House.* Urbana: University of Illinois Press.

—— (1912/2002). "A Modern Lear." In *The Jane Addams Reader.* Ed. Jean Bethke Elshtain. New York: Basic Books. 163–76.

—— (1916/2002a). "Women's Memories—Transmuting the Past, as Illustrated by the Story of the Devil Baby." In *The Jane Addams Reader.* Jean Bethke Elshtain. New York: Basic Books. 382–91.

—— (1916/2002b). "Women's Memories—Reaction on Life, as Illustrated by the Story of the Devil Baby." In *The Jane Addams Reader.* Ed. Jean Bethke Elshtain. New York: Basic Books. 392–403.

—— (1935). *My Friend Julia Lathrop.* New York, Macmillan.

Bentley, Arthur F. (1908/1949). *The Process of Government.* Bloomington, Ind.: Principia Press.

Berlin, Isaiah (1970). *Four Essays on Liberty.* New York: Oxford University Press.

Brown, Wendy (2003). "Neo-liberalism and the End of Liberal Democracy." *Theory and Event* 7.1. Project MUSE database.

Elshtain, Jean Bethke (2002a). *Jane Addams and the Dream of American Democracy.* New York: Basic Books.

——, ed. (2002b). *The Jane Addams Reader.* New York: Basic Books.

Cochran-Smith, Marilyn (2004). *Walking the Road: Race, Diversity, and Social Justice in Teacher Education.* New York: Teachers College Press.

Dewey, John (1871–1918/1999). *Correspondence of John Dewey, Volume 1: 1871–1918.* Ed. L. A. Hickman. Electronic Edition. Carbondale: Center for Dewey Studies, Southern Illinois University.

—— (1894/1999). Letters from John Dewey to Alice Chipman Dewey, October 9 and 10. In *Correspondence of John Dewey, Volume 1: 1871–1918.* Ed. L. A. Hickman. Electronic Edition. Carbondale: Center for Dewey Studies, Southern Illinois University.

—— (1899/1983). *The School and Society.* In *The Middle Works, 1899–1924, vol. 1.* Ed. Jo Ann Boydston. Carbondale: Southern Illinois University Press. 5–109.

—— (1916/1988). *Democracy and Education.* In *The Middle Works, 1899–1924, vol. 9.* Ed. Jo Ann Boydston. Carbondale: Southern Illinois University Press.

—— (1927/1988). *The Public and Its Problems.* In *The Later Works, 1925–1953, vol. 2.* Ed. Jo Ann Boydston. Carbondale: Southern Illinois University Press. 238–372.

—— (1938/1963). *Experience and Education.* New York: Macmillan.

Fink, Leon (1987). "Labor, Liberty, and the Law: Trade Unionism and the Problem of American Constitutional Order." *Journal of American History* 74.3 (December): 904–25.

Forbath, William E. (1991). *Law and the Shaping of the American Labor Movement.* Cambridge, Mass.: Harvard University Press.

Freire, Paolo (1972/2002). *Pedagogy of the Oppressed.* New York: Continuum.

Giroux, Henry A. (1988). *Schooling and the Struggle for Public Life: Critical Pedagogy in the Modern Age.* Minneapolis: University of Minnesota Press.

Greene, Maxine (1988). *The Dialectic of Freedom.* New York: Teachers College Press.

Harvey, David (2005). *A Brief History of Neoliberalism.* Oxford: Oxford University Press.

hooks, bell (1994). *Teaching to Transgress: Education as the Practice of Freedom.* New York: Routledge.

James, William (1907/1995). *Pragmatism.* New York: Dover Publications.

Jefferson, Thomas (1820). Letter to W. C. Jarvis, September 28. In *The Writings of Thomas Jefferson*. Ed. H. A. Washington. New York : H. W. Derby, 1861.

Knight, Louise W. (2005). *Citizen: Jane Addams and the Struggle for Democracy*. Chicago: University of Chicago Press.

Lemann, Nicolas (2008). "Conflict of Interests." *New Yorker*, August 11. Accessed March 4, 2014. http://www.newyorker.com/arts/critics/atlarge/2008/08/11/080811crat_at-large_lemann.

Lichterman, Paul (2005). *Elusive Togetherness: Church Groups Trying to Bridge America's Divisions*. Princeton, N.J.: Princeton University Press.

Lippmann, Walter (1925/1993). *The Phantom Public*. New York: Transaction.

Martin, Jay (2002). *The Education of John Dewey: A Biography*. New York: Columbia University Press.

Menand, Louis (2001). *The Metaphysical Club: A Story of Ideas in America*. New York: Farrar, Straus, and Giroux.

Michael, Vincent L. "Recovering the Layout of the Hull House Complex." Accessed March 4, 2014. http://tigger.uic.edu/htbin/cgiwrap/bin/urbanexp/main.cgi?file=new/show_doc_search.ptt&doc=834.

Pratt, Mary Louise (1991). "The Art of the Contact Zone." *Profession* 91: 33–40.

Putnam, Robert D. (1996). "The Strange Disappearance of Civic America." *American Prospect* 24 (Winter).

——— (2000). *Bowling Alone: The Collapse and Revival of American Community*. New York: Simon and Schuster.

Rorty, Richard (1982). *Consequences of Pragmatism*. Minneapolis: University of Minnesota Press.

——— (1999). "Ethics without Principles." In *Philosophy and Social Hope*. New York: Penguin Books. 72–92.

Russell, Bertrand (1972). *A History of Western Philosophy*. New York: Simon and Schuster.

Sandberg, Carl (1914/1980). "Chicago." In *Anthology of American Literature*. 2d ed. Vol. 2. Ed. George McMichael. New York: Macmillan. 115–16.

Stern, Deborah (1994). *Teaching English So It Matters: Creating Curriculum for and with High School Students*. Thousand Oaks, Calif.: Corwin Press.

2 "To Learn from Life Itself"

Experience and Education at Hull-House

BRIDGET K. O'ROURKE

Even before Jane Addams and Ellen Gates Starr founded the Hull-House settlement in 1889, the former Hull mansion occupied a place in Chicago's history. Built on a prairie southwest of the Chicago River in 1856 by the industrialist Charles Hull, the house had survived the Great Fire of 1871 that swept the city and paved the way for Chicago's phenomenal growth as an industrial center. As development sprawled west of the river, the former residence was converted from house to warehouse. Its first floor was occupied by offices and storerooms when Addams and Starr rented its second floor to establish the social settlement that would bear Hull's name. The building was surrounded by factories and tenements that housed growing numbers of immigrants streaming into the city from Southern and Eastern Europe. These so-called new immigrants, from Italy, Greece, Russia, Poland, and Austria-Hungary, tripled Chicago's population between 1880 and 1900: by 1910, first- and second-generation immigrants comprised more than three-quarters of the city's total population (Smith 43). As hundreds more immigrants arrived daily on the Near West Side from nearby Dearborn Street railway station, factories and sweatshops sprouted up in the area around the Near West Side to exploit this source of readily available and cheap labor.

As Addams herself affirmed in her 1910 autobiography, *Twenty Years at Hull-House,* the Hull mansion had already passed through many changes when she and Starr arrived in 1889 to settle among the working poor in an effort "to make social intercourse express the growing sense of the economic unity of society and to add the social function to democracy" (76). Over the course of the next two decades, their "experiment in cooperative living" would transform the Near West Side: By 1920, Hull-House had expanded to a nineteen-building complex that offered educational and social services to nearly nine thousand neighbors each week. The settlement offered a nursery and kindergarten, clubs and classes, libraries and cultural exhibits, and public lectures on topics from astronomy to women's suffrage. Many labor unions organized in rent-free rooms at Hull-House, including the Chicago Women's Trade Union League and the Dorcas Federal Labor Union. Settlement residents documented the living and working conditions in the neighborhood, conducted investigations into labor and sanitation standards, and documented infant mortality and the spread of infectious diseases such as typhoid fever and tuberculosis. Hull-House introduced the city's first public playground, gymnasium, swimming pool, and public baths.

Yet Jane Addams insisted that these institutional accomplishments did not define the settlement's mission. Addams came to define the value of the settlement in terms of the form of its activities—the ongoing expression of a reciprocal social relationship. In *Twenty Years at Hull-House,* she suggested that this form of expression proceeded from (but was not identical with) the founders' a priori ideals: "I am not so sure that we succeeded in our endeavors 'to make social intercourse express the growing sense of the economic unity of society.' But Hull-House was soberly opened on the theory that the dependence of classes on each other is reciprocal; and that as the social relation is essentially a reciprocal relation, it gives a form of expression that has particular value" (76). After the first two decades of her experience at Hull-House, Addams was less concerned with the settlement's success at having achieved a predetermined end (such as economic unity) than the character of its activity, the collaborative *process* of its making and remaking that gave rise to diverse and unpredictable forms of expression.

As a learning community and a flexible site of civic engagement, Hull-House enacted a model of experiential education in which the outcomes of learning were inextricably tied to its social processes. Hull-House's experiment in "social democracy" entailed conflict as well as cooperation among diverse classes of people with different goals, expectations, and values. Jane Addams came to identify the settlement's mistakes and missteps with its educational mission: after four decades of experience, she wrote that she and her fellow residents "came to define a settlement as an institution attempting to *learn from life itself* in which undertaking we did not hesitate to admit that we encountered many difficulties and failures" (*Second Twenty Years* 408; emphasis added). Setbacks and failures were not unfortunate by-products of teaching and learning at Hull-House; those experiences were grist for the mill.

As the essays in this volume demonstrate, Addams's autobiography continues to inspire the narrative reconstruction of teaching and learning in a democratic society. Contemporary readers may read *Twenty Years at Hull-House* as a narrative model of "learning from life itself"—a narrative reconstruction of experiential learning, through which past experiences may be integrated with present social realities.

Hull-House as Learning Community

Jane Addams's autobiography offers a historical model of Hull-House as a learning community—a social organization governed by a continuous and recursive, flexible but systematic model of trial, error, and subsequent correction. As Morris Berger has observed, settlement residents were educators by instinct and by training (15). Addams characterized the settlement itself as a "protest against a restricted view of education"—a flexible site of civic engagement that could potentially transform more permanent institutions of civil society, such as the public schools (*Subjective Necessity* 10). Indeed, many of the programs and services initiated at Hull-House—including kindergartens, adult education, vocational training and guidance, medical services, and community-center programs—were later incorporated into the progressive model of the school as social center. While John Dewey often receives credit for theorizing this transformation, Hull-House served as an early inspiration and testing ground for Dewey's theories of comprehensive public education.

Addams characterized the many educational activities sponsored by the settlement as "but differing manifestations of the attempt to socialize democracy" (*Subjective Necessity* 10). According to Ellen Condliffe Lagemann, who collected Addams's major writings on education, the model of teaching and learning at the settlement presumed that "individually and socially enhancing life experiences were the vital sources and telling marks of a society in which democracy was a way of life, not merely a political creed" (5). Addams conceived of education broadly, as a process both tested and refined by "the conduct it inspired" in the daily lives of adults and children (*Twenty Years* 67). Like Dewey, Addams understood the testing of experience by its consequences as the *process* of education itself. Hull-House enacted civic education through daily experiences of cooperation and conflict among different classes, races, and ethnic groups, as they negotiated and attempted to reconstruct the industrial and social life they shared.

The diverse learning community of Hull-House, and its collective experiment in social democracy, grounded John Dewey's educational theories. Dewey was a frequent visitor and occasional lecturer at Hull-House who served on the settlement's Board of Trustees. As Charlene Haddock Seig-fried has pointed out, Dewey's claim that "the very process of living together educates" was based on his participation at Hull-House and the Lab School at University of Chicago (Dewey, *Democracy and Education,* cited in Sei-gfried, "Socializing Democracy" 207). Dewey's daughter, Jane (named after Addams), said that her father's "faith in democracy as a guiding force in education took on both a sharper and deeper meaning because of Hull-House and Jane Addams" (30). In short, Dewey's experiences at Hull-House both informed and transformed his theories of democracy and education.

Addams in turn claimed that Dewey's philosophical insight illuminated her understanding of the relationship between inquiry and action, experi-ence and knowledge. Addams was particularly adept at translating theory into practice and testing theoretical principles by practical consequences: in this way, she transformed generalizations into "unusually incisive expe-riential interpretations of social situations and problems" (Lagemann viii). As Jill Conway has observed, Addams "wrote with the simple directness of someone who had personally confronted the problems which concerned her. Hers was not an abstract or doctrinaire position . . . for she wrote from experience . . . about her own confusion and puzzlement and their resolu-tion" (257). In this way, Addams's narrative reconstruction of experience in *Twenty Years at Hull-House* fleshed out the philosophical abstractions of Dewey's educational theory. Read in this light, Addams's memoir of "the experiences through which various conclusions were forced on me" reveals the limits of individual action and the necessity of collective efforts to sup-port the continuous process of "learning from life itself."

Experience and Education in *Twenty Years at Hull-House*

When Jane Addams's autobiography was published in 1910, Addams (at age fifty) was a national celebrity, the public persona of the settlement movement. That year, readers of the *Ladies' Home Journal* voted her the most respected woman in America, and eighty thousand copies of the autobiography were sold during her lifetime. Nearly a century since its initial publication, it remains the most enduring and popular account of the twentieth-century social settlement. Despite its popularity (or maybe because of it), *Twenty Years at Hull-House* never achieved canonical status in the history of American education. Lagemann suggests that the narrative arrangement of the text has made it easy to dismiss as "'mere autobiography,' nothing more than stories from one person's life" (Lagemann viii). Recently, however, scholars have recovered Addams's autobiography as an important text in progressive educational philosophy.

Addams's use of storytelling rather than objective analysis to develop her educational philosophy exemplifies her philosophical position that abstractions are best defined by daily actions. The autobiographical narrative recounts the diverse events and actions of a life, including accidents and unintended consequences. Narrative not only entertains but also enlightens: "[A]s individuals and societies we can come to know ourselves, Addams suggests, *only* to the extent that we realize the experience of others" (Elshtain 9). Like other art forms, storytelling serves to "warm us with a sense of companionship with the experience of others" and satisfies the "universal desire for the portrayal of life lying quite outside of personal experiences" (Addams, *Twenty Years* 265). Narrative enlightens the collective imagination and illuminates the relationship between the actual and the possible that Dewey associated with engaged learning. Following Dewey, Seigfried has defined imagination as "the capacity to creatively explore inherited structures from past experience in light of the future as a horizon of possible actions, and so of possible meanings" ("Socializing Democracy" 208).

By situating the personal experiences and anecdotes recounted in *Twenty Years at Hull-House* in a social framework (i.e., in "companionship with the experience of others"), Addams was able to "shift the focus of her thought and energy from self-analysis to the analysis of the society in which she lived" (Lagemann 21). Like her 1892 analysis of *The Subjective Necessity for Social Settlements,* the early chapters of the autobiography emphasize the moral struggle of a generation of college-educated, middle-class young men and women seeking an outlet for a "sense of universal brotherhood . . . which the best spirit of our times is forcing from an emotion into a motive" (6). When external conditions or social prohibitions inhibit the desire to translate altruistic feeling into action, these young people (women in particular) may remain mired in "unnourished oversensitive lives . . . shut off from the common labor by which they live" (6). Unlike the 1892 essay, however, *Twenty Years at Hull-House* narrates rather than explicates the "lack of coordination between thought and action" of the educated middle-class woman (67).

This gap between the actual and the possible was portrayed through Addams's struggle to enact the cooperative ideals of Rockford Female Seminary after her graduation, in the years before she founded Hull-House. "The Snare of Preparation," the metaphoric title of the chapter that concludes the account of her life before Hull-House, emerges as an important theme for social analysis: "[W]e spread [the snare of preparation] before the feet of young people, hopelessly entangling them in a curious inactivity at the very period of life when they are longing to construct the world anew and conform it to their own ideals" (74). By founding Hull-House in 1889, Addams successfully evades "the snare of preparation": "[W]hatever perplexities and discouragement concerning the life of the poor were in store for me, I should at least know something first hand and have the solace of daily activity . . . the period of mere passive receptivity had come to an end" (74). In the chapters that follow, the autobiography shifts from self-reflection to social analysis, and from a passive to a more intentional pattern of action.

The transition in Addams's narrative from passive to active experience corresponds to Dewey's conception of the continuum of experience from "undergoing," in which events merely occur, to "trying," which characterizes an intentional relationship between past human activities and an individual's future action: "On the active hand, experience is trying—a meaning which is made explicit in the connected term experiment. On the passive, it is undergoing. When we experience something we act upon it, we do something with it; then we suffer or undergo the consequences. We do something to the thing and then it does something to us in return: such is the peculiar combination. The connection of these two phases of experience measures the fruitfulness or value of the experience" (*Democracy and Education* 139). As David Carr has pointed out, this relationship is crucial to theorizing transformative education. Undergoing the consequences of the active side of experience prompts critical reflection on future possibilities and opens up the potential for "deliberate restorying," or reconstruction of experience, which characterizes transformative education (Carr; Clandinin and Connelly). Reflection connects the active and passive aspects of experience, transforming experience into learning.

Addams explicitly cited Dewey's principle of the "continuing reconstruction of experience" in her discussion of the educational function of the Hull-House Labor Museum. The Labor Museum exhibited traditional crafts such as spinning and weaving in order to "interest the young people working in the neighborhood factories in these older forms of industry, so that, through their own parents and grandparents, they would find a dramatic representation of the inherited resources of their daily occupation." Addams proposed: "If these young people could actually see that the complicated machinery of the factory had been evolved from simple tools, they might at least make a beginning toward that education which Dr. Dewey defines as 'a continuing reconstruction of experience.' They might also lay a foundation of reverence for the past that Goethe declares to be the basis of all sound progress" (*Twenty Years* 172). Through the Labor Museum and other efforts at progressive education, Addams sought to enable immigrant men and women to reconstruct the continuity of their experience from the Old World culture to industrial society (Deegan 251).

For Dewey, the criterion of continuity—that is, the quality of an experience that lives "fruitfully and creatively in subsequent experiences"—was essential to "genuine experience" (*Experience and Education* 28). Complementing this theme of continuity—the relationship of experiences over time—was the relationship between objective conditions (the external factors that control experience) and internal preparation for experience, which Dewey referred to as "interaction" (42). These two principles, Dewey wrote, "intercept and unite": "They are, so to speak, the longitudinal and lateral aspects of experience. Different situations succeed one another. But because of the principle of continuity something is carried over from the earlier to the later ones. As an individual passes from one situation to another, his world, his environment, expands or contracts. What he has learned in the way of knowledge and skill in one situation becomes an instrument of understanding and dealing with the situations that follow" (*Experience and Education* 44). Experience is not wholly subjective. As discussed earlier, every genuine experience has an active side that which in some measure changes objective conditions: "In a word, we live from birth to death in a world of persons and things which in large measure is what it is because of what has been done and transmitted from previous human activities" (39). Continuity situates experience in time, while interaction places individual experience in the context of social and material conditions that may enable or constrain personal needs, desires, and purposes. For Dewey, experience is the relationship between the past (what has been transmitted from past human activities) and the potentiality of future action.

Time, in Dewey's thought, is characterized not only by continuity—an endless sequence of experiences—but is also experienced cyclically and rhythmically. Cyclic repetition is one of the bases for rhythm, and both play a role in the "aha!" moment of genuine learning: "[T]hat sudden magic that gives us a sense of an inner revelation brought to us about something we have supposed to be known through and through" (Dewey, *Art as Experience* 170–71). In Addams's narrative, this experiential model of time supplanted a strictly chronological one: as she explained in the introduction to *Twenty Years at Hull-House,* it was necessary to "abandon the chronological order in favor of the topical, for during the early years at Hull-House, time seemed to afford a mere framework for certain lines of activity and I have found in writing this book, that after these activities have been recorded, I can scarcely recall the scaffolding" (18). Topical organization enabled the author to shift from recounting a personal narrative to tracing cooperative "lines of activity" and collective undertakings.

Implications for Contemporary Community-University Partnerships

In many ways, the cooperation between Jane Addams's Hull-House and John Dewey's interdisciplinary-studies department at the University of Chicago represents an ideal community-university partnership. Their collaboration serves as a historical model for what is known in contemporary higher-education circles as "community engagement," defined by the Carnegie Foundation as "the collaboration between institutions of higher education and their larger communities (local, regional/state, national, global) for the mutually beneficial exchange of knowledge and resources in a context of partnership and reciprocity" (qtd. in Driscoll 39). Many discussions of successful university-community partnerships (including the University of Pittsburgh's Community Literacy Center) cite Addams and Dewey as historical forebears for collaborative efforts at community engagement and service learning (Flower; Mathieu; Moore and Lin; Morton and Saltmarsh).

During her lifetime, however, Jane Addams expressed principled resistance to the institutionalization of partnerships between universities and social settlements. Although she frequently collaborated with academics, Addams saw a fundamental distinction between the institutional function of the social settlement and that of the university. As early as 1899, she wrote, "The settlement stands for application as opposed to research; for emotion as opposed to abstraction, for universal interest as opposed to specialization" ("Function of the Social Settlement" 187). The role of the settlement was to "test the value of human knowledge by action," while the university was concerned with the discovery of knowledge for its own sake. Charlene Haddock Seigfried has noted that Dewey and like-minded colleagues at the University of Chicago challenged this prevailing model of university knowledge "by holding it to account according to whether it contributed to the quality of life of individuals in communities and by directing it toward resolving problematic situations outside the academy" ("Socializing Democracy" 218). While Addams continued to seek flexible and pragmatic engagement with scholars, she avoided commitment to any institutional partnership that might threaten the unity of theory and practice at the settlement or subordinate the community-based organization to the male-dominated academy. Moreover, Addams sought to put knowledge at the service of the community "rather than using the community merely as a source for data for research projects unconnected to its welfare" (Seigfried 218).

The exploitation of community-based knowledge by universities remains a concern in contemporary institutionalized community-engagement programs. Paula Mathieu and others have expressed concern that informal, grassroots service-learning projects and partnerships may lose their flexibility when subsumed to the strategic objectives of institutionalized programs. Echoing Dewey and Addams, Mathieu emphasizes the importance of continuity and appropriate timing in reciprocally engaged community-learning projects. She cites many stories of "service learning gone wrong"—cases of failed engagement from the point of view of those being served. Mathieu sees the problems of poor timing, discontinuity, lack of follow-through, and mismatched objectives as inimical to institutionalized programs: "The rhythms of the university do not necessarily harmonize with the rhythms and exigencies of community groups. If the impetus driving service learning is a desire to promote the university as a site of good work, how likely is it that universities will do multiple, meaningful service projects semester after semester, classroom after classroom, in exactly the amount of time a semester allows?" (99). Even the best intentions of service-learning participants do not always lead to good outcomes, as the "second wave" of scholarship on service learning suggests.

So, what transforms such contemporary perplexities and discouragement into genuine learning? What transforms challenges and contradictions like those Mathieu describes into what she calls "tactics of hope"? For one thing, the historical model of Hull-House suggests that a community of learners is needed to transform setbacks and failures into genuine learning. Service-learning projects that rely on the passion and conviction of individual instructors may be unsustainable without support, reciprocity, and genuine partnership. Furthermore, those who are genuinely committed to building authentic community-university relationships must redefine "success" in local and contingent terms, "devising timely and spatially appropriate relationships in the streets where we work" (Mathieu 20). Like Addams and Dewey, Mathieu envisions a method of evaluating social action in light of its consequences in the daily life of the community, rather than by strategic objectives. Authentic community-university partnerships demand "the kind of hope that doesn't offer a predetermined blueprint for future practices but demands a critical interrogation of the present to accompany any action that results" (Mathieu 134). Moreover, participants must *hope*—an active verb that conveys among its many meanings "the ability to recognize the radical insufficiency of any actions, be honest in assessing their limitations, imagine better ways to act and learn, and despite the real limitations, engage creative acts of work and play with an eye toward a better not-yet future" (Mathieu 134).

The story of Hull-House as a community institution ended in 2012, when the Jane Addams Hull-House Association closed its doors due to financial difficulties. One of the longest-running social-service agencies in the country, the Hull-House Association continued to operate in decentralized sites around Chicago long after the original social settlement and much of the surrounding neighborhood was demolished in 1963. Today, only the original Hull mansion and the former coffee house remain, now overshadowed by the imposing modernist structures of the University of Illinois at Chicago. Despite the relative obscurity of the former buildings on the physical landscape, Hull-House remains embedded in the history of Chicago's Near West Side—and in the historical tradition of American education. As long as educators engage students in the continuous process of transforming the conflicts and mistakes of the past into meaningful collective action, the model of "learning from life itself" will endure well into the twenty-first century.

Works Cited

Addams, Jane. "A Function of the Social Settlement" (1899). In *The Social Thought of Jane Addams.* Ed. Christopher Lasch. Indianapolis: Bobbs-Merrill, 1965. 183–99.

———. *Second Twenty Years at Hull-House.* New York: MacMillan, 1930.

———. *Subjective Necessity for Social Settlements* (1892). Reprint ed., Chicago: Jane Addams Hull-House Museum, n.d.

———. *Twenty Years at Hull-House* (1910). New York: Penguin, 1981.

Berger, Morris. *The Settlement, the Immigrant, and the Public School: A Study of the Influence of the Settlement Movement and the New Migration upon Public Education, 1890–1924.* New York: Arno Press, 1980.

Carr, David. *Time, Narrative, and History.* Bloomington: Indiana University Press, 1986.

Clandinin, D. Jean, and F. Michael Connelly. "Narrative and Story in Practice and Research." *ERIC* (1988): ED309681.

Conway, Jill Ker. "Jane Addams: American Heroine." In *The Woman in America.* Ed. Robert J. Lifton. Boston: Houghton Mifflin, 1965. 247–66.

Deegan, Mary Jo. *Jane Addams and the Men of the Chicago School, 1892–1918.* New Brunswick, N.J.: Transaction, 1988.

Dewey, Jane M. "Biography of John Dewey." In *The Philosophy of John Dewey.* 2d ed. Ed. Paul Arthur Shilpp. LaSalle, Ill.: Open Court, 1951. 20–40.

Dewey, John. *Art as Experience* (1934). New York: Perigee, 1980.

———. *The Middle Works, 1899–1924.* Vol. 9: *Democracy and Education* (1916). Ed. Jo Ann Boydston. Carbondale: Southern Illinois University Press, 1980.

———. *Experience and Education: The Kappa Delta Pi Lecture Series* (1938). New York: Collier Books, New York: Macmillan, 1963.

———. "The School as Social Center" (1902). In *The Middle Works, 1899–1924*. Vol. 2. Ed. Jo. Ann. Boydston. Carbondale: Southern Illinois University Press, 1976. 80–93.

Driscoll, Amy. "Carnegie's Community-Engagement Classification: Intentions and Insights." *Change* 40.1 (2008): 39–41.

Elshtain, Jean Bethke. "Power Trips and Other Journeys: *Essays in Feminism as Civic Discourse*." Madison: University of Wisconsin Press, 1990.

Flower, Linda. *Community Literacy and the Rhetoric of Public Engagement*. Carbondale: Southern Illinois University Press, 2008.

Lagemann, Ellen Condliffe. Introduction to *Jane Addams On Education*, by Jane Addams. Ed. Ellen Condliff Lagemann. New Brunswick, N.J.: Transaction, 1994. vii–41.

Mathieu, Paula. *Tactics of Hope: The Public Turn in Composition Studies*. Portsmouth, N.H.: Boynton Cook, 2005.

Moore, Mary, and Phylis Lan Lin, eds. *Service-Learning in Higher Education: Paradigms and Challenges*. Indianapolis: University of Indianapolis Press, 2009.

Morton, Keith, and John Saltmarsh. "Addams, Day, and Dewey: The Emergence of Community Service in American Culture." *Michigan Journal of Community Service Learning* 4.1 (1997): 137–49.

Peaden, Catherine. "Jane Addams and the Social Rhetoric of Democracy." In *Oratorical Culture in Nineteenth-Century America*. Ed. Gregory Clark and S. Michael Halloran. Carbondale: Southern Illinois University Press, 1993. 184–207.

Seigfried, Charlene Haddock. "Socializing Democracy: Jane Addams and John Dewey." *Philosophy of the Social Sciences* 29.2 (1999): 207–28.

Smith, Carl. *The Plan of Chicago: Burnham and the Remaking of the American City*. Chicago: University of Chicago Press, 2006.

3 Problems of Memory, History, and Social Change

The Case of Jane Addams

PETRA MUNRO HENDRY

> History is perpetually suspicious of memory and its true mission is
> to destroy it.
> —Pierre Nora

That Jane Addams is one of the twentieth century's most radical thinkers and
pioneering pragmatist philosophers seems without question. While numerous academic works in political science, philosophy, sociology, history, and
English continue to examine her unique contributions, she remains on the
margins of educational philosophy and history. The reasons for this are part
of a much larger project that includes an analysis of the ahistorical nature
of education as well as the ongoing deintellectualization of our field. The
ongoing "presentism" within the field of education obscures the role of history and more importantly, I will suggest in this essay, the role of memory in
the constitution of the subjective self. For Addams, the pragmatist principle
that experience is knowledge was predicated on the belief that all experience is memory. She saw the past not as something distant or "other" but as
constituted through both a collective and individual self. For teachers and
educators, it is this self, constituted through experience *and* memory, that
becomes a critical site for reflection. It is thinking through memory that
becomes the site for what Addams calls "disturbing conventions" (qtd. in
Seigfried 2002, xxii).

Thus, I turn to memory. My interest in memory is twofold. One aim is
to re-member Jane Addams. Not that I hope to discover the "real" Addams.
Like Baker (2001), my aim is to keep subject identities in "perpetual motion."
Who Addams is is highly contested. For some she is the embodiment of the
do-gooder, the saintly social worker, the epitome of Victorian womanhood.

These sentimental readings have rendered her a heroine beyond recognition. Her impenetrability has resulted in distrust and suspicion with those who criticize her politics as assimilationist and paternalistic (Mills 1964; Lissak 1989) or as a repression of her "sexual maladjustment" (Brown 2004).[1] Others see her tireless work as a social reformer and activist, specifically her pioneering work in the social-settlement movement, as a means through which she quenched her "emotional need to be loved" (Brown 2004, 11). Never credited as a social philosopher in her own right, her activism is interpreted as "derivative" or "putting into practice" the theories of John Dewey, William James, and George Herbert Mead. While the "Metaphysical Club" has taken on almost mythical status in American philosophical circles, few consider Hull-House as "a pragmatist, feminist think-tank" (Hamington 2009, 23). More current scholarship (Deegan 1990; Munro 1999; Hamington 2010; Hendry 2011; Seigfried 1996) has focused on Addams's radical pragmatist philosophy by situating her prolific writings, including twelve books and more than five hundred published articles, through her own eyes to understand her unique contributions to theory.

To read Addams as a philosopher requires setting aside assumptions about beginning from abstract theoretical positions. As a pragmatist, her theorizing was always embedded in social life and in daily experience, and most importantly, "the human care it requires" (Fischer, Nackenoff, and Chmielewski 2009, 14). Five interrelated concepts were central to her pragmatist philosophy:

Sympathetic Knowledge: The only way to approach any human problem, best understood as a form of social ethics, sympathetic knowledge maintains that it is the responsibility of members of society to know one another for the purposes of caring and acting on each other's behalf. Knowledge is not propositional but gained through disrupting one's perceived experience and understanding. This disruption—or, as Addams calls it, "perplexity"—is central to social empathy.

Lateral Progress: This notion of progress as going "sideways" rather than forward was a direct challenge to dominant notions of social change at the turn of the century in which Darwin's theory of evolution viewed change as evolving in a linear fashion. Progress is not about moving forward but about spreading the connections and networks that will ensure the fuller economic and political participation of all members of society. Addams's unflagging commitment to pacifism was due to her belief that conflict and violence are the natural enemies of social progress.

Pluralism: Contrary to the dominant fear of "the decline of white civilization" at the time, Addams saw diversity not as something to be feared but as something that is critical to democracy. In contrast to the dominant ideologies of the time, which argued that immigrants and African Americans were uncivilized and responsible for the decay of the moral fiber of America, Addams maintained that it was the "common lot" who would regenerate a decaying America.

Social Democracy: For Addams, democracy is a mode of living and a social morality. Democracy is social ethics; ethics is the science of social relations. Social relations, in Addams's view, are reciprocal and interdependent. She rejected a universalistic or "equality" view of democracy as functioning to obscure difference. Democracy is based on community networks, not individual rights.

Fallibility: For pragmatist theorists, truths are beliefs confirmed in the course of experience and are therefore fallible and subject to further revision. Mistakes are inevitable when engaged with human beings across multiple differences. Humility becomes central to pragmatism. For pragmatists engaged in the cycle of action and reflection, humility is a prerequisite to social change.

While these central concepts of Addams's pragmatist philosophy are relatively well known and theorized (Hamington 2010), her work on memory and history as it relates to social change remains on the margins. While Brown (2004) maintains that she "used reminiscences to illustrate her social philosophy" (8), I would maintain that her use of reminiscence was not mere illustration but was critical to her social philosophy. Experience, while grounded in our "lived social relations," is embedded in history and memory. As Winfield (2007) reminds us, "it is at the juncture of memory and context that individuals both recognize and construct reality" (12). Memory for Addams plays two important functions: first is its role in interpreting life for the individual, and second is its activity as a selective agency in social reorganization. For Addams these two functions of memory were not mutually exclusive and were in fact interdependent. She ultimately believed that "experience eventually is nothing but memory" (Seigfried 2002, xx). This is her unique contribution to pragmatist philosophy.

Addams's theory of memory is best articulated in her book *The Long Road of Woman's Memory*. Perhaps the least well known of her books, it has remained on the margins of theoretical analysis. While Addams wrote this work in 1916, at age fifty-six, it was not her first attempt to articulate the important role of memory in social transformation. In reading Addams's work with an eye toward memory, it is apparent that a common rhetorical feature she engaged was framing her writings within her own memories, or the collective memories of others, as a means to address contemporary social issues and injustices. I turn to three of her writings to illuminate and examine the ways in which she takes up memory. The first is "Cassandra," written at age twenty-one, her commencement address at Rockford Seminary in 1881; the second is "The Modern Lear," written in 1894 as a response to the Pullman strike; and third, written at age fifty-six, is "Women's Memories—Transmuting the Past, as Illustrated by the story of the Devil Baby," a chapter in *The Long Road of Woman's Memory*. I would argue that these essays were not written across time but through space. Spatially, they circle again and again through human experience, outside time, to help us understand our fundamental responsibilities to each other. Engaging memory and history as a form of social ethics is essential to rethinking the role of social justice in education.

Cassandra: Memory as Myth

The valedictorian of her graduating class, Addams began her commencement speech invoking the memory of Cassandra. In Greek mythology, Cassandra (she who entangles men) is the daughter of King Priam of Troy. Her beauty inspires Apollo to give her the gift of prophecy or "prescience." However, because she rebukes Apollo's love, he places a curse on her so that no one will ever believe her predictions. Although Cassandra foretells the Greek victory over Troy and the destruction of her father's city, she is mocked by her father's warriors. Unable to forestall this tragedy, she goes mad. "This," claims Addams in her speech, "was the tragic fate of Cassandra—always to be in the right, and always to be disbelieved and rejected" (Addams 1881/2002, 10). We might interpret her invoking of Cassandra as the arrogance of youth— Addams has gotten it right, and the world has gotten it wrong. But while Addams was clearly self-confident and ambitious, her goal is not to chastise Cassandra for her failure but to remember that failure is inevitable when we limit our understandings of the complex and contradictory ways in which we come to know.

Addams is determined to avoid the fate of Cassandra, and her speech skillfully analyzes how women of the nineteenth century can be taken seriously as shapers of culture. Her focus is on Cassandra's profound "knowledge": "Three thousand years ago this Trojan woman represented pure intuition, powerful and God-given in itself but failing to accomplish." This was not a valorization of intuition or essentializing of women's way of knowing. While the gendered nature of the myth is significant, myth is not meant to be taken literally. In effect, myths "tell us how to be human, and their powers lie in the fact that they can be used to address matters of meaning in ways that logic and reason cannot" (Davis 2004, 27). For Jane Addams, the myth of Cassandra is a warning of the tragic consequences when we are not radically open to the other and the human condition we share.

According to Brown (2004), the appeal of this myth was its explanatory power for women of her own era. "Women . . . were, mistakenly, being ignored because the modern age was so dazzled by the 'power and magnificence' of scientific knowledge that it treated intuitive knowledge with contempt" (92). For Addams it was time to convert this "wasted force" to the highest use through the scientific and scholarly training of women. Only then, Addams insisted, would women achieve what Cassandra had not gained, "what the ancients called *auethoritas,* the right of the speaker to make themselves heard, and prove to the world that an intuition is a force in the universe" (Addams 1881/2002, 11).

As her audience listened, they were likely quite comfortable with Addams's claims about the value of intuition. The notion that women are endowed with intuition was widely accepted and central to the "cult of domesticity." Interestingly, she blames neither men nor women for not being heard. As Brown (2004) suggests, she threaded the needle of her brief argument very carefully: "If she went too far in one direction, her speech would be just another sentimental paean to intuitive femininity; if she went too far in the other direction, it would be a diatribe against male supremacy; neither position was a comfortable one for the mediating Jane Addams" (93). Seeking a middle ground that would not alienate, her claim was that women lacked an education, not that they had "failed to make themselves intelligible." It is not personal failure but a societal one that has restricted women.

Having made the claim for more women's education, Addams comes to her final point. When the force of intuition is recognized, women must bring this force to bear throughout morals and justice. While the essay might be understood as a cry for individual self-recognition and voice, the cautionary tale of Cassandra is one of interdependence. Addams writes: "Actual Justice must be established in the world by trained intelligence, by broadened sympathies toward the individual man and woman who crosses one's path, only an intuitive mind has a grasp comprehensive enough to embrace the opposing facts and forces" (Addams 1881/2002, 12). Knowledge, whether physical or intuitive, is to be engaged for the purposes of broadening one's sympathies. This requires the ability to embrace opposing facts and forces—in other words, to understand the complex and contradictory nature of experience. For Addams, science and intuition are two sides of the same coin. Both are necessary to understand the human condition.

At the cusp of young adulthood, Addams is ready to enter the whole of history. She ends her commencement speech with the following injunction:

> The opening of the ages has long been waiting for this type of womanhood. The Egyptians called her Neith; the Hebrews, Sophia, or Wisdom; the Greeks, Athene; the Romans, Justicia, holding in her hands the scale pans of the world; the Germans called her Wise-woman, who was not all knowing, but had a power deeper and more primordial than knowledge. Now is the time for a

faint realization of this type, with her faculties clear and acute, from the study
of science, and with her hand upon the magnetic chain of humanity. Then the
story of Cassandra will be forgotten, which now constantly meets and stirs us
with its proud pathos. (Addams 1881/2002, 12)

Drawing on the memory of women in the past to understand her own predicament as a young woman, Addams acknowledges that to have a voice and
to be heard requires not only the ability to employ a rhetoric of mediation
but also "memory"—in Addams's words, a "hand upon the magnetic chain of
humanity." As an educator, I am reminded of the important role of honoring
myth and memory, as well as history, in understanding teaching as a form
of social ethics. Not only can students benefit from "remembering" stories
of the past to understand their own experience, but drawing on and honoring students' memories is critical to helping them situate their own lived
experience within a larger social context. Drawing on students' memories
can also promote an ethics of listening, as well as an appreciation for the
role of vulnerability that is essential to understanding the human condition.

A Modern Lear: Remembering Conflict

In 1894, thirty-four year old Jane Addams had already distinguished herself
as a public figure. It would prove to be a year that would test her abilities as
well as provide her greatest challenge in articulating her pragmatist philosophy of social ethics. This challenge would come in the form of the Pullman
strike. Already deeply involved in labor issues, Hull-House was at the center
of responding to this crisis. Addams's skills as a negotiator were already well
established, and she was called on to mediate between the railway-car workers
and their employer, George Pullman. She failed, unable to bring both sides to
a mutual understanding. This failure haunted her and provided the opportunity to clarify her own ideas with regard to the nature of conflict, specifically
class struggle and how vast differences could be negotiated. Once again she
would draw on myth, memory, and history to "suspend" space and time as
a means for understanding human relations. Drawing on Shakespeare's *King
Lear*, Addams's "A Modern Lear" warns the reader that tragedy is inevitable if
we forget our connectedness and interdependence. Madness and chaos will
be the inevitable consequence if we shun a social ethics for an ethics based
in individual morality.

The Panic of 1893, the most severe economic crisis in the nation's history,
brought 40 percent unemployment in Chicago. By April 1894, the families
living in the Pullman company town were struggling to pay rent, and some
were starving. Forty-five minutes from downtown Chicago, the Pullman

town, erected in 1881, was called by a London reporter the "most perfect city in the world" (Miller 1996, 25). Built after the labor strikes of the 1870s, known as the Great Uprising, this company town was applauded by many as the solution to "labor." This assertion was now being tested. In light of the depression, the company stood firm—they could not pay higher wages—though they continued to pay stockholders the same dividends as before the depression. After failed attempts to negotiate, the workers went on strike. Arbitration broke down when Pullman refused to make any concessions and would not even meet with Addams. The strikers, under the leadership of Eugene Debs, called for a national boycott of the Pullman cars; it was to be the largest coordinated work stoppage in the nation's history. Unrest in Chicago grew, and federal troops were called in. The settlement workers at Hull-House were confronted with desperate poverty, homelessness, and eventually "madness" as workers failed to bear the shame of appearing as paupers. Hull-House came under severe attack for its support of the workers, and Jane Addams was personally criticized for betraying her class.

By the end of the year, Addams lamented, "I longed for the comfort of a definite social creed that could explain the social chaos" (Addams 1910, 187). She immersed herself in a range of theoretical explanations, from the liberal, laissez-faire argument that promoted patience and thriftiness, to Christian socialism as articulated by Richard T. Ely's *Socialism and Social Reform* (1894), which favored "soft" socialism, to Marxian socialism. She had read Karl Marx's *Capital* several times and was engaged often with the Hull-House resident Florence Kelley, who had translated Friedrich Engels's *The Condition of the Working Class in England*. Surrounded by many German and Russian Jewish working-class socialists, Addams engaged in endless conversations as to the causes of poverty. However, she was suspicious of any totalizing social theory. In the case of Marxist-socialist thought, she critiqued the theory of class conflict as solidifying a monolithic, static view of class that oversimplified and obscured differences among the working poor and the middle/upper classes.[2] Marxism denied the possibility of cross-class consciousness and the possibility that anyone could go beyond his or her own class perspective and understand another's point of view (Knight 2005).

When the strike ended, the questions remained: Are class antagonisms inevitable? Is antagonism useful? What are the obligations of employers and employees to each other? Who had been disloyal? Who had been betrayed? What are the moral responsibilities of each to the other? Both sides had held grudges; both were rigid in their positions. Addams turned again to history and memory. She began "A Modern Lear" by reflecting, "It sometimes seems as if the shocking experiences of that summer, the barbaric instinct to kill, roused on both sides, the sharp division of class lines, with the resultant distrust and bitterness, can only be endured if we learn from it all a great ethical lesson" (Addams 1912/2002, 163).

This lesson came in her analysis of the familial claim of fatherly indulgence by both George Pullman and Shakespeare's King Lear. She wrote: "[W]ithout pushing the analogy too hard may we not compare the indulgent relation of this employer to his town to the relation which existed between Lear and Cordelia? He fostered his employees for many years, gave them sanitary houses and beautiful parks, but in their extreme need, when they were struggling with the most difficult question which the times could present to them . . . he lost his touch" (Addams 1912/2002, 169). Like Lear, Pullman suffers the indignation that his paternal benevolence is not appreciated. Pullman could not perceive himself as in the wrong or grow beyond his controlling habits, which saw the workers' independence as a "personal slight." Unable to understand why their children reject their generosity, Lear and Pullman become angry and lose the "affectionate intelligibility" necessary for understanding the "child's point of view." By comparing Pullman to Lear, Addams not only makes clear the connection between the tyranny of domestic and industrial paternalism, she argues that social disorders are the result of continued allegiance to personal ethics, when social ethics is needed.

While Addams spends three quarters of "A Modern Lear" critiquing Pullman (the primary reason the article didn't get published until 1912), in the last pages she turns her attention to Cordelia and the workers. She reflects: "In reading the tragedy of King Lear, Cordelia does not escape our censure. Her first words are cold and we are shocked by her lack of tenderness. Why should she ignore her father's need for indulgence, and be so unwilling to give him what he so obviously craved?" (Addams 1912/2002, 173). Likewise, Addams maintains that Cordelia, like the workers, "failed to include her father in the scope of her salvation and selfishly took it for herself alone, so workingmen in the dawn of the vision are inclined to claim for themselves, putting out of their thoughts the old relationship" (174). She continues, "[I]t seems to us a narrow conception that would break thus abruptly with the past, and would assume that her father had no part in her new life. We want to remind her that 'pity, memory and faithfulness are natural ties'" (173). Ultimately, the tragedy of the Pullman strike was one of the inability to forgive. Holding on to an *absolute* moral position, neither side had the capacity to take in the other's pain and make it their own. Addams's social ethics rejected absolute theories of right or wrong. In other words, no particular moral value is universal; for example, goodness is not an intrinsic property. It must become good or valuable through a process of shared experience—of vulnerability (Seigfried 2002, xxii). Absolute positions ultimately result in conflict.

For King Lear, relying on his individualistic ethic of women's subordination, Cordelia does not fulfill her moral obligation to obey. Cordelia, however, is fulfilling what she understands as her larger social duty. Addams writes in "A Modern Lear" that "this older tragedy implied a mal-adjustment between individuals. . . . This modern tragedy in its inception is a mal-adjustment between two large bodies of men . . . it deals not with personal relationships, but with industrial relationships" (Addams 1912/2002, 165). Drawing on this domestic tragedy, Addams uses the familial claim to illustrate the consequences of Lear ignoring the "common ancestry" of Cordelia and himself. Workers and employers had to be full economic and social partners. While she was critical of Pullman, she also cautioned labor against the capitalist focus of material wealth as the sole measure of social value. And according to Brown (2004), she urged her union and socialist friends to abandon the "heroic romance of class conflict, just as men like Pullman had to abandon the heroic romance of philanthropy" (291). Social ethics requires that all members of a community recognize their interconnections. Addams urged that we need to see the individual in relation to the family, and the family in relation to society, according to a code of ethics that deals "with these larger relationships, instead of a code designed to apply so exclusively to relationships obtaining only between individuals" (Seigfried 1996, 232).

Social ethics was based in cooperation, not conflict. For Jane, conflict, including the Marxist notion of class struggle, impeded sympathetic knowledge. Shortly after Dewey moved to Chicago in 1894, he and Addams discussed the role of conflict in social progress. Dewey argued that "antagonism was necessary . . . to growth . . . and a requisite step toward the reconciliation of opposites" (Brown 2004, 203). For Addams, opposites were merely "unity in its growth." Antagonism was only misunderstanding, a tension in the progress toward a common outcome. Addams wrote that antagonism was always unnecessary; "it never arose from real objective differences, but from personal reactions" (Menand 2001, 313). Later, Dewey wrote to his wife, "I can see that I have always been interpreting the dialectic the wrong end up, the unity as the reconciliation of opposites, instead of the opposites as the unity in its growth" (qtd. in Menand 2001, 313). Addams was convinced that antagonism always "functioned to block movement toward unity, conferring personal belligerence with a philosophical legitimacy that served no common end" (Pinar 2009, 73).

For Addams, the Pullman conflict represented a collision of an old set of values based on individualism and paternalism with a new set of values based on mutuality and cooperation. This "industrial tragedy" represented a rupture in the cultural system. In the end, she makes clear that the individual virtues that enabled Lear or Pullman to succeed are no longer suitable. "Being good to people in a paternalistic way is not the same as trying to understand them" (Elshtain 2002, 112). One year after the strike, Addams made a speech to charity workers in New York in which she declared, "[T]here is nothing so dangerous as being good to people." Do not be "good to people" but be "good with people." Pullman, like Lear, had confused paternalism with generosity; they had "used kindness to acquire power, not to redistribute it" (Brown 2004, 1).

Addams's analysis of the Pullman strike is an example of how she understood social ethics as well as how she illuminates experience through memory. By bringing Lear and Pullman into conversation, she moves not only back in history but also across space to make connections that illuminate the web of human relations. Her brilliant analysis of two seemingly unrelated figures draws on memory to highlight the need for a radical shift from an individual to a social ethic. This social ethic must be grounded in an understanding of social change not as the result of conflict, but as a process of growth through interaction. This growth requires openness, humility, and listening. To approach all human beings (parents, students, administrators, and policy makers) with the disposition of "being good with people" requires that we attend to others as if they were experts in their own lives. And, if mistakes have been made, they require forgiveness. This is in stark contrast to the deeply authoritarian and punitive educational system that is the current reality (Pinar 2012). For Addams, social change is a cooperative endeavor in which she applies "sympathetic knowledge by refusing to pass judgment and listening carefully" (Hamington 2009, 57). Without forgiveness, there is madness. We need only remember King Lear.

"The Devil Baby": Memory as Transmuting the Past

Imagine Jane Addams sitting quietly in the parlor of Hull-House, reading the morning *Tribune* and collecting her thoughts for the day, when suddenly three neighborhood women burst through the front door demanding to see the "Devil Baby." The elderly Italian women began fervently searching behind curtains, couches, and under desks for the baby "with his cloven hoofs, pointed ears and diminutive tail" (Addams 1916/2002, 7). This "sighting" was the beginning of a stream of thousands of women and men (some from as far away as Milwaukee) who in the spring of 1916 came to Hull-House, day and night, over a period of six weeks in search of the mythical Devil Baby.

In the Italian version of the Devil Baby story, the key protagonists are a "pious Italian girl" and her atheist husband: "[T]he husband in a rage had torn a holy picture from the bedroom wall saying that he would quite as soon have a devil in the house as such a thing, whereupon the devil incarnated himself in her coming child. As soon as the Devil Baby was born, he ran about the table shaking his finger in deep reproach at his father, who finally caught him and, in fear and trembling, brought him to Hull House" (Addams 1916/2002, 8). In the Jewish version of the story, a "father of six daughters had said before the birth of a seventh child that he would rather have a devil in the family than another girl, where upon the 'Devil Baby' promptly appeared" (8).

The fascination with the Devil Baby brought to Hull-House not only immigrant peasant women but also "persons of every degree of prosperity and education, even physicians and trained nurses, who assured Addams that they were there only out of scientific interest" (Addams 1916/2002, 8). Soon there were lines out the door. People even offered to pay admission, and when they were turned away they became angry. Addams first tried to ignore the commotion about the Devil Baby. Yet, when she heard the voices of old women gathered in the foyer, she could not help but pay attention. She recalled, "I was irresistibly interested and left anything I might be doing in order to listen to them. As I came down the stairs, long before I could hear what they were saying, implicit in their solemn and portentous voices came the admonition: 'Wilt though reject the past / Big with deep warnings?' It was a very serious and genuine matter with the old women, this story so ancient and yet so contemporaneous" (9). According to Addams, the story had aroused an active force in human nature "which does not take orders, but insists only upon giving them" (10). It did not take long for Addams to realize that despite the mythical or irrational nature of the story, or perhaps because of it, she needed to pay attention to and take seriously the old women's fervor in believing it. As Marilyn Fischer (2010) suggests, "Addams interpreted the devil baby tales, not as evidence of superstitions held by ignorant, backward folks, but as a form of moral instruction that had evolved and been refined through a long historical development" (83). The Devil Baby story became the catalyst for Addams's book *The Long Road of Woman's Memory* (1916), in which memory becomes the basis for philosophical reflection and socially transformative action.[3]

Addams begins by invoking the Mother of the Muses, Mnemosyne, the personification of memory in Greek mythology: "Memory, that memory who is the Mother of the Muses, having done her work upon them . . . it was the Muses again at their old tricks—the very mother of them this time—thrusting their ghostly fingers into the delicate fabric of human experience to the extreme end of life" (Addams 1916/2002, 3). Memory was at work in the Devil Baby story, bringing the past into the present, and the present to the past: this ancient tale had thrust itself into the present. As the elderly women came to Hull-House, day in and day out, she invited them to sit for tea and became spellbound by the stories she heard. Through listening sympathetically, she began to understand the power of this narrative in women's lives. She wrote:

> It stirred their minds and memories as with a magic touch, it loosened their tongues and revealed the inner life and thoughts of those who are so often inarticulate. They were accustomed to sit at home and to hear the younger members of the family speak of affairs quite outside their own experiences, sometimes in a language they did not understand. . . . The Devil Baby story evidently put into their hands the sort of material with which they were accustomed to deal. They had long used such tales in their unremitting efforts at family discipline, ever since they had first frightened their children into awed silence by tales of bugaboo men. (Addams 1916/2002, 10)

According to Elshtain (2002), "[T]he Devil Baby story was a kind of triumph, as it showed that tales and metaphors were alive and well as a form of moral instruction and social control" (178). Not only did this story give evidence of the survival of folklore, but it revealed to Addams that to be "cut off from such telling and listening kills the spirit" (Elshtain 2002, 179).

The hundreds of immigrant women who came to Hull-House looking for the Devil Baby had lived long, tragic lives filled with poverty, pain, abuse, and disappointment. It pained Addams to see the profound disappointment in their eyes when they were told that there was no Devil Baby. It was a revelation for her to realize that for these women the past had more significance than the present, and myth had more power than fact. As Addams suggests, what means did women have in ancient times save the "charm of word?": "The vivid interest of so many old women in the story of the Devil Baby may have been an unconscious, although powerful testimony that tragic experiences gradually become dressed in such trappings in order that their spent agony may prove of some use to a world which learns at the hardest; and that the strivings and sufferings of men and women long since dead, their emotions no longer connected with flesh and blood, are thus transmuted into legendary wisdom" (Addams 1916/2002, 15). One of the functions of memory is to "transmute" the tragic experiences of lives lived in extreme hardship into something of value. Not only did this tale function to reward women's virtue, but as their Americanized daughters and granddaughters listened to the story and understood its value, the alienation between the generations was lessened. For Addams, wisdom consists in understanding that no myth that consoled earlier generations can lose all significance for later generations.

In seeing how the power of memory reconciled human relationships and revealed new understandings, Addams's pragmatist thought was enriched. She recalled: "My mind was opened to the fact that new knowledge derived from concrete experience is continually being made available for the guidance of human life; that humble women are still establishing rules of conduct as best they may" (Addams 1916/2002, 19). By seeing beyond the "ignorance and gullibility" of these women, Addams pays attention to some of the most marginalized members of society, taking seriously their lived experience (Fischer 2010). In a patriarchal culture in which women's experiences were distorted or denied, Addams extended pragmatic thought to the most disenfranchised by valuing their stories. Among the pragmatists, only Addams concretely demonstrates what ordinary women have contributed to human understanding and how they did so. She draws attention to this transgressive aim by expressing her surprise that it is working-class women in the harshest, most monotonous, industrial circumstances who have used their memories to successfully integrate individual experiences with broader, more impersonal insights (Seigfried 2002, xxv). Addams comes to the realization of the sifting and reconciling power inherent in memory itself.

Addams takes seriously what the lives of ordinary women have contributed to human understanding and how they did so. While pragmatists like Dewey focused on everyday experience as a site of knowing, experience in and of itself was not enough. For Dewey, experience only becomes meaningful when it is reflected upon in relation to more formal theories of inquiry. For Addams, the "power inherent in memory itself is the catalyst for transformation. Memory is not mere recall, but a new, constituting act of consciousness" (Seigfried 2002, xxx).

This understanding of memory was in contrast to Dewey, who explained in a discussion of memory that "students of the primitive history of mankind tell of the enormous part played by animal tales, myths and cults" (Seigfried 2002, xviii). Dewey (1920) distinguishes between past ways of life and modern civilization by maintaining that "the primitive life of memory is one of fancy and imagination, rather than of accurate recollection" (81). For Dewey, memory, unless abstracted and then juxtaposed against the complexity of life, is not knowledge. For Addams, memory does not serve a utilitarian goal. Her understanding is not disembodied but active and dynamic; memory serves to transform and challenge social conventions and bring about social change.

For Addams, the Devil Baby story is not sheer reminiscence but an act of reflecting on experience and learning from it. Because this event created such perplexity and did not fit into any rational explanation, Addams was prompted to new modes of thought, through which she began to understand how these women use their memories to explain their beliefs, values, and actions. These stories are not merely "objects" to be analyzed by the sociologist, or events to be "witnessed," but the context for reflective analysis in a dialogic process of engagement between two persons. Memory is not passive but a dynamic factor "in making sense of often painful experiences and radically changing one's own core beliefs in the process" (Seigfried 2002, xiv). Transgressing notions of the individual, Addams recognized the role of memory in a dynamic educational process whereby two persons engaged in dialogue emerge from the process of listening forever changed in their understandings. Memory is thus not only an act of reminiscing but of active engagement in meaning making.

The story of the Devil Baby resulted in a renewed appreciation for the knowledge of elderly, immigrant women acting as a mechanism of social control. Legends, folktales, myths, and superstitions are not reflections of a primitive past, mere stories, but are themselves experience. Ultimately we are transformed through our interactions and experiences with others. But unlike mainstream pragmatists, Addams redefines the concept of experience as memory. According to Seigfried (2002), Addams believed that "experience eventually is nothing but memory" (xx). While the epistemological implications of this are profound (especially in the field of social studies), the pedagogical imperative that we attend to memory as experience is just as profound. This requires a radical shift in our pedagogical understandings. Educators need not only begin with students' experiences (traditional progressive pedagogy) but with their memories and stories. This requires the deep listening and sympathetic understanding that are critical to the reciprocity and growth necessary for social change. It is difficult to imagine a curriculum that calls for individual and collective memory as lived through story, folktale, myth, and legend as the heart of social transformation. Like the difficulty of accepting the Devil Baby, though, I believe that this is what Addams is calling us to consider.

Memory as Social Change: Disturbing Conventions

Cassandra, King Lear, and the Devil Baby—each of these narratives draws on the rhetoric of memory to fold history back into space. Unlike time, space has no point of transcendence and thus defies total revelation. Putting history back in space, enfolding it, brings it to life. Consequently, Addams is able to make more complex issues of knowledge, ethics, memory, social change, and history and their interrelationships. Memory is thus not mere nostalgia or sentimental reminiscence but an interpretative, political, and creative process of becoming. For the early Greeks, as Addams reminds us through Cassandra, memory was not a means to situate events within a temporal framework but a way to understand the whole process of becoming. History, as a function of time, loses the poetic, the imaginative, and the power to evoke. History was not read by the ancients as "sequences of events that were linked causally, but as manifestations of timeless realities that were expressed as repetitions and themes" (Davis 2004, 29). Repeating, going back over and over again, in and through time and space, not only establishes connections but is central to resisting the logic of identification or representation. Memory as repetition, as recursion, as reflexivity is both the doing and undoing of representation. Thus conceived, memory becomes a site for "disturbing conventions." For Addams, memory as experience is a network of interconnections that provides ruptures and unexpected conjunctures. In essence, any past experience would offer a point of advantage from which to get at a problem presented in a new experience.

Experience (or memory) is a web of relationships, or social ethics, that defies the logic of time as linear, of knowledge as representation, and of social change as predicated on the resolution of conflict. Clearly, these premises defy dominant individualistic perceptions of education as rational, knowledge as a commodity, and change as inevitable progress. Memory, as Addams suggests, requires a pedagogy that attunes us to education as listening to the other, knowledge as memory, and social change as a web of human relations based in humility and forgiveness. This pedagogy of memory is central to understanding our humanity and can provide the foundation for a democratic education.

Notes

1. Brown (2004) elaborates on scholarly interpretations that configure Addams's choice of career over marriage as a sign of maladjustment requiring explanation (11). Rather than acknowledge her same-sex attachments to Ellen Starr Gates and Mary Rozet Smith, biographers have chosen to cast her instead as lacking any personal life. This has contributed to an image of her as impersonal and impenetrable.

2. In the end, it was her abiding faith in the working classes and her rejection of the concept of "false consciousness" that resulted in her rejection of Marxism. The idea that members of the working class were ignorant of their oppression and its causes reinforced an image of the working classes as disempowered and thus ultimately reproduced the very hierarchies that Addams was contesting.

3. Dewey (1920) does note that moment-to-moment lived experience is too taken up with the task at hand to be fully conscious and human. "Only later do the details compose into a story and fuse into a whole of meaning" (81).

Works Cited

Addams, Jane (1881/2002). "Cassandra." In *The Jane Addams Reader*. Ed. Jean Bethke Elshtain. New York: Basic Books. 10–13.

———(1910). *Twenty Years at Hull-House*. New York: McMillan.

———(1912/2002). "A Modern Lear." In *The Jane Addams Reader*. Ed. Jean Bethke Elshtain. New York: Basic Books. 163–76.

———(1916/2002). *The Long Road of Woman's Memory*. Introduction by Charlene Haddock Seigfried. Urbana: University of Illinois Press.

Baker, Bernadette M. (2001). *In Perpetual Motion: Theories of Power, Educational History, and the Child*. New York: Peter Lang.

Brown, Victoria Bissell (2004). *The Education of Jane Addams*. Philadelphia: University of Pennsylvania Press.

Davis, Brent (2004). *Inventions of Teaching: A Genealogy*. Mahwah, N.J.: Lawrence Erlbaum.

Deegan, Mary Jo (1990). *Jane Addams and the Men of the Chicago School, 1892–1918*. New Brunswick, N.J.: Transaction.

Dewey, John (1920). *Reconstruction in Philosophy*. Boston: Beacon Press.

Elshtain, Jean Bethke (2002). *Jane Addams and the Dream of American Democracy*. New York: Basic Books.

Ely, Richard T. (1874). *Socialism and Social Reform*. New York: T. Y. Crowell & Co.

Fischer, Marilyn (2010). "Trojan Women and Devil Baby Tales: Addams on Domestic Violence." In *Feminist Interpretations of Jane Addams*. Ed. Maurice Hamington. University Park: Pennsylvania State University Press. 81–106.

Fischer, Marilyn, Carol Nackenoff, and Wendy Chmielewski (2009). Introduction to *Jane Addams and the Practice of Democracy*, ed. Marilyn Fischer, Carol Nackenoff, and Wendy Chmielewski. Urbana: University of Illinois Press. 1–20.

Hamington, Maurice (2009). *The Social Philosophy of Jane Addams*. Urbana: University of Illinois Press.

———, ed. (2010). *Feminist Interpretations of Jane Addams*. University Park: Pennsylvania State University Press.

Hendry, Petra (2011). *Engendering Curriculum History*. New York: Routledge Press.

Knight, Louise W. (2005). *Citizen: Jane Addams and the Struggle for Democracy*. Chicago: University of Chicago Press.

Lissak, Rivka Shpak (1989). *Pluralism and Progressives: Hull House and the New Immigrants, 1890–1919*. Chicago: University of Chicago Press.

Menand, Louis (2001). *The Metaphysical Club*. New York: Farrar, Straus, and Giroux.

Miller, Donald L. (1996). *City of the Century: The Epic of Chicago and the Making of America*. New York: Touchstone.

Mills, C. Wright (1964). *Sociology and Pragmatism: The Higher Learning in America*. New York: Paine-Whitman.

Munro, Petra (1999). "'Widening the Circle': Jane Addams, Gender, and the Re/Definition of Democracy." In *"Bending the Future to Their Will": Civic Women, Social Education, and Democracy.* Ed. Margaret Smith Crocco and O. L. Davis Jr. Boulder, Colo.: Rowman and Littlefield. 73–91.

Pinar, William F. (2009). *The Worldliness of a Cosmopolitan Education: Passionate Lives in Public Service.* New York: Routledge.

—— (2012). *What Is Curriculum Theory?* New York: Routledge.

Seigfried, Charlene Haddock (1996). *Pragmatism and Feminism: Reweaving the Social Fabric.* Chicago: University of Chicago Press.

—— (2002). Introduction to *The Long Road of Woman's Memory,* by Jane Addams. Urbana: University of Illinois Press. ix–xxxiv.

Winfield, Ann Gibson (2007). *Eugenics and Education in America: Institutionalized Racism and the Implications of History, Ideology, and Memory.* New York: Peter Lang.

4 Jane Addams

Citizen Writers and a "Wider Justice"

LANETTE GRATE

> As the years progress, what women and men will discover is that
> the most lasting and rewarding educational experiences come
> not from specific information provided in classroom lectures
> or assigned textbooks, but from the values obtained in active
> engagement in meaningful issues. We achieve for ourselves only as
> we appreciate the problems and concerns of others—and only as
> we see our own lives as part of a much greater social purpose.
> —Manning Marable

College graduates are routinely promised that during their lifetime they will earn one million dollars more than their non-degreed peers. The idea that a college education translates into economic prosperity is widespread, so much so that individual financial benefit rather than service to society has become for many the main goal of a higher education. When writing my dissertation on Jane Addams, I became increasingly convinced that spending endless hours researching and writing about her ideas without putting them into practice was antithetical to her pragmatic philosophy that modeled an active, participatory, transactional mode of experiential education capable of producing educated citizens concerned with the welfare of others, especially the less fortunate members of society.

Jane Addams often found herself questioning the values and expectations of the dominant culture. While a seminary student at Rockford Female Seminary, she withstood the containment strategies of an authoritative religious discourse system bent on relegating her and all other women to a private domestic space. She resisted by enlarging and extending the restrictive rhetoric. For example, in her Junior Exhibition speech, "Bread Givers," Addams expanded the traditional role of women in domestic labor to include the "direct labor" of educated women in the public sphere. At the seminary Addams also substituted her own educational theory, learning for the love of learning, for an inferior one: learning for reward or grades. In the process of resisting the seminary's proscribed values, she came to a better understanding of Matthew Arnold's theory that conduct is more important than culture. She reflects in *Twenty Years at Hull-House* that "[t]his is what we were all doing [in college], lumbering our minds with literature that only served to cloud the really vital situation spread before our eyes" (51). In other words, she believed that active civic participation that addresses real problems in society should be the objective of higher education. In an April 1881 editorial for the *Rockford Seminary Magazine,* she quotes Thomas Carlyle: "'For the end of man is an action and not a thought, were that of the noblest'" (Editorial 116).

The more I studied Addams, the more intrigued I became with her, not only as a person, but also with her theories of education as participatory civic action. In her view, educators have a duty to "free the powers of each man and connect him with the rest of life" (*Democracy and Social Ethics* 80). Adams believed that students could be taught not only to observe critically but also, more importantly, to apply what they observed by active involvement in "a really living world" (*Twenty Years at Hull-House* 46). In fact, not delaying civic involvement to some future date that never arrives (how often do you hear people say that they plan to join the Peace Corps when they retire?) but using the college years to become involved in the greater good *now* Addams saw as the real purpose of education.

In "Claim on the College Woman," Addams identifies two types of cultivated persons. One is the scholar who spends his or her life immersed in and becoming an expert in his or her field, attaining more and more knowledge. The other type emerges from study and desires to apply what he or she has learned in the real world. Addams says, "Emerson and Lowell both have insisted that the scholar ought to be willing to turn away from his investigations for a time and apply truths to current events. They were dissatisfied because scholars did so little for the cause of abolition and yet they were themselves engaged in the work" (60). In other words, scholars might lecture, publish books, and make money as experts discussing important issues such as abolition, all the while remaining safely removed from active involvement in ending slavery. Peter Kropotkin, a Russian anarchist and communitarian whose picture hung on the wall of Jane Addams's Hull-House office along with Lincoln's and Tolstoy's, wrote, "[H]ow cowardly are the educated men who hesitate to put their education, their knowledge, their energy at the service of those who are so much in need of that education and that energy" (Kropotkin 278).

An educated person, Addams says, "must teach the child to act . . . and to live out the larger ideas for which the world has always hoped" ("Claim on the College Woman" 62). An educated person must set aside scholastic egoism and self-aggrandizement and begin "to think of his neighbor's good" because "[t]he quickest way to save a man or a community is to get him interested in the affairs of others" (61). The educated person, she urges, must reach out beyond the circle of family and self to care for the less fortunate in society. We must change our ideas about greatness, she says. The great man is not the refined, cultured, educated scholar who knows the most in his field, nor the successful, rich college graduate earning a six-figure income in a corporation; rather, Jane Addams insists, the great man is one who can "serve the cause of all" and help those in need (60). Conduct, Jane Addams believes, trumps culture.

As a writing instructor, I am aware of the influence of academic rhetoric instruction on the shaping of young lives. According to James Berlin, "When we teach students to write, we are teaching more than an instrumental skill. We are teaching a mode of conduct, a way of responding to experience" (86). Berlin continues: "The way we teach writing behavior, whether we will it or not, causes reverberations in all features of a student's private and social behavior. . . . [R]egardless of one's approach to writing instruction, it is impossible to deny that in teaching students about the way they ought to use language we are teaching them something about how to conduct their lives" (92). In other words, if the emphasis in teaching writing is on using language to win an argument and defeat an opponent, then we are teaching a competitive way to engage others. This aggressive rhetoric can be seen, for example, in partisan political debates that lead to gridlock. If the emphasis in writing instruction is on dialogue and sympathetic understanding of another's point of view, then we are teaching an alternative way to engage with others that might lead to cooperatively solving problems such as inequality and injustice, issues that continue to plague modern society. The first method might make an individual competing in the new corporate economy rich; the second would make all of us and our society richer.

When I began teaching first-year composition classes, I required students in my academic research and writing classes to analyze and critique important societal issues, but their writing never went beyond a superficial weighing in on the usual subjects like abortion and the death penalty—subjects they chose simply to satisfy requirements for a grade. Then, while writing my dissertation and learning more about Addams's ideas on experiential, participatory learning, I began to consider this question: how could I give my students the opportunity to use their writing not only to examine societal injustice but also to work together to initiate reform? I wondered if I could, as Elizabeth Ervin suggests in her discussion of activist discourse, "reimagine rhetorical situation from a more activist perspective, and, simultaneously, . . . reimagine activism from a more rhetorical perspective" (317). I decided to experiment in my academic research and writing classes with these ideas to see if I could change the rhetorical situation in my classroom and teach writing in such a way as to encourage the development of citizen writers.

First, to change the rhetorical situation meant changing the way I teach. At the outset, I decided not to give reading assignments and lectures *about* Jane Addams, in the same way that I don't give reading assignments and lectures *about* composition. We learn to write academic prose by writing, so I assumed we would become citizen writers by applying the same theory. But I wasn't just going to ask my students to do this while I graded their efforts. I decided to emulate Addams by becoming a citizen writer/educator myself and participate *with* my students in a communal investigation and response to a social-justice issue. Becoming an active participant with my students would mean extra hours of work for myself. I couldn't use my syllabus from semesters past, which focused on a lengthy argumentative academic research paper. I would be putting together the syllabus as we went, allowing new ideas and new developments to detour or even derail class plans. I have a tendency, like many teachers, to be a tad obsessive—could I let go of the control of my classes and let their interest and enthusiasm be the guiding force in the directions we took? What if the students were resistant? What if I was asking too much of them with their busy schedules and lives? And, then, there were the inevitable *so what* questions—questions I usually applied to measure the relevancy of their writing I now had to apply to my own practice. So what if each semester eighty students encountered an activist educator in their first-year writing class? So what if this activist educator encouraged her handful of students to develop sympathetic understanding by not only writing about but also getting involved in a social-reform issue? Would it really change anything? And would I be able to teach composition in such a way that not only exposed the need for social reform but also motivated my students and myself to work constructively to create it?

I read the literature of naysayers like Stanley Fish, who warn that civic education is not the role of the college instructor. Moreover, Fish believes that civic responsibility that includes a concern for social justice cannot be taught by a college curriculum (C5). Fish says, "[D]emocratic values and academic values are not the same and . . . the confusion of the two can easily damage the quality of education" (C5). According to Fish, my role is to teach my students how to become competent academic writers—not competent citizen writers. But if encouraging and creating opportunities for civic participation is not my role, then whose role is it? How would my students learn that societal change begins with the individual working cooperatively with other concerned individuals, if I didn't provide an opportunity for them to experience it? The following quote has been attributed to Peter Kropotkin: "Think about the kind of world you want to live and work in. What do you need to build that world? Demand that your teachers teach you that" (qtd. in Lappe 154). It was the best answer I could find to Stanley Fish's objections.

Before proceeding further, however, I needed to know more about how Addams envisioned putting her theories about education into practice. While Addams supported basic education, she was greatly concerned that an American education lacked social relevance due to compartmentalization, which separated what was happening in school from what was happening in real life. She states, "The isolation of the school from life—its failure to make life of more interest, and show its larger aspects—the mere equipping of the children with the tools of reading and writing, without giving them an absolute interest concerning which they wish to read and write, certainly tends to defeat the very purpose of education" ("Foreign-Born Children" 112). While Addams is referring here to students in the primary grades, this "isolation of the school from life" is a complaint voiced by many college students who are passive recipients of their instructors' knowledge. On the contrary, Addams believes that knowledge is not delivered from teacher to student, but, rather, knowledge is discovered or created together. The philosopher Charlene Haddock Seigfried explains: "Knowledge does not exist like apples on a tree that can be picked by anyone with a ladder, but emerges in situations in which sympathetic understanding opens the way for cooperative undertakings" (42). Addams clearly advocates an active, collaborative pursuit of knowledge based on real-life experiences. And, from engagement in these real-life experiences, the "absolute interest," which she says gives meaning to education, arises. The Addams scholar Maurice Hamington notes of Addams, "In her view, a pluralistic democracy relies on an informed citizenry—informed not only in propositional knowledge (this or that fact), but informed about the entanglements of one another's lives" (162–63). Specifically, this entanglement could be encouraged by what Addams calls "education by the current event," or using a controversial news story to generate group discussion that could lead to public action. Citing examples such as the Scopes trial, the Labor party's ascension in England, and turbulent racial relations, she says:

> The newly moralized issue, almost as if by accident, suddenly takes fire and sets whole communities in a blaze, lighting up human relationships and public duty with new meaning. The event suddenly transforms abstract social idealism into

violent political demands, entangling itself with the widest human aspiration.
... At such a moment, it seemed possible to educate the entire community by
a wonderful unification of effort and if the community had been able to command open discussion and a full expression of honest opinion the educational
opportunity would have been incomparable. (*Second Twenty Years* 381)

According to Hamington, Addams's current-events pedagogy "foreshadowed
modern problem-based learning" (157).

In setting up the course, I weighed the advantages and disadvantages of
letting the students choose their own social-justice issue from a current
"controversial news story." Individual papers on different issues seemed to
defeat the purpose of collaborative effort of which Addams is such a strong
proponent: "There is no affection and no friendship so complete as that which
develops when two people merge their energies in a common cause" ("Address" 140). I decided it would be better if we worked together as a group on
one issue with the idea that the students could then transfer and apply what
they learned to other issues once the semester was over. I chose the issue of
wrongful conviction because I was familiar with the work of the Innocence
Project. Also, wrongful conviction is an issue that Jane Addams addresses
in her work. According to the Innocence Project, a nonprofit organization
that works to free innocent people unjustly incarcerated in U.S. prisons, 297
wrongfully convicted people have been exonerated using new advancements
in post-conviction DNA testing. Those exonerated include seventeen who
served time on death row. The disproportionate majority of those wrongfully convicted are minorities and/or from lower income brackets ("Facts on
Post-Conviction DNA Exonerations"). Experts believe that wrongful conviction may be the new civil-rights issue of this century. The issue of wrongful
conviction concerned Jane Addams as well. In *The Second Twenty Years at
Hull-House,* Addams writes, "[T]he love of justice which exists in the heart
of man is the distinguishing mark of his humanity," and it is "the supreme
obligation of each generation to find the means by which it may be purified
and still further increased" (304). Addams devoted much of her time and
effort to bring about what she terms a "wider justice" (305). One chapter
in *The Second Twenty Years at Hull-House* is entitled "Efforts to Humanize
Justice." Addams says, "Of all our spiritual efforts, it [justice] is the one that
we should watch with the greatest care and anxiety, with the most passionate
eagerness and solicitude" (305). In her discussion, she analyzes the 1927 murder trial of Sacco and Vanzetti, which she calls an "acid test" for instituting
a "wider justice" (333). She views the Sacco and Vanzetti convictions, as well
as the Dreyfus Affair in France, as similar instances of trying people not on
facts or evidence but on the basis of racial and cultural stereotypes. Addams

says, "[P]eople all over the world were to be aroused because they believed men were being tried on their religious, political or racial affiliations, which they instinctively realized has been the historic basis of intolerance" (334). In both the Dreyfus and the Sacco and Vanzetti cases, concerned citizens rose up and challenged the courts. "Apparently," Addams says, "such cases occur from time to time and take shape in men's minds as an epitome of the problem of justice itself" (334–35). The "possibility of error," she writes, is a secondary concern in cases such as these once the community is set on enacting a severe punishment.

In other words, Addams accurately notes the communal psychology at work: what the community expiates is its own fear—whether or not the real perpetrators are found is secondary to the all-encompassing need to mete out the punishment—and the wrongfully convicted serve as communal scape-goats. She had no doubt that Sacco and Vanzetti, though innocent, would be executed. People sent petitions to the governor of Massachusetts from all over the world, but they did no good because, as Addams says, "the officials in Massachusetts had grown confused between justice and the machinery of the law" (338). She believes that challenging this type of injustice and setting up a "wider" type of justice is of primary importance in order to establish "a universal type of just dealing which alone is stable and secure" (339).

Intrigued with Addams's insights about wrongful conviction as a failure of a democratic ideal tied up with historical intolerance of cultural others, collective societal delusion, and a misuse of language, I thought that the issue of wrongful conviction, the "epitome of the problem of justice itself," might be one that would interest my students, motivate them to research and write, and allow for a transactional learning experience with the real world. But how could I get the issue of wrongful conviction to "take fire," as Addams describes in her advocacy of "education by the current event"? My students would probably not thrill to researching and writing about the ancient history of the Dreyfus Affair or the Sacco and Vanzetti case. I needed a current example—one with which they could identify and empathize. After a little research, I located one in our home state.

In May 1993 in West Memphis, Arkansas, three eight-year-old boys were brutally murdered. The victims were found naked, hog-tied, and submerged in a creek in a wooded area off Interstate 40 just across the Mississippi River from Memphis, Tennessee. The little boys often played in the woods near their homes after school. The terrified community and the insistent media pressured the police to solve the crime. Rumors flew, and the reward grew. One Saturday in June, a mentally challenged teen voluntarily went to the West Memphis police department to repeat some of the rumors he had heard with the hope of getting the reward money. Twelve hours later, the teen, who had an IQ of seventy-two, had implicated himself and two other boys. The mentally handicapped youth immediately recanted his confession, but that night all three teens were arrested and charged with the murders.

Despite immediately assuring the community that the case was solved, the police had neither physical evidence that corroborated the confession nor any physical evidence that linked the teens to the victims or to the crime scene. Neither could the police establish any motive. With no evidence and no motive, Police Chief Gary Gitchell went before the public and assured the community that on a scale of one to ten, his confidence in the guilt of the three arrested registered at an "eleven." The West Memphis police department discovered that one of the accused teens had an esoteric knowledge of Wicca gleaned from books he had purchased at a public-library book sale. Going against the advice of FBI criminal profiler John Douglas,[1] who told the West Memphis detectives that there has never been a single documented case of Satanic-ritual murder and to lead with their scientific evidence, the police, having no evidence, declared Satanism to be the motive for the murders. The media picked up the idea, inflaming collective societal delusions. No one pointed out that Wicca and Satanism have no connection or that both may not have been accurately described by the press or by police. The accusation of Satanism, never substantiated, seemingly sealed the doom for all three—the other two were considered Satanists by association.

In the spring of 1994, a jury convicted the oldest teen on three counts of capital murder and sentenced him to die by lethal injection. His two younger codefendants were both dispatched to life in the state penitentiary. Damien Echols, Jason Baldwin, and Jessie Misskelley, known nationally and internationally now as the West Memphis Three, were convicted as Dreyfus and Sacco and Vanzetti, and countless unfortunate other citizens, were—on an unpopular affiliation, which Addams says is "the historic basis of intolerance" (*Second Twenty Years at Hull-House* 334). The modern case, which mirrors the pattern of other historic cases of wrongful conviction, raises serious questions about the implications of allowing testimony based on stereotypes to form the basis of judicial decisions. The case also shows how institutional structures of authority (the criminal justice system) confer legitimacy on such stereotypes in an effort to appease the public rather than actually dispense justice.

The West Memphis case is a complex and intriguing case from a scholarly perspective that crosses many academic disciplines including sociology, psychology, political science, criminal justice, journalism, religious studies, and composition. The West Memphis Three can be viewed as Addams did the Sacco and Vanzetti case, as an "acid test" to illustrate the "epitome of the problem of justice." How could a jury convict someone without evidence? What if the only evidence the state produced against the three defendants was the false accusation that they were practicing an unpopular religion? What if the juvenile who confessed, implicating himself and the two other boys, was mentally handicapped with an IQ of seventy-two? What if he was coerced by the police? What if the police lied to him and told him that he failed a polygraph when he actually passed? What if he was interrogated for over twelve hours with no parent or attorney present, and only forty-six minutes of the interrogation was taped? What if all three of the defendants were poor, and their families had no money to retain adequate counsel?

I devoted the first part of the semester to studying and researching the case with my students. At the beginning of the semester, students viewed Joe Berlinger's and Bruce Sinofsky's award-winning documentary about the case, *Paradise Lost: The Child Murders at Robin Hood Hills* (1996). Next, I asked students to pretend that they were on the jury in 1994, to review the case, and then render a verdict with evidence to substantiate their decision. The students researched and studied online police reports, the trial transcripts, and original newspaper and television-news accounts of the murders, arrests, and trials. They also conducted primary research by interviewing people involved in the case, such as public officials and journalists, their own parents, and other citizens who lived in the state at the time of the crime and the trials. During the primary research stage and in an effort to find repeating patterns, the students also studied other wrongful-conviction cases from Salem to the present. In class discussion, students analyzed the specific causes of these wrongful convictions, seeking commonalities with the West Memphis case. The overt correlations between the historical cases and the West Memphis case engaged the students' prior assumptions about authority and the criminal-justice system. Their thinking about justice became destabilized; they began to question their own prejudices and tendencies to stereotype; they learned the difference between hearsay testimony and scientific evidence. And they became more aware of how language can be manipulated by those with power. During this information-gathering and sharing phase, the facts of the particular case we chose to study stimulated their curiosity and led to intense research, discussion, and debate.

I then asked the students to research and write a paper in some way related to the issue of wrongful conviction and this case. Since the case involved citizens of our state, the students had access to numerous primary research opportunities. For example, one student was granted an interview with the lead prosecutor, John Fogleman. Another interviewed one of the lead detectives, Mike Allen. One student interviewed her mother, an attorney, who worked for the defense team. Several students researched newspaper archives and television news reports about the case from 1993–94, writing a paper about cultural stereotyping and media bias. Other students compared the West Memphis case to historical cases such as the Salem witch trials or the 1983 McMartin Day Care case.[2] Some researched juvenile coerced confessions after listening to the forty-six minute taped confession of seventeen-year-old Jessie Misskelley. One student researched the trial transcripts of the case and then wrote a paper about logical fallacies committed by Fogleman in his closing arguments. After sifting through the timeline of events the night of the murders and reading police reports of other possible suspects, several students wrote papers that advanced theories of whom they thought actually committed the murders. Once written, the papers were continuously revised through numerous peer revisions and instructor conferences. At the end of the semester, all students were required to turn in a writing portfolio with twenty pages of polished writing and revision drafts.

In the second half of the semester, besides researching, writing, and revising their research papers, students also brainstormed ways to make their voices heard beyond our classroom in regard to wrongful conviction and the West Memphis Three case. They designed and distributed flyers, brochures, and posters and manned tables at the student center to obtain signatures for petitions to be presented to the governor. They participated in letter-writing campaigns to the governor and attorney general. They started a West Memphis Three Facebook group. As we brainstormed ways to take the message of wrongful conviction to a wider audience, one student volunteered that she had a family connection to one of the original defense attorneys from the 1994 trial, Dan Stidham. The student contacted Mr. Stidham and invited him to speak to the classes. As we worked on the logistics of the visit, another student suggested that we make it a campus-wide presentation. Then, another suggested that we send out a national invitation on the WM3.org Web site. The classes worked together to organize the presentation. They scouted out auditoriums on campus and reserved one for the presentation; they designed, printed, and posted flyers; they advertised on Facebook; they contacted Little Rock television stations and newspapers to let them know about the event; they set up the sound system and computer hookup in the auditorium prior to the presentation.

On the night of the presentation, a large crowd gathered in Doyne Auditorium on the University of Central Arkansas campus in Conway. The audience consisted of students from Arkansas and the surrounding states of Missouri, Texas, and Tennessee. These out-of-state students, who were also studying or writing about the case in their college classes, had seen our advertisement on the WM3.org Web site. Other notables in the audience included the investigative journalist Mara Leveritt;[3] Damien Echols's wife, Lorri Davis; and three activists from Los Angeles, Burk Sauls, Grove Pashley, and Lisa Francher,[4] who were in Arkansas visiting the three convicted men. A Little Rock television crew arrived. Dan Stidham, Jessie Misskelley's defense attorney, spoke for over three hours about the case. Near the end of his presentation, Stidham introduced the Los Angeles activists and invited them to join him on the stage, where they took questions and comments from the audience.

Student response to meeting these activists, models of citizen civic empowerment, confirms the importance of providing students with positive community role models. In end-of-semester reflection papers, one student said, "I was star struck." Another wrote, "The coolest part of the semester was the fact that we got to actually meet the main people in support of this case at the Dan Stidham lecture. That lecture was freaking awesome and I will never forget that moment for the rest of my life." As for myself, the "coolest" part of the semester was that although they wouldn't realize it until later, my students had become activists themselves that night by organizing the presentation and speaking out against the wrongful conviction of innocent citizens in our state.

How do students feel after completing such a course? One student wrote:

College Writing II has been the most productive class with which I've ever been involved. We studied stereotypes and biases . . . and the infamous West Memphis Three case. I learned so much about that case that I feel I am an expert in my own right. . . . I've written a letter to the governor. I've written songs about it. I've rented movies and checked out books about it. I've also learned so much about other topics as well as through my research . . . and consequently, my writing has improved. The writing process never really meant much to me. I never put much thought into anything I wrote, because I was only doing it for a grade. I told the instructor what he or she wanted to hear and nothing more. This class has compelled me to go out and do my own independent research, something I would have never done before. . . . I can pick apart logical fallacies as if they were nothing. Since attending this class, I have joined UCA's debate team, because I think I have the reasoning skills to help out and have a good time while learning. The workshop style of our class was extremely beneficial, and got everyone involved in a way that I had never experienced. I've never had a problem voicing my opinions in front of a class, but also never really had the opportunity to do so on a regular basis. I have learned to never accept what is given to you. I'm asking questions and thinking for myself. . . . I have enjoyed this class more than any other in my first full year of college, and have learned invaluable lessons.

Another stated:

> The West Memphis Three case was the thing in the class that I liked the most
> . . . it is an Arkansas case and a lot of people in Arkansas don't even know about
> the case, which is sad. The West Memphis Three case . . . is still very much
> alive and I feel that I can be a big part [in] setting them free if it comes down
> to a clemency appeal or not. I also know that the day they are set free will be
> the day that I'm in Grady, Arkansas, watching at last Damien come out of the
> penitentiary. I know it will happen too, and I thank you for giving me the chance
> to support these men in their journey to freedom. All in all I enjoyed my time
> in this class and would not have wanted to take any other writing course unless
> they studied the West Memphis Three case in-depth like we did.

Another student wrote:

> I have to say, at first I was a little confused as to why the entire semester was
> dedicated to some strange murder mystery that I had never even heard of. I
> now see that our papers, unlike meaningless fiction you write in other classes,
> actually made a difference. Our interest sparked interest in others and now
> I really feel like you and all your students are, and will hopefully continue
> to make a positive difference in the community. I know I am a better writer
> for having taken this course. I learned how to cite properly, and I was able to
> practice my writing a lot over the course of all the drafts I made. I like the fact
> that you made us keep revising our papers over and over, because I feel like that
> is probably the best way to get the most out of your topic. I also learned how
> powerful and useful writing can be. I respect the fact that you gave the effort
> to create a curriculum that wasn't limited solely to the classroom. Our papers
> had a purpose and truly had an impact on many different people. I think we
> did a great job of creating awareness for a great cause.

Some students reflected about my involvement with the class. One wrote,
"This has been the first year that a writing teacher of mine has got themselves
[*sic*] involved with the class." Another added, "Most professors take every
minute that we are in their class and jam information into our heads. It is
different in this class." And a basic writing student said:

> I loved the class. It wasn't no [*sic*] stupid class where the teacher assigned you a
> lot of work that don't make any sense. I really did learn a lot in this class. And
> I would like to thank you for teaching us about the West Memphis Three case
> because the case is a very important case. In most classes you wouldn't learn
> about what really happens but we did in here. I hope the boys finally get a fair
> trial someday and the world knows what really happened.

Analyzing the instructor-evaluation comments written by my students at
the end of each semester indicated that the overwhelming response to the

class was enthusiastic and positive. Several students voiced a desire to move on to explore and get involved in other social-justice issues in addition to wrongful conviction during the semester. For example, one student wrote, "Change it up a bit more on to a different case or issue besides the WM3." And, "I would rather write about more of a variety of issues."

After completing the course, many students appeared to be more sensitive about the power of writing to influence public opinion. At the end of the semester, one student wrote, "Throughout this semester, I finally began to grasp the concept that opinions, injustices and society's misconceptions can be affected by the written word. This has helped me to see the point in learning how to express myself with pen and ink instead of just verbally. To think that I could influence someone with my writing is a sobering thought and it occurs to me that authors must take certain responsibilities for their words." Students who completed the class also reported sharpened critical thinking skills: "I learned to look at problems, situations, basically everything from more than one standpoint, just in case something makes more sense once it's looked at in a different light."

After learning about wrongful convictions in their first-year academic research and writing classes, many students wanted to continue to pursue the issue of wrongful conviction and work to overturn the convictions of the West Memphis Three. To further this aim, I created a student panel, the UCA Demand Justice Student Panel, and invited former students to join. Bridging the classroom and the community, the all-volunteer panel conducted open-forum public discussions to raise awareness about wrongful conviction. I chose a panel approach because it is a form of collaborative, nonviolent direct action that creates constructive tension by inviting dialogue and discussion. The panel experience promotes individualized, interactive, and interdisciplinary learning while allowing students to research, write, and present information in public settings. The UCA Demand Justice Student Panel is offered here as a model—the focus of a student panel could just as easily be bullying, homelessness, hunger, addiction, violence, crime, health care, or environmental sustainability.

The UCA Demand Justice Student Panel offered an organized and thoughtful opportunity to discuss a case that stirred intense local and national interest by offering presentations on campus for classes, clubs, and groups. The panel received a three-thousand-dollar UCA Foundation grant to support its work. Besides conducting open-forum discussions, student panelists also researched legislation for creating an Innocence Commission in Arkansas and participated in rallies in the state to raise awareness about wrongful conviction. Students on the panel organized a protest rally called Steps toward

Justice[5] at the Little Rock State Capitol. They invited professional and student speakers, as well as musicians, and arranged an open-microphone session at the end of the program. Students in my composition classes helped with and attended the rally. In an end-of-semester reflection paper, one student wrote: "My favorite part of the semester was . . . the WM3 rally at the State Capitol in Little Rock. . . . Knowing that there are other people in Arkansas that want to help with this case and that we all came together to do it is like a scene in my head that I can't shake out."

In 2011 the Arkansas State Supreme Court granted a new hearing to determine if the West Memphis Three should be given a new trial after post-conviction DNA evidence testing showed no link to the convicted men. Faced with a weak case, the prosecution offered an Alford plea,[6] and the three convicted men were released on the condition that they not sue the state. On August 19, 2011, after eighteen years in prison, Damien Echols, Jason Baldwin, and Jessie Misskelley were freed. Echols is the first Arkansan to ever walk off death row. The release of the West Memphis Three successfully completed one goal that engaged my composition students for many years. However, since Echols, Baldwin, and Misskelley were not officially pardoned, and since they were not given any monetary compensation by the state of Arkansas, there is still work to be done on this particular injustice. My students and I have now shifted our attention, research, and writing to advocating for a full pardon for these men with compensation for time served. Another angle we continue to research is the establishment of an Innocence Commission in our state to prevent future wrongful convictions.

Jane Addams challenged me to reenvision and reorganize the way I teach writing. By working together to address an injustice in our state, my students and I became entangled in the lives of three wrongfully convicted men. This entanglement prompted us to lend our voices and our writing beyond abstract ideals to demand justice in concrete ways. A familiar narrative of higher education is that a successful college graduate will earn a degree that will open the door to a comfortable middle-class lifestyle and a financially rewarding job in the corporate world; or, if you ascribe to the government's version, the successful graduate will be equipped to compete in the global economy. Addams asks us to imagine a larger meaning of the word "success." In her definition, "success" is not so much an individual accomplishment as it is a creative, collective endeavor to address and correct the problems of modern life. Marilyn Fischer, Carol Nackenoff, and Wendy Chmielewski claim that "Addams models for us how to transcend traditional disciplinary boundaries and how to make daily experience, and the human care it requires, central to our theorizing" (3). Maurice Hamington agrees, saying, "Her century-old work at Hull House continues to inspire and provide insight into an alternative approach to education not dependent on traditional concerns about programs and disciplines that mark the politics of academia" (165). Addams's alternative approach is based on genuine concern for others, combined with collaborative efforts to make society a better place for all, the ingredients necessary to create not only a pluralistic, participatory democracy but also citizen writers whose powerful prose and compassionate actions can change our world.

Notes

1. John Douglas spoke at the Legal Defense Team Press Conference on November 1, 2007, at the University of Arkansas at Little Rock Law School.

2. In the McMartin Day Care case, several members of a family who operated a preschool in California were charged with sexually abusing children under their care. The initial accusations, investigations, and arrests occurred between 1983 and 1987. The trial ran from 1987 to 1990. No one was ever convicted, and all of the charges were dropped in 1990.

3. Mara Leveritt, an award-winning investigative journalist, wrote *Devil's Knot: The True Story of the West Memphis Three,* a detailed account of the case. A movie based on Leveritt's book was released in 2013.

4. Burk Sauls, Grove Pashley, Lisa Francher, and Kathy Bakken of Los Angeles created WM3.org, a Web site that provides information about the West Memphis Three case.

5. See Leveritt, "Arkansas University Students Demand 'Steps toward Justice'"; and the following video clips of the April 20, 2007, rally: "Friend of the Devil," April 28, 2007, accessed January 29, 2014, http://www.youtube.com/watch?v=7OLSeuepggw; "Legalization," April 28, 2007, accessed January 29, 2014, http://www.youtube.com/watch?v=IFrZ_D62Rw4; and "Ozark Mountain Plateau," April 28, 2007, accessed January 29, 2014, http://www.youtube.com/watch?v=iufKWTQq9lM.

6. An Alford plea is a plea bargain that allowed the men to maintain their innocence while at the same time acknowledging that the state might have had evidence to convict them in a new trial. It appears to have been a way for the state to avoid being sued for wrongful conviction.

Works Cited

Addams, Jane. "Address." National Council of Women Voters. St. Louis. November 13, 1919. Typed ms. 6. *Jane Addams Papers Project,* ed. Mary Lynn McCree Bryan. Microfilming Corporation of American and University Microfilms International, 1984–85. 48: 138–49.

———. "Bread Givers." In *The Jane Addams Reader.* Ed. Jean Bethke Elshtain. New York: Basic Books, 2002. 8–9.

———. "Claim on the College Woman." *Rockford Collegian* 23.6 (June 1895): 59–63.

———. *Democracy and Social Ethics.* Urbana: University of Illinois Press, 2002.

———. Editorial. *Rockford Seminary Magazine* 9 (April 1881): 113–16.

———. Editorial. *Rockford Seminary Magazine* 9 (May 1881): 151–55.

———. "Foreign-Born Children in the Primary Grades." National Education Association's *Journal of Proceedings and Addresses* 36 (1897): 104–12.

———. *Newer Ideals of Peace: The Moral Substitutes for War.* Ed. Paul Dennis Sporer. New York: Anza, 2005.

———. *Twenty Years at Hull-House.* New York: Penguin Books, 1998.

———. *The Second Twenty Years at Hull-House.* New York: Macmillan, 1930.

Berlin, James. *Writing Instruction in Nineteenth-Century American Colleges.* Carbondale: Southern Illinois University Press, 1984.

Bryan, Mary Lynn McCree, ed. *The Jane Addams Papers Project.* Microfilming Corporation of American and University Microfilms International, 1984–85, 82 reels. Waldo Library, Western Michigan University, Kalamazoo.

Douglas, John. "Legal Defense Team Press Conference." University of Arkansas at Little Rock Law School. November 1, 2007. Accessed March 9, 2014, https://www.youtube.com/watch?v=3DezJoSUFgc.

Ervin, Elizabeth. "Rhetorical Situations and the Straits of Inappropriateness: Teaching Feminist Activism." *Rhetoric Review* 25.3 (2006): 316–33.

"Facts on Post-Conviction DNA Exonerations." *The Innocence Project* Fact Sheet. Innocence Project, July 27, 2012.

Fischer, Marilyn, Carol Nackenoff, and Wendy Chmielewski, eds. Introduction to *Jane Addams and the Practice of Democracy.* Urbana: University of Illinois Press, 2009. 1–18.

Fish, Stanley. "Aim Low: Confusing Democratic Values with Academic Ones Can Easily Damage the Quality of Education." *Chronicle of Higher Education* 49.36 (May 16, 2003): C5.

Hamington, Maurice. *The Social Philosophy of Jane Addams.* Urbana: University of Illinois Press, 2009.

Kropotkin, Peter. *Memoirs of a Revolutionist.* London: Smith, Elder, 1899.

Lappe, Frances Moore. "Asking the Right Questions: Education as Dialogue on Social Values." In *Rethinking the Curriculum: Toward an Integrated, Interdisciplinary College Education.* Ed. Mary E. Clark and Sandra A. Wawrytko. New York: Greenwood Press, 1990. 151–63.

Leveritt, Mara. "Arkansas University Students Demand 'Steps toward Justice.'" Mara leveritt.com, April 3, 2007. Accessed January 29, 2014, http://maraleveritt.com/2007/04/arkansas-university-students-demand-steps-toward-justice/.

———. *Devil's Knot: The True Story of the West Memphis Three.* New York: Atria Books, 2002.

Seigfried, Charlene Haddock. "The Courage of One's Convictions or the Conviction of One's Courage? Jane Addams's Principled Compromises." In *Jane Addams and the Practice of Democracy.* Ed. Marilyn Fischer, Carol Nackenoff, and Wendy Chmielewski. Urbana: University of Illinois Press, 2009. 40–62.

5 Student Stories and Jane Addams

Unfolding Reciprocity in an English Classroom

BETH STEFFEN

The teenagers who have bounced, slouched, fidgeted, slept, doodled, sulked, laughed, cried, or just sat in the circled desks in classrooms where I've taught—whether in southern Wisconsin's small city, Beloit, or in Madison's La Follette High School—are white, African American, Asian, African, Latino, Native American, mixed with blended ethnicities, male, and female. Many have had part-time jobs; some have been homeless. Some have been parents; a number have been parentless. Many have been athletes; a few have been wheelchair-bound. Some have been drug addicts, while others have never tasted alcohol. Some have been spoken-word poets and celebrated singers; others have been deaf. Some have been academically brilliant, bound for division-one colleges with full scholarships; others have landed in prison. All have been literate, but how their literacy has been expressed is as rich and varied as the students themselves. After seventeen years as a high-school English teacher, shifting rooms and buildings, I have lived among students and their stories intensely; the worlds students inhabit touch each other's and mine in ways I cannot discern in a linear, tidy analysis.

A new semester begins. Eighty-three students comprise my two sections of English 12 and one of English 11. Within three days, reading a couple of journal entries from each child, I learn that six mourn deceased fathers and one a deceased mother, that several use casual sex to assert their identities, that dozens ache for the attention of absent, negligent, or too-busy parents, that another seeks a compatible lover, though homosexuality's stigmas constrict his open searching. One's ventilator motor, running the machine that keeps him alive, rattles the classroom space. A couple boldly insist that they hate the girl or boy sitting in the next seat and are distracted from learning by loathing rooted in some long-past encounter. Among the twenty or so students with disabilities are several so skittish about writing "wrong" that their pencils stutter across their notebooks, yielding tentative phrases rather than fluent paragraphs. In one section are eight immigrants: two from Mexico, one from Kosovo, one from India, one from Honduras, one from Latvia, and two Hmong refugees from Thailand. Forging distinctive communities of mutual respect and understanding from the divergent perspectives and disparate needs of these eighty-three students is the task at hand this new semester, as it is every semester when fresh bodies, stories, and needs arrive again. Finding energy, sustaining stamina, and keeping my focus on the pieces of their lives that students share is a work in progress. Jane Addams's writings, from another century and another city, offer sometimes wise, often practical, and always humane perspectives.

In Chicago's Nineteenth Ward, beginning in 1889 until her death in 1935, Addams's evolving quest was to help her neighbors to help themselves. Her texts are comprised of story after story about the people with whom she lived and worked at Hull-House, the settlement she cofounded. She met immigrant children ashamed of their parents' old-country styles and customs. She met working mothers reeling from sweatshop shifts that compelled absence from sick children. She met strained grandparents, bewildered by the new country's lax values. Addams shared others' narratives to present the complexity of human circumstance, morality, and the interplay of conflicting ethical systems that can claim equal validity and are therefore harder to disentangle. Even as she supported creating efficient systems to manage her neighbors' urgent and varying needs, Addams cautioned against losing individuals amid "scientific" (that is, empirically measurable and inflexible) "methods."

She wrote in *Twenty Years at Hull-House* of a man who came for aid to a relief committee on which she served during the terrible depression of the early 1890s. Following her "carefully received instructions" from the Bureau of Organized Charities with which she was affiliated, Addams gently but firmly told the man to get a job before asking for help and informed him of a canal-digging position when he said he was suited for indoor work and could find none. After she sent him away, he worked for two days on the canal and died a week later of pneumonia. Addams wrote, "I have never lost trace of the two little children he left behind him, although I cannot see them without a bitter consciousness that it was at their expense I learned that life cannot be administered by definite rules and regulations; that wisdom to deal with a man's difficulties comes only through some knowledge of his life and habits as a whole" (108). For Addams and for modern teachers, the complexity of individuals' lives defies streamlined policies and standardized assessments.

Twenty-first-century public schools are under intense governmental and media scrutiny. Test scores are analyzed and interpreted and curriculum streamlined, all in the interest of accountability. In Wisconsin, adolescents' performance on the Wisconsin Knowledge and Concepts Exam (WKCE) and on the ACT are celebrated or bemoaned as indicators of a school's success. Bureaucratic and administrative pressure often dissuades educators from developing student-centered practices and instead emphasizes tidy, measurable instruction geared toward high WKCE and ACT scores. In English/ Language Arts courses, the nuances of individuals' lives and space for learners to construe meaning through innovative thinking are often sacrificed in teacher-monopolized classrooms.

Addams cautioned against lecturers' egos steamrolling over learners: "The habit of research and the desire to say the latest word upon any subject often overcomes the sympathetic understanding of his audience which the lecturer might otherwise develop" (*Twenty Years* 281). Arthur Applebee diagnoses teachers' emphasis on "knowledge out of context," noting that prompts for writing and discussion tend to be "dominated by questions that focus on details of plot and vocabulary that are assumed to have one right answer" (29)—an answer that the teacher possesses. American democracy, as Jane Addams conceived it, is undermined by such narrow conceptions of curriculum and by such rigidly defined learning environments. Addams argued that teachers should prioritize students' experiences and individual "special contributions" as a means to a fully realized democratic society: "We are gradually requiring of the educator that he shall free the powers of each man and connect him with the rest of life. . . . [W]e are impatient to use the dynamic power residing in the mass of men, and demand that the educator free that power" (*Democracy and Social Ethics* 80). For social progress, Addams was convinced that widespread learning and a "subtilty [*sic*] of intercourse" leads to improvement in the human condition (80). In Addams's social philosophy, each individual's recognition of and commitment to valuing human interconnectedness is the critical basis for democracy. For teachers committed to developing students' literate skills, the imperative is to be attuned to students' perspectives and experiences, to set a context where students can connect with each other despite their apparent differences, and to facilitate students' muscle-flexing with reading, writing, and thinking for dynamic audiences and for significant purposes.

Many twenty-first-century educators, including those in my district, are confronted with demographic changes and exploding achievement gaps, yielding pressure to become culturally responsive or culturally relevant— though what that means, exactly, is nebulous. Consultant Sharroky Hollie writes, "If you were to take all the books, research articles, and presentations on culturally relevant teaching and put them in one area, you could probably fill a hotel room from the floor to the ceiling," while the number of materials on "classroom practices for culturally relevant teaching" would fill the bathroom (44). Addams's writings are more richly illustrative of culturally responsive practices than many theoretical tracts.

Addams compiled perspectives, details, and wisdom—from the aged, the working, the adolescent, the lazy, the lost, the criminal, the intellectual, the immigrant, and the craftsman. In her writings, Addams stakes no claim to moral superiority, as she describes endless learning in her textured neighborhood. She fosters connections to enhance learning, and her layered examples model an effective educator's disposition. Placing desks in a classroom circle decenters the instructor, whose seat changes daily. Every voice is equally privileged so that the drone of Charlie Brown's incomprehensible teacher doesn't prevail. Addams describes several students who came to see her and complained about their principal because "'he never talks about life. . . . He never asks us what we are going to be; we can't get a word out of him, excepting lessons and keeping quiet in the halls'" (*Spirit of Youth* 160). Lucid contemporary research indicates that for students to learn, their background knowledge and experiences must be integrated with new learning. In the influential *How People Learn,* John D. Bransford writes that learners "come to formal education with a range of prior knowledge, skills, beliefs, and concepts that significantly influence what they notice about the environment and how they organize and interpret it. This, in turn, affects their abilities to remember, reason, solve problems, and acquire new knowledge" (10). Bransford and his colleagues' findings insist that if teachers do not engage students' background knowledge, students cannot learn.

In the twenty-first century, as in Addams's Chicago, student-centered practices are not only educationally valid, they are critical to keeping students in school. Human beings want to be valued, heard, and recognized in the social spheres where they expend their time and energy. The dropout rate in the United States hovers around 25 percent, even in the 2010s. Parents and grandparents who never found school a helpful path to changing their social and economic realities often permit their children's truancy tickets to pile up, keep children home to help with child care, or send children to work for extra income rather than fight to compel them to attend schools that are viewed dubiously as providing the means to prosperity in a floundering economy. Describing the inability of schools to engage the active minds of the kids in her diverse neighborhood, Addams depicted the challenges of pressing a representative boy to attend school: "His parents are not deeply interested in keeping him in school, and will not hold him there against his inclination. Their experience does not point to the good American tradition that it is the educated man who finally succeeds" (*Democracy and Social Ethics* 83). The work available to Addams's neighbors was not furthered by lecturers' monologues or by compliant students answering teacher-driven questions. The past century has not changed that reality. Many students will not suffer through tedious instruction—in their perspective, there is no payoff to earning a diploma.

A classroom that acknowledges the valid contributions of every member is one where learners thrive, and as students share stories and experiences, they are able to "usefully and intelligently connect" to each other and to have power over the lives they are in process of defining (*Democracy and Social Ethics* 81). There isn't a how-to manual, a recipe, a formula for forging space for learning grounded in respect and intellectual challenge between students and between a teacher and her students, but dynamic, thoughtful classes lead to educated kids.

Reciprocity of understanding in a classroom unfolds incrementally, over time. Many students are self-conscious: about their experiences, about their voices, about their clothes, about their bodies. In a circle, students can't hide. Everyone can be seen, and when one speaks, all are watching. We read aloud, and everyone takes a turn. No one may pass. While reading a paragraph is requested, reading a sentence is fine. If someone doesn't know a word, we talk about the word and don't snicker at a mispronunciation. Students hear their voices out loud. Students gain public courage.

We get into groups with different configurations often. I ask each student to name the others in his or her group. Students roll their eyes at my obtuseness, but student names are known. Anonymity dissolves. Journal entries can be on any topic, though possibilities relevant to a day's issues are suggested. Journals are returned promptly, and my comments are in pencil—nonjudgmental and informal—ranging from "yikes" to "holy smokes" to lengthier interactions with writers' concerns, often, but not always, connected to course literary themes and social issues. Trust emerges. Students write about overbearing bosses, athletic frustrations, parental skirmishes, love-life stumbling blocks, adolescent pranks, violence administered and sustained, and shameful missteps. An always-open invitation to share orally from journals begins to be accepted.

When papers are due, anyone can read aloud for extra credit. I tell students that their pieces contain so much insight and rich experience that for me to be the only reader would be a travesty; because students are shy, extra credit is the incentive to share, but really, I want everyone to benefit from each other's written voices. Students hear bits and pieces of their classmates' lives, deeper connections to literature, and social critiques. Communal ownership of the classroom space develops. I create and share a piece too, not for extra credit, but from the sheer joy of writing. The feedback they receive from a writer, passionate about words, matters to them in ways that critique from a teacher with a red pen seldom could.

On occasional Fridays, a current-events game claims thirty minutes or so of the class's ninety. Students' expertise with popular culture enhances our competition as kids compose questions—at least one per child—about sports, movies, television, music, video games—to supplement mine, which focus on international, national, state, local, and school issues. As the class members giggle about celebrity foibles or hum snippets of top-forty tunes, even the most shy or isolated child finds an area of expertise; the community coalesces a little more. As the days progress, some who never previously watched the news bring up headline issues for discussion. Laughter and teasing creep into spaces where initially awkward silence or insider whispering used to predominate. Two who never spoke before the class see each other at a gas station, and the future Wal-Mart employee gives a consoling hug to the Vassar-bound girl who's shedding a blue day's tears.

The matter-of-fact approach to teaching and learning that we're all in this meaning-making venture together almost always lurches and bumps along. Consistent awareness of the value of a collective, group identity is precarious because of the frequent assertion of individual egos' demands. One of the greatest challenges of teaching is working with students to overcome isolation, judgment, and the defense mechanism of labeling and pinning down those who are different so as to have a tidy understanding that can be controlled and therefore does not threaten. Class, race, gender, and disability are borders between students that defy crossing; as misunderstandings flourish, school as a place for building deeper knowledge of the shared human condition flounders. According to the philosopher Maurice Hamington, "Addams values interactive education as preparing good citizens with sufficient resources to sympathetically understand others. A robust education, then, becomes an imperative of democracy" (152). The sympathetic understanding Hamington recognizes as a central tenet of Addams's social philosophy does not come easily to fruition.

A girl whose journals are full of white supremacy fumes in large, curly writing at the officious pronouncements of her black-history-spouting classmate, one day denouncing him at the top of her lungs with the nastiest of racial slurs, to which he responds with the most foul of sexist slander. A bipolar, emotionally volatile girl says that a fence should be built around the school district's ghetto, and then the buildings there should be torched. The students who live in "the hood" gasp and unleash a torrent of venom. An autistic boy whose grasp of social etiquette is tenuous hears a film's racist character say that minorities are lazy and exclaims, "He's right." Initially shocked, kids from minority backgrounds find every opportunity to verbally taunt the one who stereotyped them. A group of preppy students creates a project unmistakably depicting the class's most idiosyncratic and corpulent boy as Piggy, the bullied outcast from *Lord of the Flies,* pushing him to the brink of tears. Calming the storm that follows such outbursts and small acts of cruelty takes time and lots of deep breathing. Class members take sides; the classroom seethes with undercurrents of dislike and intimidation.

Without what Addams calls "sympathetic knowledge" of each other, literate development is stunted. Rather than ignoring tension between students or sending kids whose behaviors instigate pain and strain to administrators for discipline, I say, "If we can't coexist in a public school, one of the few places in the world where different races and social classes mix daily, how will our American society survive? In this room we have to be able to speak what's on our minds and not cower, afraid to express thoughts, or fester, harboring passive-aggressive resentments." Working through the bitterness to recoup mutual tolerance and then acceptance is a day-by-day enterprise. We reshuffle groups, switch partners, find common ground in a favorite junk food or childhood cartoon, or in the sorrow of a beloved pet's or grandparent's death, or in fury directed toward a literary bully, and slowly we erase each grim feud by re-creating a new dynamic. The classroom community is often stronger after weathering such emotional intensity together, and that strength fosters students' powerful literacy. For many, it's the first time in a public space that they have pushed past superficial tolerance to function with others in a way of being that models interactive democracy.

While we make slow progress, the proliferation of media in the twenty-first century sometimes undermines civility. Celebrity hotheads mouth off, and their verbal flatulence reverberates in school. Talking-head shouting matches predominate on key "news" networks, and students perceive loud dismissals of alternate points of view and securing the last word in argument as successful debate. Public slanders—whether a radio personality labeling collegiate basketball players "nappy-headed hos" or a comedian spewing racial slurs—reveal fissures among students. When common understanding erodes, deep resentments emerge. Chief among the hostilities are African American students' bristling at racist labels and white students' indignation that African Americans can say the N-word among themselves while it's off limits to non–African Americans. As an ardent student of the civil-rights movement and someone who is passionate about the nuances of language and the power words carry, I cringe to hear white kids carry on about the embargo on the N-word for them. Still, I know that many urban, white students are huge consumers of African American music, and hip-hop and rap stars create N-word-laden lyrics to which white kids drive, dance, bump, and grind. Historical perspective is lacking for many white students, who see racism as a throwback to slavery and civil-rights issues as obsolete, in these Barack Obama/Oprah Winfrey/Kanye West–dominated days. When African American students raise their voices and say, "Y'all never got held down being called 'nigger' like we did," white kids get angry. Many are descended from immigrants who weren't in the United States during slavery days, they say, and this "y'all" business assumes that all white people are the same, which of course the white kids resent as much as African American students do when they are denounced because of their skin color.

I turn to stories, proffering the nuance of other people's experiences to enhance students' understanding. Addams said, "Intellectual life requires for its expansion and manifestation the influence and assimilation of the interests and affections of others" (*On Education* 55). Too many white kids don't perceive the insidious prevalence of anti–African American racism, and to help them understand requires more than strident lecturing about sensitivity or cursory minilessons on diversity. A few years ago, I tell them, one of my classes was reading *A Raisin in the Sun* by Lorraine Hansberry. The strongest character, matriarch Lena Younger, is a self-respecting African American woman who thinks that blacks' use of the N-word is demeaning to African Americans as a whole. The first-hour sophomores reading the play were predominantly white, though several Hmong and Latino students were enacting parts. A highly at-risk and mischievous African American boy, Daniel, stormed out of the room, protesting his white classmates saying the N-word as they read Hansberry's scene.

I followed him to the hall and told him he should raise his concern *inside* the classroom so we could discuss the power of language, and I also told him he was a goofball for not knowing that the whole point of the scene he was protesting was how objectionable the N-word is—a point made by an African American writer and expressed by an African American character! Because of his truancy issues, Daniel had been unaware of the scene's context, but he engaged in a prolonged temper tantrum that involved a security guard, his assistant principal, and two other teachers. During the course of Daniel's histrionics, one of the African American staff members who knew him well pointed out that Daniel listened to rap songs blaring the N-word that he also often used to banter with his friends. The more Daniel hollered, the more clearly his outburst revealed delight in creating havoc rather than a principled opposition to a fictional scene in a class about which he could not have cared less. In subsequent years, Daniel made sure his English classes were with me, and I grew to appreciate his sly humor, his intelligence when he was engaged with curriculum, and his perceptive commentary on current events.

That first semester, though, Daniel's rage about white kids reading African American drama led to a conference involving his mother, his grade-level principal, and me. I explained to Daniel's mother what we were reading, and while she hadn't read the play, she exclaimed that she'd seen the movie and that she'd thought it was really good. Daniel's mother went on to share her perspective on the N-word. She said that she works at a nursing home where often the residents whose bedpans she's emptying or whose noses she's wiping call her a "nigger." She said, "I keep telling Daniel he can't get mad at that word. When he goes into the world, he will hear it, and he can't lose his temper about it." Her story was a jolting revelation of the N-word's lingering toxicity. When I retell her story now, white students who have been arguing that the N-word doesn't mean anything anymore sit silently abashed. I tell them of my African American roommate in my freshman year at the University of Wisconsin–Madison who came home from a bus ride across town enraged because an old white man had spat on her and called her a "nigger bitch." She was a tough cookie, my roommate, but she told me that she didn't punch the old man because he looked weak and frail. Her tears were frustrated tears, and feisty kids of all races share her sense of impotence and the blend of anger and decency that held back her furious fist.

Daniel's eruption and the subsequent learning it spawned illustrate the openings that students' and their families' experiences and perspectives can bore into curriculum. As course outlines, syllabi, units, activities, and lesson plans are developed, each teacher's philosophy of why and how he or she is teaching affects his or her instructional choices. In my 1994 methods class at the University of Wisconsin, Professor David Schaafsma shared the observation of an area teacher: "Curriculum is the enemy of true learning." While mandated curriculum cannot be completely ignored, and while my students spend time with the obligatory *1984, Hamlet, Of Mice and Men,* or whatever canonical texts are department-required for a given course, Jane Addams's comment rings true: "We are impatient with the schools which lay all stress on reading and writing, suspecting them to rest upon the assumption that the ordinary experience of life is worth little, and that all knowledge and interest must be brought to the children through the medium of books. Such an assumption fails to give the child any clew [*sic*] to the life about him"

(*Democracy and Social Ethics* 81). As Addams suggests, "the life about" us provides rich material for learning.

No two sections of any course I have taught have ever been the same. Each class has a personality, a set of interests, issues, and concerns that emerge as the time we share unfolds. One class had a high level of arrests; we did a project on teenagers and the law. Another class felt more extremely at risk than they perceived their peers to be; we did a project mentoring younger students about how to survive high school as guided by real students, not by the usually selected panel of successful students whom my students felt were too perfect to speak to them meaningfully. Another class loved eating; they proposed a class feast and compiled essays about their family cooking traditions. True learning occurs when students' minds are working on issues about which they are curious, passionate, interested, and concerned. As we read, write, and talk, we are building skills Applebee enumerates, "to develop a new interpretation, to analyze a new situation, or to muster evidence in support of new arguments and unexpected opinions" (33). The vastly different circumstances of students' lives engender diverse perspectives that are raw material for learning and that promote democracy. Hamington characterizes Addams's "hopeful" belief in democracy's potential, able to "flourish in an educative atmosphere of inquiry and meaningful exchanges" (181). While English curricula typically emphasize the study of literature to promote learning about human experience, ethics, conflict, and the potency of figurative language, ensuring that literary study also encompasses students' lives enables the "meaningful exchanges" that characterize Addams's "sympathetic knowledge."

Socially sensitive issues emerge frequently. Candid dialogue across gender lines can be as elusive as conversation across race, ability, and class boundaries. For example, in class discussion, many boys represent themselves as funny, immune to physical or emotional pain, and adept at wooing any girl. Sincerity flounders in class interchanges, shyly emerging in journals and papers. Movies, popular television programs, and music lyrics encourage male bravado too often. In the summer of 2006, *Time* magazine devoted a cover and a large feature story to adolescent males. The creators of a new study had been shocked to discover that teenaged boys are sensitive, feel their romances deeply, and are not just sex-starved critters on the prowl. Addams describes an encounter at a public dancehall with a young man who asked her to introduce him to a "nice girl" (*Spirit of Youth* 12), and while she perhaps too sternly dismisses the potential of dancehalls as meeting places for "nice" girls, the earnest young man's sincere desire to find someone "nice" resonates. The *Time* article that posited all-encompassing horniness of teenaged boys is irritatingly shallow.

The boys who have populated my English classes are more often than not sensitive and searching, despite the identities they sometimes project. One painfully shy junior wrote in a journal about a girl he thought to be pretty and smart and wondered if he should ask her out, though he acknowledged, "I really have no idea how to go about that." After reading *The Perks of Being a Wallflower,* Stephen Chbosky's epistolary novel about a deeply reflective boy, a witty, class-clownish junior wrote about sharing the protagonist's desire to find an "unconventionally pretty" girl, and he filled his journal with Dave Matthews lyrics that connected with his unconventional beauty ideal. Another boy who was desperately lonely filled his journals with anguished longing to meet someone, as the holidays approached, with whom he could play the piano, bake cookies, and snuggle in front of a fire. That this young man was gay in a high-school climate infused with homophobic rants made his loneliness more extreme. Another young man wrote about his girlfriend and his decision to postpone sex until after high school, feeling that their lives were complicated enough without laying on a whole added layer of confusion.

Male posturing certainly makes the more sensitive side of boys' curiosities, concerns, and desires harder to express. Addams wrote of teenagers' emerging sexuality, which she describes as "groping"—not in a physical sense of fumbling hands on bodies but in an intellectual sense of trying to grasp elusive ideas or impressions: "This period of groping is complicated by the fact that the youth's power for appreciating is far ahead of his ability for expression" (*Spirit of Youth,* 26–27). She perceives that physical and social stimuli confuse kids whose sexuality is a work in progress. In one memorable senior class, a popular, athletic boy named Stan reported his frustration with his mother who had purchased a box of condoms for him to ensure safe sex—yet he was a virgin, and he knew that his mother was cleaning his room and peeking into the condom box to monitor its contents and by extension his sexual practices. A male classmate one day said, "I know I'm a virgin, and so is Stan, but how many other people here are virgins?" The question arose in the midst of a discussion of a short story that included issues of promiscuity, and as seven of the twenty-three kids present extended their hands, the members of that class looked around the room at the raised and lowered hands (two girls in that class were mothers; one delivered her second child during our semester together) and proceeded to have an eighty-minute conversation about sex that defies every study of teen sexual attitudes and experiences I have ever read. Several of the sexually active students told the "virgins" how lucky they were. One girl said that her boyfriend would have sex with her, climax, and leave the room to sleep elsewhere. Another girl, one of the mothers, said that a hot shower was more sexually fulfilling than actual intercourse. A mouthy boy who always postured as a "playa" admitted that he'd had sex with two girls in his life but said that he hadn't wanted to sleep with the second except that she was egging him on with all sorts of erotically suggestive comments. I don't know if the students present in that Beloit classroom in the fall of 1999 remember the essence of their discussion as vividly as I do. Subsequently, when sexual issues have come up in discussion or when kids have written about confusion or concern that their sex lives are warped, abnormal, or out of sync with those of other teenagers, I have invoked the words from that past class of seniors to offer perspective so that the isolation of humans, locked in their own minds, can be eased.

Addams wrote early in *Democracy and Social Ethics* about the importance of awareness of others: "We have learned as common knowledge that much of the insensibility and hardness of the world is due to lack of imagination which prevents a realization of the experiences of other people" (8). Sometimes teenagers' stories reveal self-consciousness, selfishness, and even disturbing tendencies to exploit others for personal gain. Teaching requires an unflinching acceptance of the attitudes and experiences students bring to school, repugnant as sometimes those realities may be. Addams explored the power of popular culture on the "youth" of her acquaintance and worried about the destructive influence of the theater and of dancehalls on young people's creativity and morals. She wrote of "overworked girls" who "stream" down the streets, seeking an outlet from the tedium of their factory days, and who seemed to more stable adults to possess a "self-conscious walk . . . giggling speech" and "preposterous clothing." Addams saw through the veneer of flash put on by these girls filled with longing for glamour: "And yet through the huge hat, with its wilderness of bedraggled feathers, the girl announces to the world that she is here. She demands attention to the fact of her existence" (8). What is troubling, then as now, is the outlet for expression that adolescents, seeking to have power and to be noticed, sometimes grasp.

One of my male students, P.J., described his sexual initiation in middle school, where he asked a girl what she would do to show how much she cared for him. "Anything," she replied. After P.J. had experienced this young woman for himself, he pushed her devotion to unspeakable limits, selling her sexual favors to his friends. She began to go into the bathroom at movie theaters or into changing rooms at the mall to earn the money that my student gladly spent. P.J. was a special-needs student with an IQ of 120 whose bipolar diagnosis led to high doses of medicine that left him frequently woozy. He dictated his papers to me, and I typed them. His cavalier narration of "pimping" sickened me because I imagined the young lady who was turning tricks to prove how much P.J. meant to her would have a very different version of events than the one he blithely shared.

During the course of the year that P.J. was in my class, I spent a considerable amount of time with his mother and grandmother, strong, articulate women who emphatically advocated for their child's success. "What on earth would your mother and grandmother think of the way you're treating this young woman?" I asked, as he gloatingly continued his tale. "What would you think if the girl were your eight-year-old sister in a few years?" P.J. shrugged and said, "Well, I'm not pimpin' now." He explained that the girl he'd been exploiting stopped turning tricks when she accused a friend of his of rape, and both the accused and P.J., the procurer, had to go to court. In his paper P.J. expressed no remorse or consideration for the girl's perspective. When he read his paper out loud to his classmates, many dropped their jaws, stunned. Students often react to shocking texts very one-dimensionally and dismissively, exclaiming "gross" or "that's sick"; to unfold the impact of intense stories requires the critical thinking that comes from reading against the grain. Students responded to P.J.'s pimp paper by talking about what they would have thought, said, or felt if the girl in his story was their daughter.

Though P.J.'s narrative constructed the girl as a pawn for his profit, when students considered his story from her perspective, the objectification of girls as sex objects that many of P.J.'s female classmates have struggled with came to the fore, and P.J. himself said that if the girl in his story was his daughter he would have "whooped her" for her behavior. The ensuing discussion about sexual morals, parental influence over children's behavior, and double standards in parental expectations for sons and daughters is one that P.J.'s class revisited often, working to disentangle complicated threads of gender identity. Morally grotesque as P.J.'s story was, writing it was his entry point to curriculum, to standards, and to the development of thinking like a writer. His connection, through the writing he shared with his peers, led to reflection and growth, breaking his pattern of interacting only with a few, chosen friends. Addams describes the challenges inherent in engaging kids who have experienced "the streets": "The school has to compete with a great deal from the outside. . . . Nothing is more fascinating than that mysterious 'down town'" (*Democracy and Social Ethics* 84). P.J. and his friends, who were in other sections of English with me, were fascinated with parties, fighting, marijuana, and sex, and school was a bore to them. Becoming an academically viable student, P.J., who'd been expelled from a cross-town high school for violence, read, wrote, and earned high-school credit requisite for graduation.

While P.J.'s paper openly depicted one noxious example of female debasement, what girls put themselves through for acceptance is often disturbingly covert. The destructive lure of glamour for young women is not new. Addams told of a girl who stole some artificial flowers to decorate a hat because "she was afraid of losing the attention of a young man whom she had heard say that 'a girl has to be dressy if she expects to be seen'" (*Spirit of Youth* 80). The fifteen-year-old girl of Addams's anecdote was desperate to go to the theater and compromised her morality by stealing to ensure that she could go again. Addams lamented individuals cheapening themselves to conform to social conventions as shallow and destructive. In the decades that separate Addams's world from ours, young women's attempts to beautify themselves have grown increasingly desperate, and their despair at failing to measure up to glamorous media images sometimes yields alarming practices of self-destruction.

One student's misery had many sources: her father's suicide in prison the previous June, her self-defined obsession with marijuana, her relocation from her small hometown to live with a strict aunt in Madison who was supposed to be preventing her from hurting herself, and most intensely for Sherry, a daily urge to cut. She visited me a few times a week outside of class to talk about her drug use and cutting, and she was also in constant contact with the school social worker and an outside therapist. Sherry explained that she hated her looks and that cutting was the only relief she found from her self-loathing. She is one of many, many students with whom I have worked who take refuge in self-mutilation, but her situation was the most extreme; Sherry spent the two days of finals and the subsequent weeks institutionalized due to depression. After her release from in-patient psychological treatment, she moved back to her hometown several hours away. She came back to say goodbye one bright winter morning and emailed subsequently to describe her class schedule, drug-addiction therapy, and excitement to graduate and to move to a nearby city. Cutting was still a daily activity, though, and ending that bad habit had to be up to Sherry. The adults who work with kids can't fix students' sad lives. We must try to help them to find the means to fix their own.

Just as teachers work with students to learn from literature and from each other to reconfigure the versions of reality they conceive as viable, teachers also learn from students. Addams said, "[N]ew knowledge derived from concrete experience is continually being made available for the guidance of human life" (*Long Road* 19). Perhaps the most difficult issue for people to explore, the issue where guidance is most sorely needed, is the scariest: death. A few years ago a colleague was confronting the first death in his family—a cancer-ridden grandmother was fading through her last days. My colleague said, "I'm like my dad. I don't do death well. It makes me uncomfortable." His perspective is pretty universal. Knowing what to say when death encroaches into one's circle of acquaintance is tricky business. Grief and loss are bewildering, and for observers to wrangle words of comfort often feels trite or hollow. As with all other human issues, death and subsequent struggles to cope affect students at some time or another, and teachers fumble to provide consolation or to help a classroom community function through the baffling pain of loss. In the winter of 1997—February 7, to be exact—Tony, a senior at Beloit Memorial where I was then teaching, went home for lunch and killed himself. His English teacher was my friend, and she came to me with tear-filled eyes to tell me of his passing. Soon the halls echoed screams and moans as students who knew the young man, many who had been with him in classes that very morning, literally tore their hair and writhed in agony. One of my creative-writing students, a shy young woman named Olivia, wrote a piece trying to imagine how Tony's girlfriend might feel:

Sympathy Pains

Hearing about the death of "Tony" made me hurt for all those who were close to him, but especially for his girlfriend. Although I do not know her personally, frightening thoughts of "what if . . ." rattle my bones in sympathy for her. What if my boyfriend made the decision to take his own life? Would I feel guilty? Would I too feel the need to take my own life? What if his smile, his laughter, his love for me were trapped in a "box in the church"? I would reach out to touch him, awaiting his returning touch, but instead of warm, it would be cold and chilling. I would want to kiss him, but his lips would be lifeless. I would stare at him, waiting until I could see his beautiful smile and hear his teasing laughter. Waiting to see his big, brown eyes open up and wink at me. Waiting for his voice. Waiting forever.
In loving memory of "Tony" (1979–1997)

Reading Olivia's piece didn't make much of an impression on me at first. She was sensitive, and the "rattle my bones" line was strong, but the latter part was a bit clichéd, the cloying sentimentality of teenaged love. But a little over a month later, on March 19, Olivia's boyfriend Dwayne and another young man were shot to death in a car in the middle of the night. Beloit is a small city, and while the cliché "everyone knows each other" is not quite accurate, the whole community was rocked by the double homicide.

The day after the murder was our creative writing final meeting, during which students would share from their portfolios, and never for one moment did I expect to see Olivia. She walked in, though, eyes nearly swollen shut, sat down and placed a box of Kleenex and a photograph of Dwayne on her desk. Everyone stared silently at her. She started to sob. I asked her if she wanted to go to the bathroom, and she did. I followed her there and said, "I don't know what you need right now. No one really does. Everyone in that room is sad for you, and no one knows what to say. Do you know what you need? Do you want to go to a counselor?" She said that she didn't know what she needed either, but that she wanted to come to class for a small reprieve from the grief that choked her at home. We went back into the room, and I told the class what we'd said in the bathroom. I asked if anyone had anything they wanted to say to her. One misanthropic boy said, "I'd wish this on a lot of people, but you're not one of them." Olivia faintly smiled. Two girls told her how sorry they were, and we quietly, falteringly went on with class. Several students shared pieces from their portfolios. Then, for the first time that term, on the last day of the course, Olivia asked to read one of her writings aloud. She read the above piece that she'd written after Tony's suicide. What had seemed like corny teenaged love earlier now was eerily, shockingly powerful. A number of students started to cry, and Olivia passed Dwayne's photograph around the room. Her written image of his cold body in a church's box overshadowed the vibrant, smiling young man we all touched as he circulated the room in Olivia's silver frame.

As unspeakably painful as Olivia's ordeal was, her classmates' compassion created a safe context for her to begin to find her voice. That Olivia first shared her writing on the day after her boyfriend's murder is a testament to the dynamic of that classroom of writers. Addams urged that educators "give the child's own experience a social value" and teach a child to "direct his own activities and adjust them to those of other people" (*Democracy and Social Ethics* 81). Learning environments that insist upon mutually created understandings have measurable power for students. Though Olivia's rebound from her boyfriend's murder was a long and complex process (she was with me again the following year in her senior English class, and to suggest that she jumped from pain to Pollyanna in a matter of months would be vacuous and inaccurate), Olivia is now an accomplished businesswoman whose connection to a classroom of learners was one step on her road to success.

Ten years later, in another city, Kub, a Hmong senior beset by grotesque disabilities, found the chance to be part of a community of writers who *really* knew him, to transform his perfunctory completion of reading and writing assignments into rich, analytical literacy that was a springboard for college success. Kub's and his classmates' mutually enriching experiences depict Addams's social philosophy in action. When Kub wrote, shared orally, and published his final piece, "I've Come a Long Way," his writing revealed not only his own evolution from an unconscious child disabled by a freak disease to a bright, engaged survivor, but also provided indirect commentary on his class's development into a close-knit learning community, a group that came a long way.

Kub was familiar to many of his classmates, who had been in school with him for the past couple of years. Raised by polite parents and kind teachers, they were conditioned to be friendly to the "sick" boy and always greeted him with hale courtesy. They'd sunnily say "hi Kub!" and he'd nod, and that was the extent of their interaction. When he walked into class the first day of his senior year, I only knew him from a grim, front-page story in the school newspaper the year before. Kub had been the victim of cruel harassment in a boy's bathroom, where a couple of freshmen hurled wet toilet paper and vicious insults at the defenseless junior. The article focused on Kub's forgiveness of the bullies, and his large and mature spirit were notable.

That first day of school his senior year, he made his slow way into the classroom. Abnormally small and stunted in growth, he appeared to have a hunched back. Walking, he leaned dramatically to one side. His face contorted into a permanent and twisted grimace. He was accompanied by a nurse at virtually all times (he did use the restroom alone). He listed to one side as he walked because he carried machinery with him, and the weight of his load dragged him down. One device was a ventilator sprouting a tube with a mouthpiece into which Kub would discharge saliva periodically throughout the hour so he wouldn't choke to death. The tracheotomy he'd undergone made effective swallowing impossible and also prohibited clear speech. Thus his other machine: a Dynavox into which he would type thoughts or comments. Pushing a button enabled the device to "speak" for him in a robotic man's voice.

Writing first-week journal entries, Kub was minimally engaged in class—he preferred science to English and was present because he had to be, but he was under no illusions that English 12 could be of use or value. He had always found English to be a waste of time—literary study based on books, disconnected from experience, and tedious to endure. Within a few days, though, the first extended writing assignment engaged his critical thinking and reflection. Inspired by Kevin La Plante, a Detroit teacher who was a colleague through a national literacy project called Write for Your Life, I asked students to write letters to their childhood selves, using photographs to anchor their reminiscences. Kub brought a picture of himself as a serious, handsome boy standing erect in a crisp, white shirt. That photograph shattered a misconception: Kub's disabilities were not birth defects. At age twelve, he had fallen from his bike and been infected with Entero Encephalitis, which led to a four-month coma that had savaged his life.

Because the childhood letters come early in the course, they are tools to build trust and community. On the day that letters are due, students are offered the opportunity to share aloud for extra credit. Even before the first letter is shared, each of us shows the whole class our photo and tells the story of the pictured image. We then gingerly pass the photographs around the room, oohing and ahhing at very young versions of ourselves. Because every photo is shared, and every one of us is honored, even for a moment, communal acceptance of and respect for each class member is enacted. Students who have never shared a word of written text before feel empowered to share their writing. Kub was not one of them. With his Dynavox as a speaking assistant, in fact, he found class participation burdensome and cast his eyes down to avoid joining any conversation.

But no one is allowed to skulk or erase him- or herself. As described earlier, we periodically all read aloud, going around the circle, everyone taking at least one sentence, though a paragraph is preferred. When his turn came, Kub would aspirate his sentence, panting as he exhaled the words in a manner that was at first a bit shocking. Those who want to avoid awkwardness squirm when someone is clearly struggling. But a given in our class was accepting each other, limitations and all. Practice with speaking was one of Kub's Individualized Education Plan (IEP) goals, and so, though at first class members were unaccustomed to Kub's labored speech, as time went on, he persevered through his reading turn while we all listened patiently. When we got into groups to crack open themes or discussion issues, Kub tentatively began to participate. No one rolled their eyes or displayed impatience as he pecked out the letters of the words that comprised his thoughts on the Dynavox. His comments were apt, and his intelligence was on public display.

Expanding our exploration of literature's relevance by connecting to current events was a priority. Addams consistently sought ways to find common ground with folks from divergent backgrounds and wrote, "because with the best will in the world it is impossible to get the entire community centered upon any given theme, we gradually discovered that the current event is valuable beyond all other means of education" (*On Education* 223). In Kub's class, contemporary issues were a catalyst for new understandings of the wider world. Every few weeks we'd play the previously described trivia game, which would pit students against each other in teams. Members of the class formed three large groups, each with a spokesperson, to answer questions about international, national, state, local, sports, and entertainment-industry events. When the course started, the majority of the kids did not watch or read the news and were clueless about Middle Eastern battles, political contests, and public policies. After the first time or two, Kub's sophisticated knowledge about contemporary issues led classmates to argue about whose team would include him. As kids half-jokingly/half-seriously would protest, "No fair! You have Kub!" knowing that whatever team he was on could answer virtually every question, his existence as the pitiable boy who struggled to breathe was eclipsed by his reputation as the well-informed, crackerjack brain.

By the final days, our class had gelled. Though truancy had bedeviled a handful of students, a clash between a privileged boy and an economically strained girl had erupted into scorn and tears, a studious boy had a heart condition diagnosed and treated, and more typical adolescent drama had distracted several others, every single student wrote every single paper, and the number who chose to share their work increased steadily. On the days papers were due, attendance was high, and respectful silence dominated as thoughtful, deeply personal essays were read, whether in response to themes in *Hamlet, 1984,* Gloria Naylor's *Mama Day,* or Barbara Kingsolver's *Bean Trees.* Students had several choices for their final writing project in high-school English. Kub decided to write his "explaining ceremony," inspired by an image in Diane Glancy's poem "The Share of the Stair." The assignment encouraged students to reflect on Glancy's use of memory and family culture as they compiled their own images and insights. Kub seized the opportunity to consider a range of questions: What experiences have shaped you? Which have scarred you? What memories, people, adventures/misadventures, trips, excursions, jobs, or crises remain and do not fade with the passage of time?

Kub's piece, "I've Come a Long Way," was a rich exercise in extending metaphors. As successful writers do, Kub designed his own method to try to illuminate his topic: his life-threatening, life-altering experiences and his resilience. He began with an explanation of his illness: "I caught the contagious monster Entero Encephalitis. That monster shut down the power grid system in my body. The blackout crashed the computer lightbulb in my head. I was in an unconscious state for a long time, totaling four months stay at the Milwaukee Children's Hospital." Depicting his anatomy as a machine attacked by a monster, Kub elaborated, "All personnel in the speaking and swallowing departments died from the monster's havoc, so I lost the ability to speak and to swallow." How his sick, sick mind and body overcame the four-month coma that ensued seems excruciating. Kub explained that he was compelled to obtain "nutritional support through Gastrostomy." Because of his tracheotomy, he had to eat through a tube in his stomach. He went on to suggest the intensity of his slow healing, "The road to recovery felt like going around in an endless circle until I broke away as a tangent line. I had to work with occupational and physical therapists to build my balance. . . .

Training felt as if I was an infant learning to walk, balance and build up my strength and stamina over again." A non-native speaker, Kub had not mastered verb tenses or agreement, but his imagery was strong, and the dire quest for stamina was especially haunting for those familiar with the loud grind of his ventilator engine every few minutes, a constant reminder of his tenuous breathing.

The opportunity to flex writing muscles connected to his life's challenges was a powerful motivator for a young man who had previously eschewed writing. *Telling* the horrors he'd endured would not have been effective; Kub's continued use of metaphor *showed* what he wanted readers to know. For example, he wrote of his junior-high difficulties, "In 7th grade, I had to drag the ventilator which gives me breaths around school in a weakened state. That's like a truck which could break down any time hauling a trailer. Walking from class to class made me feel like an old man because my back hurt, and I was hunched over as I walked." He went on to describe his first days of high school, navigating through the herds of "blue wildebeest through the Africa safari" that comprised La Follette's hallways. A universal complaint of those who spend time at La Follette is unmoving bodies congesting public spaces. Later, when his classmates heard Kub's piece, many loved his original imagery of stampeding wildebeests. With a depleted oxygen supply, Kub felt "like I was high on drugs because everything I look at seems fuzzy." Constant medical care alleviated some of his physical duress, and by junior year, Kub emerged into alertness: "The fog in my head had cleared making way for the trucks in the road in my thoughts to drive without getting into thought crashes." The metaphor of a mind full of traveling thoughts avoiding collisions evokes Kub's increasingly focused consciousness of the world around him.

He described his science class's tour of an area wetland and wrote of a field trip to a wildlife sanctuary: "Standing quietly, I could hear the voices from the wind chanting spells to connect me with the earth. With my eyes closed, I inhaled and relaxed, connecting my spirit to the earth. . . . I am glad to have gotten out of the bird cage that I locked myself in so long and explore and enjoy life." Enjoying life brought him to his senior English class, of which he wrote, "I would not mind taking this class again because I was bored from all my English classes since freshman year. In this class, I began using my communication device more and spoke up more, unlike in years before." Vibrant and connected to his peers, Kub finished on a highly reflective note:

I'm so proud of myself for coming so far. Looking back at the horrible days, I try to forget them. Then I realize that my past memories and experiences made me who I am today. I can't run from my past because my past is part of me.

Rejecting those horrifying memories sends the message that those memories
of the past never happened. That is like saying racism, discrimination, rape,
bullying, dropping of atom bomb, genocide, holocaust, torture, war and more
bad memories never happened. I had to learn to overcome my memories of
not being disabled and not being able to do what I used to. That was hard and
not easy to do. Sometimes in my dream, I would dream about being normal
again like everyone else, but I know that I can never go back in time to change
what has already happened.

When Kub's classmates heard a short excerpt from his piece, they clamored
to hear its entirety.

Kub noticeably beamed as a classmate read his piece aloud, observing his
peers hear his evocative metaphors of his body's machine crashing, of the
trucks derailing within the roads of his thoughts, and of his embrace of the
unspeakable hardships he'd endured. The power of his words to move his
classmates encouraged him to apply for a scholarship, and the personal statement he crafted earned him a fully funded education at Madison College. He
earned an A+ in his first-year economics course and passionately engaged
with the social-justice concepts in sociology. He wrote me long, involved,
thoughtful emails, interacting with academic ideas.

In July 2011, Kub's sister emailed to tell me he had died in his sleep. She
knew from his papers that he'd loved his high-school English course and
that he'd kept in touch with me. He was twenty. Though his logic-defying
physical afflictions were insurmountable, Kub embodied the intelligence, the
skill, the voice, and the insights that lurk within each student. Because his
English 12 experience connected him to a vibrant community of learners,
his literate growth opened life-enriching opportunities for him. Kub is an
extreme example of Jane Addams's social philosophy in action. Connected to
his peers, finding and relishing the power of language, Kub wrote and spoke
his way to full participation not only in a high-school class but in the wider
world.

There is no "right" way to teach curriculum or to foster literacy. There is
a group of people, sharing a space, forging understanding, through fits and
starts and lurches and bumps. Writing and talking are meaning-making
acts, explorations of many possibilities. Addams suffered deeply from public excoriation as her steady pacifism was resented by the war-rabid masses
during World War I. Refusing to compromise in her conviction of the war's
immorality left her lonely and frustrated; she knew that her position was
principled and right, and all her years of experience had developed in her
the very rare gift of not taking herself too seriously. Emphasizing the faith
in human potential that supported her and her like-minded friends, even

in the lowest point of her public life, Addams wrote, "[W]hat after all, has maintained the human race on this old globe despite all the calamities of nature and all the tragic failings of mankind, if not faith in new possibilities?" (*Peace and Bread* 151). When our students glower at each other across races, when they squirm within the parameters of socially constructed gender identities that don't quite fit, when they hurt each other or themselves, when death penetrates the community we share, when their challenges defy logic, we may be winded, knocked off balance, bewildered.

What grounds us in the promise of our practice for a progressively more just future are our stories. Naming and claiming the realities that have defined or confined us helps us to alter the way we conceive our social dynamic. A student's mother, working in a nursing home and bathing the bodies of patients who call her "nigger"; a young man boasting of his power as a pimp; a girl showing and telling the murder of her boyfriend; a student whose intellect is obscured by physical disabilities—over and over our learning is shaped by student stories. Each unfolding story takes us in a direction that could not have been foreseen at the semester's outset. As we construct, share, and listen to our own and to each other's stories, the worlds we inhabit overlap and touch, helping us to move forward from isolation and confusion to a realm where progress as individuals and as a society emerges, enriched by empathy, infused with possibility.

Notes

Special thanks to Andrea Anderson, Debbie Kinder, Mary Mowers, John Oestreicher, Scott Pichelman, and Chad Wiese for reading and for responding to drafts of this text.

Extra special thanks to James Fitzpatrick, a later-generation, Chicago-bred educator whose passion and principle motivate and inspire enduringly.

Works Cited

Addams, Jane. *Democracy and Social Ethics*. Urbana: University of Illinois Press, 2002.
———. *The Long Road of Woman's Memory*. Urbana: University of Illinois Press, 2002.
———. *Peace and Bread in Time of War*. Urbana: University of Illinois Press, 2002.
———. *The Spirit of Youth and the City Streets*. Urbana: University of Illinois Press, 1972.
———. *Twenty Years at Hull-House*. New York: New American Library, 1961.
Applebee, Arthur N. *Curriculum as Conversation*. Chicago: University of Chicago Press, 1996.
Bransford, John D., Ann L. Brown, and Rodney R. Cocking, eds. *How People Learn: Brain, Mind, Experience, and School*. Washington, D.C.: National Academy Press, 2000.
Elshtain, Jean Bethke, ed. *The Jane Addams Reader*. New York: Basic Books, 2002.
Hamington, Maurice. *The Social Philosophy of Jane Addams*. Urbana: University of Illinois Press, 2009.

Hollie, Sharroky. *Culturally and Linguistically Responsive Teaching and Learning.* Huntington Beach, Calif.: Shell Education, 2012.

Knight, Louise W. *Citizen: Jane Addams and the Struggle for Democracy.* Chicago: University of Chicago Press, 2005.

Kub. "I've Come a Long Way." In *B-One-4 Diversity.* Madison, Wisc.: La Follette High School, 2007.

Lagemann, Ellen Condliffe. Introduction to *On Education,* by Jane Addams. Ed. Ellen Condliffe Lagemann. New Brunswick, N.J.: Transaction, 1994. 1–42.

Olivia. "Sympathy Pains." In *Let Me Clear My Throat.* Beloit, Wisc.: Beloit Memorial High School, 1997.

6 Scaling Fences with Jane, William, and August

Meeting the Objective and Subjective Needs of Future University Students and Future Teachers

DARREN TUGGLE

In *Citizen,* her biography of Jane Addams, Louise W. Knight relates the story in which Addams has a moment of epiphany after attending the bullfights in Spain and realizing that she was somehow immune to the suffering of animals because her love and pursuit of "culture" had somehow "cut her off from feeling compassion from suffering" (163). It was at this moment that Addams realized she had "fallen into the meanest type of self-deception" (*Twenty Years at Hull-House* 56), that she had stepped into the trap of preparing to do important work rather than actually doing important work. It was then that she determined that "action was the only solution" (Knight 163); eight months later she found herself in Chicago scouting locations in which she would make her dreams of opening a social settlement a reality.

In my life I had a similar epiphany, but, alas, it was not nearly as romantic. After dropping out of college, three classes away from graduating with a double major in political science and psychology, and spending the next ten years of my life jumping from one restaurant job to another, I found myself sitting across the table from my then girlfriend (now my wife of more than ten years) who gently suggested that I might be more likely to overcome my constant state of ennui if I were to get a life. Okay, she might not have used those exact words, but the sentiment was the same. At that moment, I probably had more in common with the bulls from Addams's story than the matadors or Addams herself, but it was then that I realized I had spent the greater part of my adult life running away from the fact that I knew that my true calling was to become a teacher. My true path had been there all along. I had always taught in some way or another, whether as a martial-arts instructor, a music-camp counselor and section leader, or even as a wine-service trainer for restaurants; teaching had always been a part of who I was (and am), but I had fallen into my own "meanest type of self-deception." A few months later, I found myself in the same neighborhood that Addams had settled in many years before working on my degree in English education at the University of Illinois at Chicago. Five years (life is not a race) later, I graduated with highest honors and was ready to enter the world of education with my flaming sword of literature and my impenetrable shield of class-room management. Without really knowing it, I saw myself as a crusader or missionary who was going to (arrogantly) save the children of Kelvyn Park High School from themselves. Perhaps I should have read *Twenty Years at Hull-House* and studied Addams's evolution from crusader to writer before I mounted my fiery steed.

Kelvyn Park High School is an open-enrollment, neighborhood school (this is a nice way of saying that we take everyone . . . a claim that magnet and charter schools cannot make) in Chicago's Logan Square neighborhood. The student body is approximately 90 percent Latino with a growing Afri-can American population. The Latino population is a blend of Mexican and Puerto Rican students, as well as students representing several other Central and South American countries. In the hallways, you are likely to sense the faint scent of *mangoes con chili* and the sounds of *bachata* and *salsa* wafting through the air. Nearly 100 percent of our students qualify for the reduced lunch program, and we have a large population of students whose families have recently immigrated.

In spite of the challenges that are often faced by schools in neighborhoods that are full of families struggling with poverty, over the last few years Kelvyn Park High School has gone through a renaissance of sorts, making significant gains in attendance, graduation rate, college placement, and academics. The students and staff have won many awards for academics, athletics, and the arts. The school has a thriving drama club, the Kelvyn Park Drama Society, which is dedicated to bringing the works of William Shakespeare to friends and families in the neighborhood. The club, which I am proud to sponsor, invites students from our feeder schools to live performances that include post-show discussions with younger students. In addition, the school has a thriving social-justice academy that has done amazing film projects on topics like the effects of gentrification on neighborhoods like Logan Square. Kelvyn Park also offers adults from the community continuing-education programs in language, literacy, and technology. These and many other programs are part of the efforts by the administration, staff, and students to make Kelvyn Park a community center as much as a school.

Kelvyn Park students have had great success of late in the realm of college admissions, gaining entrance to outstanding universities in Chicago and across the nation. In 2006, Kelvyn Park was second only to North Side College Prep, one of the nation's top urban public schools, in the number of financial awards given to Chicago Public School graduates. The problem has not been getting the students *into* universities; it has been *keeping the students enrolled in the universities until graduation*. Sadly, the graduation statistics for Kelvyn Park students attending four-year universities are as appalling as the national averages for minority students who attend public schools. According to a 2000 study by the U.S. Department of Education, the percentage of 1992 twelfth graders who were likely postsecondary participants who completed a bachelor's degree or higher by 2000 by ethnicity were: 51 percent Asian/Pacific Islander; 49 percent white, non-Hispanic; 31 percent black, non-Hispanic; and 24 percent Hispanic (U.S. Department of Education). These statistics become even more real for me each time I run into a former student who tells me he or she has dropped out but plans on "going back" after taking a "semester off." As a person who took a "semester off" and did not return to the university until ten years later, I understand the reality of the situation. Sometimes the short-term necessities of life keep us from pursuing the long-term goals that could possibly afford us a better future. But I came back; will most of them be able to do that? It's not clear.

As alarming as these statistics are, the statistics related to the attrition rate for new teachers are similarly disturbing. According to a 2001 report by the Illinois State Board of Education, teachers with less than five years of experience leave the profession at relatively high rates—between 8 and 11 percent per year. Related studies indicate that Illinois loses about 30 percent of its teachers in the first three years on the job. The reality is, as educators we are getting our high-school students into college but not keeping them there, and universities are getting new teachers into schools but not keeping them there. The answers to these problems may lie in reevaluating the ways in which both institutions attempt to meet the educational needs of their respective students. It is my assertion that both institutions have failed to attend to students' objective *and* subjective needs, thus failing to acknowledge their full and complex nature and needs as human beings.

In her introduction to *On Education*, Ellen Condliffe Lagemann asserts that Jane Addams believed that "settlement work should simultaneously fulfill 'objective' and 'subjective' necessities. Effort merely to relieve poverty, disease, malnutrition, and alienation—the 'objective' needs—so evident right outside Hull House's front door would have less long-term benefit, Addams thought, than efforts that combined assistance to the needy with opportunities for effective altruism among privileged youth in search of ways to enact their ideals" (3). Like the social work done at Hull-House, curricular activities should be designed to meet both the "objective" and "subjective" needs of students. The objective needs tend to be easier to identify and measure. For high-school students, objective needs are tied to grade-point averages, standardized test scores, literacy skills, and graduation rates; for teacher candidates, objective needs are tied to criteria like learning to develop lesson plans, mastering strategies for literacy instruction, completing practicum, and passing basic-skills tests. Assuming that both college-bound high-school graduates and teacher candidates have had their objective needs met, why are so many high-school graduates not able to "handle" the university experience, and so many new teachers are leaving the teaching profession after a few years? One possible answer is that, in helping all of our students to meet their objective needs, we may often forget to address our students' subjective needs.

The subjective needs of our college-bound students and teacher candidates are those not found in the pages of No Child Left Behind or through questions found on a basic-skills test. For the future college students, subjective needs are those that will allow them to feel that they have the opportunity to succeed in the university setting, which is often completely alien to urban students and their families. Unlike many of their suburban counterparts, urban students often do not have family traditions and/or expectations of post-secondary education. In addition, many urban minority students never really understand what it is like to be a minority until they begin taking university-level classes. Students from Kelvyn Park, for example, live in a Latino neighborhood, go to a Latino school, and are surrounded by Latino culture. It comes as a great surprise to the students when they travel to the university and find themselves vastly outnumbered by students who do not eat their food, dance their dances, or speak their language. A former student of mine who is currently attending the University of Illinois at Urbana-Champaign reported to me that it was not the work that made her want to drop out of college, it was the fact that she "could not find fresh tortillas anywhere." While there is little that educators can do about the state of ethnic food offerings at university dining halls, there is much that we can do to emotionally prepare our students for the university life.

The subjective needs of teacher candidates are tied to gaining a genuine understanding of the talents and skills of urban students. Todd DeStigter, professor of English education at the University of Illinois at Chicago, points out that most of his students "come from the [Chicago] suburbs and, unfortunately, bring with them very low expectations of what so-called urban students are willing and able to do as readers and writers" (DeStigter). These preconceptions about the abilities of urban students need to be amended before teacher candidates enter the schools in order to keep them from contributing to the cycle of low expectations that is, sadly, prevalent in many urban school districts. This is not to deny that there are many academic challenges facing urban students; it is, however, vitally important that teacher candidates learn about these issues through genuine experiences with students rather than dealing with hearsay and preconceptions. As Jane Addams points out, "[T]he wisdom to deal with a man's difficulties comes only through some knowledge of his life and habits as a whole" (Addams, *Twenty Years at Hull-House* 108).

So the challenge comes for high-school teachers and university education programs to create curricular activities that will meet the objective and subjective needs of our respective constituents. In *Twenty Years at Hull-House*, Jane Addams states her belief that "the dependence of classes on each other is reciprocal; and that as the social relation is generally a reciprocal relation, it gives a form of expression that has a particular value" (59). The needs of the various participants in Addams's social settlement seem to be the same as those of our high-school classrooms and university education programs. We need to design activities that will help to create and strengthen already existing reciprocal relationships between secondary schools and university programs. It is through these relationships that we will be able to meet many of the previously identified subjective needs of our students.

One such reciprocal relationship-building project that I am extremely proud to be a part of is the Kelvyn Park High School/University of Illinois at Chicago Multi-genre Writing Project. This project teams the students from my Advanced Placement literature and composition class with students from Professor DeStigter's University of Illinois at Chicago English education program. This project began five years ago when DeStigter, a former professor of mine, and I talked about how exciting it would be to have my senior AP students take part in a collaborative writing project with students who were enrolled in his Teaching of Writing course.

From the beginning, DeStigter and I wanted this project to look and feel very different from the collaborations, like student teaching, that normally occur between universities and secondary schools. We decided that we wanted to create a situation in which the high-school students and teachers-to-be would engage in a collaborative relationship rather than the typical student/teacher relationship. We knew that this would be a challenge for all involved, because many current models of education do not encourage teachers and students to collaborate as equals. We acknowledged that most of the participants had years of experience in teacher-centered classrooms where the student role was to receive information from the teacher and then regurgitate the information in tests or essays.

We also decided that we wanted to base our writing project on the reading of a specific text that our students would share. For the first three years, these texts were all Shakespearian plays. We chose Shakespeare because we felt that my students would greatly benefit from collaborating with university students on challenging texts. In addition, we felt that this project would allow the university students to approach the teaching of Shakespearean text through writing.

We agreed that our goal for the project would be for our students, matched in two-person (one from each institution) teams, to create collaborative, artistic expressions interpreting classic literature to help them understand current social issues and to learn to use different types of writing to show learning and understanding through in-depth analysis and interpretation of Shakespeare's figurative language, imagery, symbolism, and tone.

The basic framework for our project came from the "multigenre" writing work that Tom Romano developed at Miami University in Ohio. For our project, writing teams developed five contextually accurate perspectives (writing pieces) utilizing five different genres. Each perspective would represent one of the five acts from the selected play. We also agreed that perspectives could be written in the first or third person and that the perspectives could be fiction or nonfiction. For each writing team, there were two required genres: a visual display (like a movie poster or a large advertisement) and, as the culminating act, a dialogue between two characters from the play. Students were encouraged to think of this assignment as act 6, scene 1.

In addition to the perspectives that each writing team was asked to create, each individual was asked to develop a framing piece that was designed to help the students to reflect on their own individual process of learning through writing. The authors were asked to include cohering devices that would make the artistic work a unified analysis of the thematic idea developed in the pieces. The cohering devices included an introductory letter, a table of contents identifying the title and genre of each selection, and a concluding piece that asked the students to reflect on the learning process. This part of the project, the analysis of literature and writing to show comprehension, was designed to meet the objective needs of the students.

For the most recent incarnation of this project, DeStigter and I decided to move away from Shakespeare and base the project on the American playwright August Wilson and his modern masterpiece, *Fences*. This decision did not come lightly, but we agreed that it would be interesting to see how the project would change if we focused on a more "culturally relevant" piece. This is not to assert that Shakespeare is culturally irrelevant, but connections between our students' lives and themes reflected in Wilson's piece are much more explicit. It was our hope that, as Addams discovered in her work at Hull-House, "culture and politics would have a much greater value if they were related by the contemporary experience of diverse groups of people than they would if they were based solely on classical or elite standards of beauty, conduct, or morality" (Lagemann, Introduction 5).

For the second incarnation, the dialogue component was amended by asking each team to create a piece of *writing that extended the play* beyond its final act. The pieces could be in the form of an additional scene that takes place after the one that currently ends the play, a series of letters between characters that explains what their lives are like after the play ends, or anything else they thought would take the play a bit further beyond its ending point.

Another addition to the project came in the form of a research requirement. This piece was added because it was agreed that the high-school students needed more work with research, and that the university students needed to think about different ways in which research can be used with students, meeting objective needs for both groups. For the research component, the writing teams were asked to create a *research piece told as a story* in which they do some research on an aspect of the play that interested them and then write about what they learned in the form of a brief (approximately two-page) first-person narrative. For example, they might decide to research Negro League baseball and write an account from the point of view of a player or fan; they might research jazz or the blues during the time of the play (1950s) and write a story from the perspective of a musician; they could look into the role of women in the civil-rights movement and write a story about what it might have been like to participate in that movement; they might like to research the role of black soldiers in World War II. The possibilities were almost endless.

In the end, students were assigned three specific writing perspectives and given one open-ended assignment in which the individual writing teams were asked to create their own piece based on how they wanted to show what they had learned through their collaborative exploration of the text. After reading our students' evaluations of the previous year's projects, we also decided to limit the number of submissions for each team to four, where we had required five for previous years. It was our hope that the students would focus more on depth of writing rather than breadth.

Once the texts and writing assignments had been agreed upon, it came time to get the two groups, the high-school seniors and the English education students, together, face-to-face. It was during this portion that the project began to address both the objective and subjective needs of our students. For the first meeting, the university students traveled to Kelvyn Park High School for introductions and pairings. By this point, the students from both groups had read the first three acts of the play, so both groups were familiar with the text and its primary themes. The students from the university were asked to arrive at the school at 7:30 A.M., a time completely alien to many university students. This, in itself, was a great way for the university students to understand the reality of urban high-school students. Because of overcrowding in urban schools, schools are often required to start early and end late in order to accommodate all of the students. The moment when the two groups met was one of great excitement, and the tension was palpable. At this point, neither group of students was sure what to expect. The high-school students were on their own turf, but faced with the intimidating reality of being teamed with a university student; the teacher candidates had the advantages of age and educational experience but were in a setting that was unfamiliar and, in some cases, intimidating. They were no longer reading about urban education; they were sitting in the front row.

As in the past, DeStigter and I made a great show of creating the writing teams, adding to the excitement that the participants already felt. You could see individuals from both groups scanning the room trying to guess with whom they would be paired. There was no great science at work here, just two lists of names pulled from hats. One by one the names were read, and the pairs were created. The sheer randomness of the pairings added to the "subjective" educational nature of the project. The pairs crossed all race, gender, sexual-preference, and religious lines. For many of my students, this was their first opportunity to work with a non-Hispanic partner; for many of the university students, the opposite was true.

Once the writing teams were created, copies of the assignment sheets were distributed, and the teams were left to figure out how to tackle this enormous project, using only the remainder of their morning and one additional meeting. What seemed to anchor the individual teams was their knowledge of the text and the desire to outdo the rest of the writing teams. As we walked around the different groups, we were bombarded with specific questions that always began with the words, "Can we . . . ?" Our response was always the same: "Go for it!"

At the end of the first frantic two-hour visit, students were asked to decide upon a "collaboration plan" for the project and determine an agreed-upon form of communication. After the university students departed, my students and I met for a short debriefing meeting. After dealing with the opening, "Man, there is no way we are getting this project done!" and "My partner is really hot!" comments, the students reported that they were very excited by the project and were eager to share their ideas with the rest of the group; they did so with a sense of pride and ownership that one does not often hear in the high-school classroom. "Pride and ownership" might be the first measurable signs that the assignment was meeting the subjective needs of my students.

Over the next few weeks, my students reported frantically working with their university partners, using email and phone calls as their primary means of communication. Some of the groups were able to meet in person, but for the most part, the communication was electronic. Although many of my students found this challenging and sometimes frustrating, they realized that they were responsible for the work and needed to find an efficient way of collaborating with their university partners. These sorts of logistical difficulties are indicative of the deeply rooted, systemic hindrances to this type of collaboration. Of course, helping students learn to overcome such difficulties is one of the values of this type of project.

For the second phase of the project, the students from Kelvyn Park traveled to UIC to continue the writing process. Once we arrived at the university, the writing teams were released from a central meeting location and went to various locations around the campus to work on their projects. Wandering around to check on their progress, DeStigter and I found the teams working in empty classrooms, coffee shops, restaurants, and study lounges all over the campus. By the end of the session, it was difficult to tell which were the university students and which were the Kelvyn Park students. For most of my students, this element of equal status was the most rewarding part of the project. Many reported that they felt like they "belonged" on the university campus after working there for only a few hours. Jane Addams reports a similar desire for assimilation into a community after years of working with the Hull-House settlement. Like Addams, my students were able "to be swallowed and digested, to disappear into the bulk of the people" (*Twenty Years at Hull-House* 203).

After two more weeks of frantic electronic communication, our students were finally ready to participate in the performance phase of the project. For our final evening, the students from both groups met at the Chicago Teachers' Center to share their creations with their peers. Within minutes of each group's arrival, the walls were covered with visual representations of the groups' readings of Wilson's text. There were posters that showed in-depth character analysis, three-dimensional sets built with amazing detail, many posters dealing with the themes of racism and gender issues, and even a table full of puppets representing the major characters from the text.

Each writing team was then given approximately five minutes to present one or more of the writing pieces that they created for the project. The self-selected genres ranged from freestyle poetry, a puppet show, a musical production of Cole Porter's "Don't Fence Me In," and (a first!) a séance where the spirits of the deceased characters from the play were "channeled." The presentations certainly challenged many of the preconceptions that the university students may have had about urban high-school students' abilities and willingness to write.

Perhaps the most amazing part of the evening came when writing teams presented their historical narrative pieces. As a result of their research, students were able to imagine the voices of jazz musicians like Miles Davis and John Coltrane, Negro League baseball players, and African American soldiers who served in World War II. One of the most amazing pieces revolved around a fictional character who sat next to Rosa Parks on her famous bus ride. This character did not have the courage to join Parks in her protest, but was so changed by the experience that she eventually joined Dr. Martin Luther King Jr. in his historic marches. Asking the students to demonstrate the results of their research through narrative allowed them to show a much more in-depth understanding of their topics than any traditional research paper that I had ever assigned. This type of writing allowed them to move from statistics and dates to a much more profound discussion of the human side of the issues being researched and the effect that these topics have had on our society.

After the presentations were completed, we ended our evening by breaking bread together. For the hour that followed, the university professor, the high-school teacher, the future teachers, and future college students were no more. In their places stood a group of people who had shared a profound learning experience and had taught and learned from one another. This seemed to be a true manifestation of the "reciprocal relationships" that Jane Addams attempted to create in her work at Hull-House.

To bring the whole project to a conclusion, my students were required to submit a writing portfolio that included all of their writing samples along with their reflections about the entire process. Without any specific prompt from me, the students' comments reflected on how their objective and subjective needs were met by the project. One of my more reluctant readers, a student who was seldom willing to see beyond the literal meaning of a text, reported that the teamed reading and writing "helped show me different things that I didn't see in the text before and to see it [the text] as more than just words from a book." Another one of my more nontraditional AP students reported that the paired reading "helped [her] to go deeper into the reading." Lucio, a student who was a reluctant writer who never seemed to grasp the difference between rough and final drafts, reported that "we learned to write together—not just divide up the work, but rather to edit, revise, and suggest new ideas to each other." These comments reveal how the objective goals of increasing the high-school students' abilities to read and write more critically before they reached the college level were met.

Other comments by the students spoke further to how the project met the students' subjective needs, the needs that would allow them to function at the university level with confidence that many urban students lack. Rosa, a Posse Scholarship award winner, reported that the project "helped me to see the 'college life,' because we were given an assignment and we were on our own from there." This sentiment was echoed by another student, Belen, who liked "the fact that we were given the trust to decide how to do and present our things." The students felt that the project encouraged them to work at the level of their university partners. One of my students, the ever-practical Ali, reported that "this experience drastically improved my skills in meeting tough deadlines and working with a partner with very few meetings." How this project met the subjective needs of my students was best articulated by Martin, who reported that he "felt like an actual college student," and Cynzabeth, who felt that the experience was "not just a school project. It was much more than that."

Similar reflections were required from the university participants. Sean O'Bra, a two-time participant in the project and graduate of the certification program in English at UIC as I had been, and now a teaching colleague at Kelvyn Park High School, reported that his participation in the project "provided insight into students' lives, work habits, favored way of communicating, and how they behaved in their own school and comfort zone as opposed to outside of it." This is understanding that one cannot possibly glean from a book or a lecture about educational pedagogy; this is the type of insight that can only be gained by walking, talking, and breaking bread with real students. O'Bra also revealed that when reading with the students collaboratively, "The conclusions that we made seemed more authentic when we were on an equal footing in a collaborative role than if we had been in more traditional teacher-student roles."

Another future teacher candidate referred to her partners (she worked with two students) as "creative forces that I know will be a success in college." Although she reported that her partners were "not as accountable as I would have hoped throughout the project, I [realized] that they are high school students and that they have a lot on their minds that they consider to be higher priorities." Again, this is the kind of learning and understanding that comes from actually interacting with students, not from reading about students in books. For all of the frustrations that came from working with her high-school partners, this teacher-to-be stated that the project was a "much and always needed, inspirational reminder of the power and possibility that high school students often possess." This is a reminder that would benefit all of us who enter into or continue in the field of secondary education. As Jennifer, one of my students, put it: "I think that it is good for them [the future teachers] so that they could have an idea what they are getting into!"

Beyond how the project benefits our mutual students, both professor DeStigter and I can trace how our participation meets our needs as educators. DeStigter relates that participation in the Kelvyn Park High School/University of Illinois at Chicago *Fences* Multi-Genre Writing Project allows him to

> address the ongoing challenge of making the work that we do in university methods classes relevant to the real world of teaching. That is to say, one of the structural/institutional problems of a methods class is that it takes place within the walls of a university classroom and away from the contexts of high school students' lives and literacy practices. This requires that in these classes we essentially create fictional students—ones who we imagine will benefit from the ideals and practices related to literacy teaching and learning that we're working through. The problem, though, is that in circumstances like these, my methods students have no way to contextualize the things that they are learning about. That is, we're talking about certain principles of language arts teaching as useful or as "best practices" divorced from actual teaching context. That's misleading to my methods students; there is no such thing as "best practices" apart from specific students. Or, to borrow from Dewey's language in *Experience and Education,* "there is no educational value in the abstract." The KPHS/UIC project has helped remove the abstraction from the "Teaching of Writing" class; it has given my students an opportunity to get to know particular students, their unique abilities, interests, and needs, and then respond to them with forms and topics of writing that are valuable to those individual kids in the context of their lives. (DeStigter)

As for me, this project allows me to stay in touch with the world of academia and allows me to borrow a wide range of authentic writing assignments generated by high-school and university students. Quite simply, the groups came up with outstanding writing pieces that I had simply never imagined might get generated from our assignments; they exceeded my expectations and taught me. Also, as a teacher who frequently serves as a mentor for student teachers, my work in this project helps me to remember what it is like to be a soon-to-be teacher who is anxious to try new ideas with students. Most importantly, this project reminds me that I must continue to keep my expectations high for my students and to persevere to "grapple with my students, not only by formal lectures, but by every hook possible," to ensure that I provide them every opportunity to fully "express and develop their talents, interests, and ambitions" (Lagemann, Introduction 3).

I close with the following memory:

> It was the night of the final presentations, and all of the writing teams were meeting for some last-minute collaboration before their final presentations. One of the university students sat looking rather dejected by the fact that his high-school partner had become very sick and was forced to miss the evening's festivities. In his hands he held three hand-crafted puppets that he and his partner had designed for the puppet scene that they had composed. One by one, the other groups presented their creations, while he quietly waited for the final presentation slot. When it was his turn to present, he read a letter that he and his partner had composed, but you could tell that he was pretty "bummed out" that the puppet show was not going to happen. Just as he was ready to leave our stage, two of the high-school students, without prompting, jumped up to offer to help him with his presentation. After a few moments of hurried, impromptu rehearsal, the puppet show went off without a hitch, and the night ended in the true spirit of collaboration. I believe that Ms. Addams would have given the puppet show stellar reviews.

Works Cited

Addams, Jane. *Twenty Years at Hull-House* (1910). Urbana: University of Illinois Press, 1990.

DeStigter, Todd. Personal interview. October 10, 2005.

Knight, Louise W. *Citizen: Jane Addams and the Struggle for Democracy*. Chicago: University of Chicago Press, 2005.

Lagemann, Ellen Condliffe. Introduction to *On Education,* by Jane Addams. New Brunswick, N.J.: Transaction, 1994. 1–42.

U.S. Department of Education, National Center for Education Statistics. National Education Longitudinal Study of 1988 (NELS:88/2000), "Fourth Follow-up," and Postsecondary Education Transcript Study (PETS), 2000.

7 A Timeless Problem

Competing Goals

JENNIFER KRIKAVA

> To provide a center for a higher civic and social life; to institute
> and maintain educational and philanthropic enterprises, and to
> investigate and improve the conditions in the industrial districts of
> Chicago.
> —Jane Addams, *Twenty Years at Hull-House*

These words, taken from the charter to Hull-House, the Chicago settlement that Jane Addams cofounded in the late nineteenth century, reveal the objectives that she and Ellen Gates Starr had set for their social enterprise. Though complementary in many ways, these goals are also quite diverse. Addams sought to improve several aspects of her new neighbors' lives: the physical, the intellectual, and the social. Such a lofty ambition is quite admirable and, as Addams would quickly discover, quite challenging.

A fundamental problem that Addams encountered in her attempts to address these different aspects of life is that they often represented competing needs. For instance, although Addams's comfortable, upper-middle-class background had allowed her the opportunity to pursue the finest of educations, the economically disadvantaged Halsted Street residents did not enjoy that luxury. For them, the necessity to work long hours to satisfy their physical needs (food, shelter) overrode any desire they might have had to cultivate their intellectual, or even their social, needs. Consequently, a major challenge that Addams faced as she began her work at Hull-House was finding ways to satisfy these conflicting needs in order to help the people that she worked with become balanced individuals and effective citizens.

Such a challenge, though different in scale, seems not at all different from the one that consumes many educators in today's society. In fact, it is strikingly similar to the challenge that awaits me as I transition between my ninth and tenth years as a public-high-school English teacher. With the memory of this year's Prairie State Achievement Exams (PSAEs) still fresh in my mind, now seems a fitting time to reflect on the work I do with the seventy-five high-school juniors with whom I have spent the past nine months before the year ends and they exit my classroom for the last time.

The annual tradition of the PSAEs is one to which I, unfortunately, have become accustomed. Each year, our staff spends two days at the end of April administering these state-mandated tests. The first day is devoted to the American College Test (ACT). It consists of four sub-tests: English, mathematics, reading, and science reasoning. Formerly reserved for college-bound students, the test is now required for all students who have earned the course credits to be considered a junior. A student's ACT score is a crucial factor in determining college admission and therefore is of greatest consequence for those planning to attend college.

The second day is devoted to an easier battery of tests called Work Keys, which are designed to evaluate students' potential success in the workplace. Taken together, the ACT and Work Keys comprise the PSAEs, and the state uses our students' combined performances on these tests to measure how well we are fulfilling the promise of No Child Left Behind. If the scores indicate that we have not met a criterion they term "annual yearly progress," our school stands to face a variety of unsavory consequences. Having suffered these consequences in the not-so-distant past, these tests now have especially high stakes for our school as a whole.

Therefore, the annual tradition of preparing students for the PSAEs is another to which I have become accustomed. Each winter, my American literature classes ring in a new year and a new semester with a new item on our weekly agenda: ACT Prep. Every Wednesday, we devote our entire class period to reviewing the content and rehearsing the strategies that will hopefully lead them to success on these tests. The first six Wednesdays are devoted to preparing for the reading test, the next seven to preparing for the English test. These days, typically marked by quiet groans as students reach beneath their desks for the outdated workbooks we've been issued, serve as hiccups in the otherwise smooth progression of our weeks together. It doesn't matter whether we are in the middle of a writing project or at the climax of a novel; each and every Wednesday our normal classroom life is temporarily suspended while we tend to other matters.

But I've been at this too long to simply complain about the unfairness of it all. The fact of the matter is that these tests are a reality of our lives as members of the public education system; my students know it as well as I do. To protest this reality is futile; to ignore it is irresponsible. And so we proceed, from one Wednesday to the next, diligently reviewing comma-usage rules, systematically improving our ability to read one page of text and answer ten related questions in the most detached, efficient manner possible. Naturally, the kids groan, but not for the same reasons I do. I'm angered by the intrusion; they're bored by the content. Yet together we forge ahead, soothed somewhat by the routine, placated a bit by our hopes that practice makes perfect.

That is, of course, until this routine is disrupted by the late-breaking news that this year our students will be asked to leap one more hurdle in this testing marathon. In addition to the English, math, reading, and science tests, our school was "selected" this spring to participate in a writing test that would be administered as the fifth part of the ACT. There is little time and few workbook pages available to prepare them for such a hurdle. After completing a three-hour test, our students will have thirty minutes to read a persuasive prompt about some hypothetical school policy, decide on a stance, think through an argument, and write a minimum five-paragraph response that is clear, coherent, and convincing. My students might object that this isn't fair, and I would have to agree. They might argue that thirty minutes is not sufficient time; I again would agree and add that such a writing task contradicts everything we've taught our students about the process of effective writing. But again, all of our protests would be in vain. This eleventh-hour announcement has forced us to adjust our reality, and what choice do we have?

And so, this past Wednesday, I stood by and watched nineteen members of my school's junior class, several of whom are students of mine, rise to meet this challenge. And just as I suspected they would, just as the task *demanded* they should, they rushed through the reading of the prompt, skipped the careful consideration and planning of an argument, and frantically wrote their hearts out for thirty minutes. In a few weeks, their individual scores will arrive, and most likely, the effect of this extra test on their composite scores will be negligible. The next time they are given a writing assignment, they will hopefully return to the process that includes time, thought, and revision. Ultimately, I don't worry too much about their experience with this test.

Instead, I look beyond these next few weeks to the beginning of the next school year, when we will meet as a faculty and as an English department to discuss our new goals. *This* prospect makes me worry. Undoubtedly, our school's scores on the PSAE will be a highly influential factor as these goals are discussed and determined. Though the results of this writing test remain uncertain, it seems inevitable that they will impact our writing curriculum, and not in a way I deem positive. Suffice it to say, I predict an amendment to next year's Wednesday routine that includes a whole slew of timed writing tests to prepare students for this new demand of the state. What's worse, I also foresee a revision to our current writing curriculum that will further limit the already narrow opportunities I have to create worthwhile writing experiences for my students.

I have been teaching primarily American literature classes since I started at Argo Community High School nine years ago. Back then, I was completely overwhelmed by the amount of literature I was expected to cover in such a short amount of time. The focus of our English curricula, for all four grade levels, has always been rooted firmly in literature, with writing viewed as supplemental. According to my department's philosophy, if reading literature is paramount, but writing instruction must also occur, the most logical and efficient approach to writing instruction would be requiring students to write essays analyzing literature. Incidentally, this approach also lends itself perfectly to the five-paragraph essay, a form championed by my department.

Naturally, my department's firm push toward literary-analysis writing has shaped the choices I have made in my classroom. Over the years, I have carefully designed my courses to suit this model. Never mind the fact that unless our students go on to become English majors (and very few of them do), they will never again be asked to write an essay analyzing Hawthorne's use of symbolism in *The Scarlet Letter*. Never mind the fact that writing of a more personal nature would likely serve the greatest number of our diverse student body, who perhaps share little in common other than the fact that, as teenagers, they are all groping along the same murky path of self-discovery. Initially, literary-analysis writing was something we English teachers all seemed to agree on. After all, it was the type of writing at which *we* had excelled, the type of writing that had led us to our place in the classroom. Literary-analysis writing was a choice made for me by my department that has inevitably become another part of my teaching reality. Now, however, in light of my evolving awareness of my students and the limited time I have to offer them opportunities to write in personally relevant ways, it is a choice I am compelled to question.

Literary-analysis writing is also a part of reality that I don't anticipate will fade to accommodate what is sure to become the next new reality: timed writing instruction. But in a curriculum already laden with literature, writing about literature, and writing to prepare for a test, something's gotta give. What troubles me most about the addition of a timed writing test to the ACT is that it will force me, once again, to split my time and focus as a teacher of writing. In honoring the part of my job that demands that I prepare students for a test, I may be forced to sacrifice the part of my job that enables me to help kids learn about themselves through writing. True, such knowledge is not tested on the ACT, but it is something that will serve my students, regardless of where they go once they leave my classroom. And while they remain there, it is perhaps the most valuable resource that I have, as their teacher, for learning about who they are. *This* part of my job is one I am *not* willing to sacrifice.

So again, it boils down to a classic case of competing goals, a kind of conflict that long precedes me and extends beyond the limits of public education. Just as I do, Addams struggled to satisfy competing demands. She wanted, as I do, to offer personally enriching opportunities to the people that she served. But always, there were the more practical needs that demanded to be met. Obviously, those needs had nothing to do with standardized tests; they were much more urgent: food, health, shelter, employment. She had to learn to strike a balance between helping her neighbors provide for their bodies and helping them provide for their spirits and minds. History shows us that, overall, she was successful. Likewise, I know that I must and will find a similar balance between the writing that prepares my students for a test and the writing that prepares them for life as reflective, self-aware individuals.

Similarly, Addams must have struggled between her desire to help the largest number of people and her desire to really get to know the people she helped. I suppose Hull-House could have been run like a clinic: people walk in, get their needs met, and walk out. This assembly-line model of efficiency over effectiveness was the standard for industry in her time, and sometimes it seems like the standard for public education today. But Addams resisted this model, just as I do. Instead, she made it a point to know the patrons of Hull-House, her neighbors. Her method was quite simple: she listened. In fact, according to her biographer Louise W. Knight, Starr and Addams "made getting to know people the first order of the day. . . . They spent a great deal of time listening as people told them their stories" (203). The more popular Hull-House became, the greater the demands made on her time, the more difficult this must have become, but Addams refused to have it otherwise. Likewise, the more my class sizes increase, the greater the demands made on my instructional time, the more difficult it becomes to get to know my students, to listen to their stories. And so, like Addams, I will continue to refuse to have it otherwise.

A Current Challenge: Balancing Demands without Compromising Ideals

Keeping this vow in mind, one of the greatest challenges that I face as I prepare to begin my tenth year of teaching will be to design a writing curriculum for my juniors that accommodates the demands being made of them from several different sources: their state, which requires them to write objective, efficient arguments; their school, which asks them to write content-based, analytical arguments; and their teacher, who wants them to use argument, as well as other modes of writing, as a method of self-expression and self-enlightenment. Such a task seems quite daunting if these various demands are viewed as strictly competitive. However, recognizing the commonalities among them, as Addams often did, makes this challenge seem much more feasible.

In considering the exclusivity and overlap among these demands, I have established four main goals that will drive my American literature writing curriculum. First, to satisfy the state, I plan to help my students become fluent in the type of argumentative writing required for success on tests like the ACT, yet have them gain this fluency by making arguments that matter to them. Second, I will rehearse with students the steps necessary to write effectively under time constraints, yet remind them that such a method is simply an abbreviated version of the writing process with which they are already familiar. Third, to satisfy the school, I will strive to create writing experiences that ask my students to analyze the literature we read, yet enable them to do so in personally relevant ways. Fourth, and most significantly, I intend to frame all writing assignments, regardless of content, mode, or method, as opportunities for me to learn about my students and my students to learn about themselves.

Designing a writing curriculum that caters to these various agendas and meets this variety of objectives will undoubtedly be a challenge. Fortunately, I am not starting from scratch. A writing unit that I attempted with my juniors this past school year meets, in some way, the four goals I have delineated for my future writing curriculum. In addition to achieving this balance, this unit also seems to be in keeping with the spirit and ideals of Jane Addams.

A First Attempt: "You Say You Want a Revolution"

About midway through the first semester of American literature, my juniors and I find ourselves in the thick of the American Revolution/Age of Reason. As we read Thomas Jefferson's *Declaration of Independence* and Patrick Henry's *Speech in the Virginia Convention,* naturally we discuss the social and political forces that compelled these men to write such stirring arguments against tyranny and in favor of revolution. We also discuss the rhetorical devices that they used to make their language, whether written or spoken, so compelling. From Henry's allusion to the "song of the siren" and his famous bold statement, "Give me liberty or give me death!" to Jefferson's masterful use of parallel structure in enumerating the colonies' grievances against King George, our founding fathers helped teach a lesson that future American writers would come to learn: *how* you say is as important as *what* you say. This lesson was one I also hoped my students would apply to their own writing. An even more significant lesson I hoped they could take from this historical literature, however, was to recognize the power of language to identify and make others aware of problems that demand change. This was certainly a lesson that Jane Addams took to heart in her career as an activist as she spoke out on issues such as women's rights and child-labor laws.

My attempt to teach both of these lessons as an extension of the literature we had spent several weeks reading took shape in a writing unit I have entitled "You Say You Want a Revolution," my own attempt at an allusion that sails clear over the heads of the majority of my students, who were born in 1990 and aren't aware that music existed before then. The idea is for them, using our founding fathers as inspiration, to identify a change that needs to be made somewhere in their world. In hopes of not limiting them or their thoughts, I tell them this change may be either personal or public. Ultimately, they will write an argument (like Jefferson) that they will deliver as a speech (like Henry) in an effort to convince their classmates of the necessity of this change.

To reinforce the process approach to writing, I make the first assignment a prewriting brainstorm activity. I give them a handout with these five categories, each followed by several blank lines: My life, My school, My community, My country, My world. I ask them to imagine the rings of rippled water created when a pebble is dropped into a pond. In this visual metaphor, they are the pebble, and each ring represents one of the five categories; some are closer to them and others are farther away, but all are connected to the pebble and its place in the pond. Their homework assignment is to brainstorm a variety of problems that fit within each category. They don't have to fill lines for every category, but their goal is to come up with at least ten problems. The caveat, of course, is that any problem they identify has to be one that they can do more than simply complain about; it has to be one for which they can offer actual, viable solutions.

The following day, we spend an entire class period merging their individual suggestions into one class brainstorm. I divide the white board that spans the front wall of our classroom into five sections, and we spend fifty-five minutes listing, explaining, and debating what our class considers to be its most dire problems. No thought is censored. Consequently, this day's discussion is usually one of the most lively and inclusive. The students benefit from an awareness of issues they had perhaps never considered. I benefit from a newfound appreciation of how aware my students are of themselves and the world around them, and how impressively they defy the stereotype of teenage apathy.

Next, I ask them to narrow their list down to focus on one problem that they wish to address. Once they've done this, they are ready to outline their ideas. I provide for them a general template to follow. Their paper should address four questions in turn: What is the problem? What is the solution? What would my opponents say? What will be the outcome of this change? I take the same template and write an outline for a sample speech. This year, I wrote about the proposed change of banning smoking in public places. Modeling the structure and progression of ideas seems to help them begin to formulate their own arguments. I collect their outlines and provide feedback to help them strengthen their arguments.

Once students have determined the focus of their arguments and know what they want to say, I again ask them to consider how they will say it. I provide for them another brainstorm activity. This one lists six rhetorical devices that we've studied in the unit's literature: bold statement, allusion, rhetorical question, parallel structure, repetition, and imagery. After each device, I provide a brief definition and a couple of examples from the pieces we've read. I ask them to brainstorm examples of these devices that they might incorporate into their own papers. Ultimately, they will be required to include one example of all six in their final drafts.

Blending the content of their argument, which they've assembled on their outlines, with the rhetoric of their argument, which they've gathered through their brainstorm activity, they are ready to write their first drafts. We review the conventions of effective essay structure: attention-getter, thesis statement, transitions, topic sentences, closing statement, and so on. The rough drafts of their papers are then subjected to a structured peer review. Here, students edit each other's writing for grammatical correctness, provide feedback on content and use of rhetorical devices, and evaluate the overall argument using the same rubric that I eventually will use to evaluate their papers. Using this response as a guide in revision, students compose their final drafts, which are neatly typed with all six rhetorical devices clearly marked and labeled.

Finally, the unit culminates with at least three days of speeches. These days are among my favorite spent with my juniors. Each year I am impressed with the levels of insight and maturity my students exhibit when asked to examine the world and their places in it. This year, many of my students chose to focus on the pond's outer rings. Some, like Pawel, addressed issues that teens stand to inherit as they cross the threshold into adulthood. He spoke about the mounting credit-card debt that most Americans accumulate each year.

Others, like Chris and Ian, discussed problems that directly affect teens. Chris spoke about alcohol abuse, a problem that can affect people of all ages, but one that he feels has most harmful consequences for teenagers. After identifying and explaining several such consequences—drinking and driving, poor decision-making, health risks—he went on to suggest several remedies for this problem. He called on the community and school to become more involved by inviting speakers whose lives have been adversely affected by underage drinking to address the student body about the dangers of alcohol use.

Similarly, Ian called on the school to provide more information to students regarding another issue that, according to his cited statistic, affects one in eight teenagers in the United States: depression. Another of his proposals was particularly eye-opening to me. In explaining the causes of teen depression, Ian discussed the amount of pressure kids his age feel from every angle. He noted that "teens can feel pressure from parents, from teachers, from work, and even from themselves. For example, especially during junior year, both teachers and parents emphasize college to no end. The pressure to achieve in grades and the ACT is overwhelming to many." Listening to the highest-achieving student in class speak these words helped me gain at least two new insights. First, the consequences of our intense ACT preparation were even more far-reaching than I had originally suspected. Second, the value of this particular writing unit, in providing students a voice and providing me an opportunity to listen to it, was greater than I had originally imagined.

This voice also resonated on issues closer to the students' lives, reverberating in the smaller rings of the pond. Michelle reminded me of how tied to their community Argo students are when she spoke about the need to renovate a local park. Founders Park was a place that she had enjoyed as a child but one her younger siblings now avoid because it has fallen into disrepair. In appealing to those in her community to volunteer their time and resources to help restore the park, she alluded to the efforts made in the aftermath of Katrina to help repair what had been ruined. Though the levels of destruction are not at all comparable, Michelle was able to parallel the power of focused, cooperative effort. She insisted that "just like the time that horrible hurricane struck and destroyed many cities, we need to work as one and create something wonderful." Next year, I intend to challenge students like Michelle to move beyond discussion of the issue. I plan to offer extra credit (magical words in any high-school classroom) to those who take action to enact a solution to the problem they address.

Still closer to home were those who spoke on issues of school policy that affect them as Argo students. Many students proposed changes that might seem somewhat clichéd: less homework, greater choice in electives, and a later start time each morning. However, when viewed in light of Ian's speech on the stress put on high-school students, these issues took on more weight.

Similarly, four students in my first-period class all decided to address the same issue, which at first I feared would lead to redundancy. Instead, it produced an engaging, thought-provoking debate on the legitimacy of Illinois' mandate that high-school students take four years of physical education. Freddy and Patty, two highly active student-athletes, argued that the health of America's youth depends on such a requirement. Patty opened with a bold statement that one-third of America's children are overweight or obese. She argued that for many teens, the only physical activity they get each day is that which is required by their P.E. class. She went on to suggest alternatives to traditional gym-class activities, such as wall climbing, yoga, and competitive racing video games, that have been successful in other area schools. Jordan and Liz then countered their classmates' claims by arguing that gym, like electives such as music and art, should be a choice for students. As Liz protested, P.E. can cause "low self-esteem, embarrassment, and, on a personal level, it's an overall unwanted nonsequitor in my day. It takes valuable time out of a student's day that he could be spending on an AP class, or another worthy subject." These four compelling speeches, delivered in close proximity to one another, helped define an issue that everyone in class had a stake in and, therefore, helped create a stirring debate.

Two other students spoke on issues much more difficult to debate. Mike and Adrian were brave enough to discuss two interrelated and long-standing issues at Argo: racial intolerance and school violence. Mike began his speech by referencing Argo's race riots of the 1960s, events that cast a shadow from which our school is still struggling to emerge. Mike's father had attended Argo at this time, and his memories helped inform Mike's speech. The intolerance is now less overt, demonstrated more by a segregated cafeteria than outright brawls. Mike called it an obstacle "we can live with, but cannot prosper with."

But school violence, according to Adrian, is a dilemma no one should have to live with. Coming on the heels of a year when our school made headlines for several instances of hazing and violence, Adrian's speech seemed to be made on behalf of many of his classmates. I think it would be illuminating for our administration to hear requests for heightened security, metal detectors, and random locker searches made not by overprotective parents but by fearful students. In fact, next year I also plan to invite our principal to visit class on a day when the scheduled speeches focus on issues of school policy. Hopefully, having the ear of the administration will further inspire my students and encourage another move from talk to action.

As brave as Mike and Adrian were to address such sensitive issues, arguably the most courageous were the few students who chose to look inward, rather than outward, in identifying a change that needed to be made. The most memorable example of such a student was Dan. In the middle of his sophomore year, Dan had been diagnosed with leukemia. As an honors student and AAA hockey player, this event turned his world upside down. Due to the amount of school he missed, he had to drop out of honors classes. Due to the physical toll the disease took on his body, he had to quit playing hockey, a passion that had consumed him since he was a small boy. Obviously, the terrible news and the resulting consequences had also taken a toll on his attitude and outlook on life. Amazingly, this sixteen-year-old had the self-awareness to realize that changing his attitude and improving his outlook were necessary if he was going to fight his disease and enjoy his life. It just so happened that his realization and our writing unit coincided.

Yet what grew out of this coincidence was ultimately more rewarding than a powerful speech. In the time that Dan's classmates were working on their speeches, he was sick and missed several days of class. By the time he returned, he had missed most of the lessons related to the speech. He began coming to my English Resource during his study hall to catch up. Discussions about his speech eventually turned into more personal conversations about his life, his cancer, and how he was managing to negotiate between them. Likewise, I shared with him details of my sister's battle with cancer, and from these conversations we got to know each other as people and became quite close. Thus, this writing experience created an opportunity for me to listen to one of my students in a way I never would have otherwise. It also provided the foundation of a teacher-student friendship that is rare and incredibly gratifying.

Overall, I would consider this writing unit a success. It allowed my students to meet the four writing objectives that I have set based upon my values, as well as those of the school and the state. First, the unit provided an opportunity for my students to practice the art of argument. They had to select an issue, take a stance, and support it with pertinent reasons and examples, while also acknowledging and refuting the counter-argument. This is the formula called for on the ACT.

Second, the unit reinforced writing as process. My students began with uncensored brainstorming, individual and cooperative, narrowed their focus to one topic, organized and outlined their ideas, received feedback on those ideas, studied a model argument, formulated a draft, received additional feedback, composed a final draft, and finally, shared this final draft with a wider audience. This process, from start to finish, consumed the better part of two weeks, but I consider it time well spent. Practicing this process will enable them to internalize it and allow them, when called upon, to modify it to accommodate other writing tasks.

For instance, just a month later, as my juniors were preparing for a timed writing test that serves as part of the English department's semester exam, I referenced our Revolution writing unit in a couple of different ways. Obviously, it served as a perfect review of argument structure. But it also helped me remind students that writing is always a process, even when certain situations require them to abbreviate that process. When allowed just fifty-five minutes to compose an effective argument (or a mere thirty on the ACT), they would need to omit or condense certain steps. For instance, cooperative brainstorming would not be a possibility, though they should certainly take a few moments to let their thoughts run wild before committing to a topic. Similarly, outside feedback would not be possible, but they should save a few moments at the end of the allotted time to quickly review and edit their own writing.

In addition to catering to the goals of the state, this unit provided an opportunity for my students to write the way their school most values: as a response to literature. Granted, they did not respond to literature in the traditional sense—their arguments were not analyses of Jefferson's or Henry's arguments—but they did respond in a way more fitting to the literature and its themes. By having the freedom to write and speak on the issue most vital to them and their world, my students perhaps gained some sense of the urgency and passion contained in these documents written centuries ago. Hopefully, they came to appreciate the courage it takes to voice and defend their convictions. Finally, by composing and delivering rhetoric of their own, rather than simply appreciating that of others, they realized the force of language and felt the power of a well-turned phrase.

Finally, this unit highlighted what I value most about writing: its power to reveal us to ourselves. I cannot speak on behalf of my students, but it is difficult to imagine that this sort of writing experience did not compel them to examine their world, their lives, or their beliefs in some new way. In fact, next year, so that I won't have to imagine, I plan to ask my students to write some sort of follow-up piece to reflect on their experiences with the writing unit.

Undeniable, however, is the insight I gained about my students. We devote so much class time to discussing literature that it almost becomes a filter through which I listen to my students. Based on Dan's interpretation of a character in a story, for example, I might infer something about his own character. But listening to him speak in first person about his personal experiences and struggles, I understand him in a way that makes me better equipped to teach him and makes me a better teacher overall. The culmination of this writing unit awarded me three hours to simply listen to my students, another rare and gratifying gift. Apart from the individual discoveries I was able to make about each of them, the collective one was most satisfying: teenagers, so often cast as self-absorbed and apathetic, have an enormous capacity to care and invest themselves when given an opportunity and a bit of guidance.

This insight was one that Jane Addams also discovered in her encounters with teens at Hull-House. In the final chapter of *The Spirit of Youth and the City Streets,* she argues that young people are not merely helpful in achieving social change, they are essential. She claims that "youth is so vivid an element in life that unless it is cherished, all the rest is spoiled.... When we count over the resources which are at work 'to make order out of casualty, beauty out of confusion, justice, kindliness and mercy out of cruelty' . . . we find ourselves appealing to the confident spirit of youth" (47–48). Addams felt that this fearless spirit of enthusiasm and optimism could serve as the impetus for little revolutions that, one by one, could transform the world. Listening to the conviction in my students' voices as they argued their beliefs, I certainly agree with her.

However, Addams also recognized that a force as powerful as the spirit of youth requires nurturing and guidance, tasks she called on public schools to provide. She worried that if "teaching is too detached from life, it does not result in any psychic impulsion at all," but that a student, "if given a clue by which he may connect his lofty aims with his daily living . . . will drag the very heavens into the most sordid tenement" (*Spirit of Youth* 52). Although this writing unit was my rather modest attempt to provide my students that "clue," at least it was a step toward making school and writing relevant to life. I believe Addams would have considered this a step in the right direction.

A New Approach: Uncovering Common Ground

In her introduction to Jane Addams's *On Education,* Ellen Condliffe Lagemann describes the transformation that Hull-House underwent in its first few years. She explains that "when Hull House first opened, its activities were based on the presumption that life could be improved by sharing the advantages of learning with the people who had not had the opportunities for study associated with a secure, American middle-class way of life" (22). Guided by this philosophy, Addams geared many of Hull-House's initial programs toward the sharing of classic literature and art with her Halsted Street neighbors.

Soon enough, however, the immigrants who visited the settlement expressed their interest in more practical concerns such as health services, day care for their children, and the maintenance of sanitary living quarters. Faced with this conflict of interests, Addams was forced to adjust her initial goals to accommodate various agendas. According to Lagemann, she met this challenge. Lagemann explains how over time, "the Hull House program broadened, becoming less pretentious and more practical in its aims. Formal cultural and instructional activities did not disappear, but they were increasingly designed in a more collaborative fashion and were combined with efforts to investigate and alleviate neighborhood health, housing, and environmental problems" (23). When Addams was introduced to a competing agenda, she did not stubbornly ignore it, nor did she carelessly abandon her own ideals. Instead, she looked for ways to adapt her existing programs to satisfy a new set of needs. Rather than drawing lines in the sand, she worked to establish common ground.

Her approach is one from which modern-day educators can certainly learn. In fact, I intend to adopt it as a model in my future negotiations between the state's demands, the school's mandates, my students' interests, and my own ideals. As I look ahead to the next school year, I expect that these conflicts will only intensify and become more complex. I may not believe in the state's idea that throwing a random, hypothetical issue and thirty minutes at a student is an effective way to measure his or her ability as a writer, just as I may not believe in my school's insistence that all students prepare to become English majors. But I *do* believe that students should know how to use writing as a tool to accomplish a variety of purposes, argument and literary analysis being just two among them. Therefore, I will seek to find new ways to integrate these two purposes with the one I perceive as paramount: writing as a means for self-awareness.

The overall success of my first attempt at providing writing experiences that bridge the gaps between the state, my school, and me prove that compromise is possible. In addition to revising and improving this writing unit, my goal for this upcoming year is to create new learning experiences that address multiple goals by continually looking for places where these goals intersect. Ultimately, my search for common ground may not leave me, nor the state, nor my school wholly satisfied. Rather, my efforts likely will serve the best interests of my students by providing them a more well-rounded education.

Finally, I look once more to Addams for guidance in my teaching, for although she may not have listed my profession on a résumé, there is overwhelming common ground between our work. In fact, her description of a successful nineteenth-century settlement in *Twenty Years at Hull-House* sounds strikingly similar to my description of a successful twenty-first-century classroom. She writes that "the one thing to be dreaded in the Settlement is that it lose its flexibility, its power of quick adaptation, its readiness to change its methods as its environment may demand. It must be open to conviction and must have a deep and abiding sense of tolerance. It must be hospitable and ready for experiment" (83–85). A willingness to bend, to adapt, to change, to tolerate, to experiment—this quality helped Jane Addams navigate a new professional frontier, and it is one I hope will help my students and me find success as we continue our own journeys.

Works Cited

Addams, Jane. *Democracy and Social Ethics*. Urbana: University of Illinois Press, 2001.
———. *The Long Road of Woman's Memory*. Urbana: University of Illinois Press, 2001.
———. *The Spirit of Youth and the City Streets*. Middlesex, U.K.: Echo Library, 2006.
———. *Twenty Years at Hull-House with Autobiographical Notes*. New York: Signet Classics, 1999.
Knight, Louise W. *Citizen: Jane Addams and the Struggle for Democracy*. Chicago: University of Chicago Press, 2005.
Lagemann, Ellen Condliffe. Introduction to *On Education*, by Jane Addams. New Brunswick, N.J.: Transaction, 1994. 1–42.

8 Surveying the Territory

The Family and Social Claims

ERIN VAIL

In Jane Addams's *The Spirit of Youth and the City Streets,* the advocate for democracy and pragmatism suggests that, because of their energy and enthusiasm, young people are invaluable in the promotion of social justice. Although not technically an educator herself, Addams displays great respect for teachers and asserts that schools play a crucial role in allowing young people to positively shape their communities. "All that would be necessary," she writes, "would be to attach this teaching to the contemporary world in such wise that the eager youth might feel a tug upon his faculties, and a sense of participation in the moral life about him" (153). Throughout my career, I have often examined the value of teaching in a private school as opposed to a public one. I have also wondered where middle-class students fit into the notion of educational democracy. In other words, what role do they have in promoting equality and social justice? Many teacher-education programs and the scholarship one reads in such programs focus on empowering students with economic and social disadvantages, and, to a practicing teacher, the notion of encouraging more traditionally "oppressed" students to actively participate in creating a more democratic society has a certain appeal. This task, however, seems a bit easier when working with students without many opportunities. My middle- and upper-middle-class students may be aware of the inequalities of opportunity experienced by their peers in their city and nation, but their personal inexperience with those inequalities makes it difficult to talk about and engage in social change separate from a concept of charity. In some sense, educational "privileges" often separate these students from "participation in the moral life about them." Addams herself experienced a similar disconnect in the "snare of preparation." As an English teacher, I feel I have a unique opportunity—indeed, a responsibility—to encourage all students, regardless of socioeconomic background, to participate in the life about us. Addams's framework of the family and social claim translates readily into my classroom as a means for embracing this challenge.

In several of her writings, Addams analyzes the impact of the conflicting family and social claims on college-educated women of the late nineteenth and early twentieth centuries. Nearly a century later, Addams's remarks on this conflict continue to resonate within the discourse of democracy. Particularly for me as a teacher in a college-prep high school, questions about what to teach young people about how best to live one's life surface constantly. My students, for the most part, are college-bound, aiming at professions that will allow them to support a family and perhaps "do better" than their parents. They also happen to attend a private, Catholic school where they are encouraged to live a life of service, characterized by compassion and justice for all in their community. Addams's struggle to negotiate the family claim and the social claim reveals interesting parallels to my students' situations, and has directly impacted the development of my own educational philosophy. In this essay, I will attempt to understand Addams's explanation of these claims, to analyze them in two recent cinematic narratives, to place them in a context with some of Addams's ideas about education and democracy, and finally to suggest a connection between these ideas and my classroom in a college-prep high school. Ultimately, I would like to show how Addams's life experience and theoretical framework represent a unity among social and educational contexts rather than a dichotomy of "haves" and "have-nots."

The Addams biographer Louise W. Knight asserts that "[t]he family-and-social-claims framework is one of Addams's most original, if too long neglected, contributions to social . . . thought" (256). Knight discusses the development of this theory, noting that it originally included both young men and young women but became a gendered theory later in relation to the specific role of the settlement women. While Addams's more complete description of the framework served her feminist purposes, its contemporary application need not be limited to women, of course. Knight paraphrases Addams's theory thus: "They [educated daughters] then become torn between two sets of duties: 'the family claim,' the responsibility the daughter feels to subdue her dreams in favor of serving the family, and 'the social claim,' the duty to society that she longs to fulfill" (255). Addams herself separates the family claim from the merely personal—condemning Henrik Ibsen's Nora for deserting her family for purely selfish reasons—but asserts that "the failure to recognize the social claim as legitimate is what causes all the trouble" (*Democracy* 37). To put it simply, the family claim is obvious because the young person has grown up with it. Regardless of sex, the young person likely sees education as a means to supporting him- or herself and his or her family. The social claim must be placed explicitly in the path of the young person who, with his or her innate enthusiasm and desire to act, will almost certainly pick it up. This challenge of honoring the family claim and illuminating the social claim is one I embrace as a teacher.

Despite the passage of a century, many of my contemporary middle-class students find themselves in circumstances not unlike Addams's: They enjoy the privilege of educational opportunity but also experience a great desire to use their education for the greater good. In fact, this intersection of ideals is the very groundwork of the settlement movement. While the empowerment and improvement of the lives of the working poor are clear objectives of the movement, Addams argues that true democracy will only materialize through cooperation and reciprocity among different economic groups. For Addams, the settlement movement is based "not only upon conviction, but upon genuine emotion, wherever educated young people are seeking an outlet for that sentiment of universal brotherhood, which the best spirit of our times is forcing from an emotion into a motive" (*Twenty Years* 75). A truly democratic society, then, arises when the privileged recognize that "the good we secure for ourselves is precarious and uncertain . . . until it is secured for all of us and incorporated into our common lives" (*Twenty Years* 76). The settlement gave Addams and her contemporaries the opportunity to participate in this common life in a deeply personal way, with the hope that all would benefit from the interaction, and democracy would blossom. American society as a whole still stands to gain from the cooperation of economically and educationally privileged individuals with others who face disadvantages. Addams asserted that the settlement residents "are bound to regard the entire life of their city as organic, to make an effort to unify it, and to protest against its overdifferentiation" (*Twenty Years* 85). One of my goals is to emulate the settlement model in the classroom by encouraging my students to participate in the life of their community in a way not unlike the young people in the settlement movement headed by Addams.

The framework of the family and social claim is inherently optimistic, as it recognizes the young person's longing to participate in the society around him or her. It is also multifaceted. The theory has close ties to Christianity, as Addams discusses the two alongside each other in "The Subjective Necessity for Social Settlements." As well as the young person's desire to *do something* with all the education he or she has acquired, "The impulse to share the lives of the poor, the desire to make social service, irrespective of propaganda, express the spirit of Christ, is as old as Christianity itself" (*Twenty Years* 80).

But the claims, while easily situated in a Christian mentality, stand outside of religious "propaganda." To put it another way, the social claim promotes an ethic consistent with Christianity without resorting to judgment or coercion of non-Christians. Knight notes also Addams's hesitation to use the word "civic," because women could not yet vote and hence were not of real political value. Teenagers reflect a similar predicament. The importance of this distinction, however, cannot be overlooked, as it creates space to legitimize the social claim without tying it to a political agenda. The family and social claims draw from a framework based on reciprocity: As a member of a family, one is expected to contribute to the group in order to share in the loyalty and identification of the group; the same notion can be applied to the citizen's role in his or her community. Political affiliation, therefore, is a personal choice, separate from the citizen's duty to contribute to the good of the larger social group.

The social claim is, rather than exclusively Christian or political, inclusive and ideally suited to the real desires of the educated young person. John Dewey, a contemporary and friend of Addams, echoes her definition of the social in similarly broad and inclusive terms:

> The child is to be not only a voter and a subject of law; he is also to be a member of a family, himself in turn responsible, in all probability, for rearing and training of future children, thereby maintaining the continuity of society. He is to be a worker, engaged in some occupation which will be of use to society, and which will maintain his own independence and self-respect. He is to be a member of some particular neighborhood and community, and must contribute to the values of life, add to the decencies and graces of civilization wherever he is. (10)

As a responsible educator, it is my moral duty to teach to the social claim of each of my students and to understand that each will respond to that claim in a unique way. In a private school, I have a duty to the parents who place a particular value on education and expect some tangible return on their investment. In this sense, my classroom must be proactively "college prep," presenting my students with the information, skills, and habits that are vital for success in higher education. I also have a duty to my students for their present needs and experiences; after all, what they learn about literature and communication should matter now as much as it matters later. Finally, at Marist High School on the South Side of Chicago, I participate in a mission that strives to "foster student commitment to the Gospel of Jesus Christ; encourage a strong dedication to living according to ethical and moral standards; provide students with the opportunities to serve family, Church, and community; [and] foster family spirit through a caring environment of love, respect and tolerance" (Marist High School Handbook). Rather than feeling constrained by these obligations, I feel a great sense of freedom to interact with my students and my subject matter in a meaningful way and to encourage them to share their experiences with others in their community.

Dramatic Illustration: *The Pursuit of Happyness* and *Half Nelson*

Addams uses Shakespeare's *King Lear* to "illustrate the situation baldly, and at the same time to put it dramatically" (*Democracy* 44). She analyzes the characters of Lear and Cordelia and explicates how their relationships and actions in the play reveal the intricacy of the family claim–social claim dynamic. In her interpretation, Lear fails to see any claim other than his own as a father, and Cordelia becomes admirable only after she has acknowledged that the family claim is one part of her duty in the world. While both characters end unhappily, Addams argues that the drama does reveal some insight into the conflict bound to arise between an exclusive adherence to one or the other claim. I would here like to follow Addams's example using two films that put the inseparability of these complex and apparently conflicting claims into a more modern context. *The Pursuit of Happyness* tells the story of Chris Gardner, a young father and salesman who, after a string of very bad luck, takes on an unpaid internship in order to improve his lot in life and care for his family, and in the process faces homelessness and the challenges of caring for his five-year-old son. In *Half Nelson*, Dan Dunne finds teaching eighth-grade social studies to be the only anchor in his cocaine-addicted life. Both movies were released in theaters in 2006, and the lead actors were both nominated for Academy Awards. Each film tells an interesting story about family claims, social claims, and popular perceptions of work, education, and the self.

The more widely received *Pursuit of Happyness* is based on the real-life experiences of Chris Gardner and stars Will Smith. With a catchy patriotic title and a big-name movie star, this movie perpetuates, in nearly every facet of its plot and characterization, the myth of the American Dream and, in doing so, elevates the personal and family claims far above the social claim, relegating it to a brief epilogue or extra to the "real story." In the film, Gardner begins as a medical-equipment salesman, living with and barely able to support his wife and child. Linda, his wife, frequently works double shifts in a housekeeping job; Christopher, his son, spends his time in day care with Mrs. Chu, watching *Love Boat* and *Bonanza* reruns. After seeing a man park his luxury sports car,

Chris asks him, "What do you do, and how do you do it?" The man responds that he is a stock broker and that one should be good with numbers and good with people to succeed in the profession. This encounter presents Chris with the motivation to become a stock broker in order to better provide for his family. In the course of the film, Chris loses his wife and his home and takes on an unpaid internship to learn the brokerage trade. With charm and fortitude, Chris eventually earns a paid position at Dean Witter and, according to the film's final comments, goes on to become a millionaire.

Chris is a sometime philosopher and sort of poster-child for the bootstraps version of the American Dream. The title for his rags-to-riches tale comes, obviously, from the Declaration of Independence, and Gardner muses in voiceover that Thomas Jefferson's word choice shows remarkable insight, as citizens have a right only to the "pursuit" and not to happiness itself. Toward the end of the film, Chris claims a very brief moment of happiness when he accepts the job at Dean Witter, but the film, of course, focuses on the quest. Gardner's educational background consists of high school and the U.S. navy and his childhood nickname of "ten-gallon head" because of his intelligence. Emphasizing his natural aptitude is his ability to complete a Rubik's cube in the midst of its 1981 heyday. While Christopher is not yet in school, his father is determined to instill educational values in his son. He expresses disappointment that the children at Mrs. Chu's are watching television reruns and, after confessing his own shortcomings in basketball, tells his son never to let anyone tell him he can't do something. Gardner's motivation is clear throughout as Christopher's well-being and future security are the driving force of each choice his father makes.

There is no doubt that Gardner chooses the family claim over the social claim and, in that sense, "makes good." While his short-term choices negatively affect his family—his wife leaves him, his son must sleep in a subway men's room and accompany his father on sales calls—Chris's decision to pursue a more lucrative career path ultimately benefits his family. The career, however, presents an interesting contradiction to the social claim, as consulting with the wealthy on their retirement portfolios does nothing to improve the lives of others like Chris, struggling to make their way in low-income, unsatisfying jobs. Gardner's story illustrates how the focus on the personal and family claim in the American Dream model serves to undermine any social claim to improve the opportunities of the multitude of working-class Americans, those whom Jane Addams desired so much to include in American democracy. It should be noted that the real Chris Gardner's life continued beyond the story of the film to include important philanthropic work, including career counseling for homeless people.

While his eventual attention to the social claim is certainly noteworthy, the story of the movie does not explore this aspect of his memoir; rather, the movie focuses on his "triumph" as an individual and as a father. This focus highlights a major difficulty for teachers whose students are bombarded by a culture that so often relegates attendance to the social claim to a postscript on a success story. To a viewer like me, Gardner's work with homeless people would make for just as compelling a tale as his rise to millionaire stockbroker. Instead, however, his individualism and ability to care for his son take the foreground and, in doing so, point out the pervasiveness of the neoliberal paradigm of twenty-first-century America. Chris Gardner, as portrayed in the film, represents the model neoliberal citizen as "one who strategizes for her- or himself among various social, political, and economic options, not one who strives with others to alter or organize these options" (Brown 43). Downplaying Gardner's later social-claim work serves to perpetuate neoliberal ideas about how individual freedom and economic growth always trump public-mindedness and social justice. The widespread acceptance of such a distinction makes it difficult to link family and social claims in the classroom in such a way that students can imagine alternatives to injustices that certainly exist in their schools and communities.

In *Half Nelson,* we meet an alternative to Gardner in the character of Dan Dunne, and also an alternative to the perception that the social claim is always secondary to the family claim. Dunne is a white teacher in a black school. By day he professes a dialectic philosophy of history, teaching his students that historical moments like the civil-rights movement exemplify a struggle between opposing forces, history defined as the study of change over time. He also coaches the eighth-grade girls' basketball team, using his sense of humor to promote self-esteem and morale among the girls. Early in the film, he is discovered by one of the players, Drey, smoking crack in the locker room after a game. This encounter is the impetus for a developing student-teacher relationship that subverts the teacher-as-savior cliché so common in Hollywood narratives of American education. Dunne continues to deteriorate further into cocaine addiction as Drey, representative of her peers, encounters the adolescent obstacles present in poor and minority neighborhoods. Her brother is in jail, and she is taken under the wing of his friend, the drug-dealing Frank. Besides his conflict with his superior for "not using the binder" (prescribed curriculum) to teach civil rights, Dunne also faces the educator's ethical dilemma of how far to intercede in the life of a student, as he anticipates Drey's entry into the "work" of drug-dealing.

The characters of Dunne and Drey reveal the complexity of the family and social claims and their inherent ties to the classroom. Dunne, for example, is portrayed as a progressive thinker and a sympathetic educator. A fellow teacher, with whom he has a sexual affair, asks him if he's a communist. When Drey sees his collection of books, she wonders why he has so many about black people. One night in a bar, the father of a former student informs Dunne that his daughter is in her first semester as a history major at Georgetown, apparently owing to his influence. The relationship between Dunne's personal/family claim and social claim, however, is fraught with tension. He helps his students to question their world and their place in it. He communicates with them in their language and leads them into the complex world of ideas and social change. In a telling scene with his family, Dunne's father mockingly asks him if he's still teaching Ebonics, revealing the apparent disapproval of his parents, whose calls Dunne ignores throughout the film. As evidenced by his drug problem and dearth of relationships, he is a miserable individual attempting to contribute to society. The narrative turns on his relationship with Drey when he attempts to prevent her from following Frank down the path of selling drugs. For Drey, the family versus social claim is perhaps even more complicated. The thirteen-year-old lives with her always-working mother; her brother Mike is in jail for an unmentioned but implied drug-related crime. Frank symbolizes the family claim as he steps in for Mike and Drey's absent father, coming to her basketball game to cheer her on. Drey finds herself caught between Frank's example as the dealer who doesn't use and Dunne's example as the addict trying to shape young lives and encourage good choices.

Each character has a distinct attitude toward the apparently disparate claims. Dunne has evidently rejected the family claim, living alone and ignoring his mother's phone messages. He also bids farewell to an ex-girlfriend who plans to marry a man she met in rehab, highlighting his apathy toward starting a family of his own. But he also iterates more than once that his students give him purpose. Even as he falls further under the influence of addiction, he continues to work with and defend his students. He asserts to his colleagues and principal that his students are learning how to think, and throughout the film he challenges them to question their world, empowering them through their education. Drey illustrates the result of this empowerment in a scene where she reclaims her stolen bike from a neighborhood boy without resorting to violence. As an adolescent, Drey's family claim is more pressing as she struggles to please her mother and protect herself. She is torn between her sibling-like relationship to Frank and her sense of compassion toward her struggling teacher. Unlike that of *Happyness,* the ending is outwardly ambivalent: Drey helps Dunne to clean up after a drug-related absence, but it is unclear whether either character will take decisive action in the future.

While there appears to be little hope for Dunne, Drey's youth and decision to help him seem to point her toward some attention to a social claim.

These stories enhance Addams's conception of the relationship between the family and the social claim as one of *both* not *either.* Like Lear and Cordelia, Gardner and Dunne lose something valuable in their disregard for the other claim. Jane Addams tells us that "in most cases the [social] is repressed and gives way to the family claim because the latter is concrete and definitely asserted, while the social demand is vague and unformulated" (*Democracy* 40). This applies to Chris Gardner and Dan Dunne, as Gardner's duty to keep a roof over his son's head is more concrete than Dunne's responsibility to teach eighth graders about dialectics. The accessibility of the two films also bears remark, as *The Pursuit of Happyness* was widely marketed and distributed while *Half Nelson* remains a "small film," seen by far fewer people. It is not surprising that an uplifting film about a father's unlikely accomplishments has more popular appeal than one that features a drug-addicted schoolteacher. These films illustrate that the tendency to privilege one claim and ignore the other seems to prevail and that Addams's hope for a "healing compromise" between the two continues to seem a distant dream. Addams asserts that "it is difficult to distinguish between the outward act of him who in following one legitimate claim has been led into the temporary violation of another, and the outward act of him who deliberately renounces a just claim and throws aside all obligation for the sake of his own selfish and individual development" (*Democracy* 37). Chris Gardner follows a legitimate family claim and becomes a stockbroker; Dan Dunne renounces an ambiguous family claim to pursue a career in teaching. Gardner is heroic; Dunne is pathetic. And yet there is something in each to be emulated, something in each that bears scrutiny, and some relationship between both and the world of education.

The stories of Chris Gardner and Dan Dunne reveal the ubiquity of the family claim–social claim conflict in our own society. Each film dramatizes a character's choice to favor one over the other and the consequences of that choice. In fact, both characters exist in a contemporary neoliberal context that further separates and complicates the claims. The anthropologist David Harvey's reference to Margaret Thatcher speaks to the conflict, as "there was, she famously declared, 'no such thing as society, only individual men and women'—and, she subsequently added, their families. [In the neoliberal state] all forms of solidarity were to be dissolved in favour of individualism, private property, personal responsibility, and family values" (23). This idea, which has taken hold in the last few decades, clearly stands in direct opposition to the philosophy of Addams, making it even harder to capitalize on the innate social enthusiasm of young people. This illustrates, I think, why Addam's conception of the family and social claims is so vital in the classroom, particularly for middle-class students who are simultaneously driven by their desire to achieve and accumulate and their desire to contribute and participate. Her framework offers an alternative to the ideology that the market, rather than human beings, should govern activity.

Direction and Adjustment: Claims in the Classroom

In a classroom, especially one that is characterized by more "haves" than "have-nots," Jane Addams's theories about these claims challenge me, particularly in my approach to curriculum, to make an "adjustment between the family and the social claim, in which neither shall lose and both be ennobled" (*Democracy* 37). As an educator with a relatively remarkable amount of autonomy, I must make decisions every year about which topics and texts will help my students "get ahead" and which will help them "get together." Not surprisingly, Addams's proposed method for such an adjustment is one rooted in experience: "The educators should certainly conserve the learning and training necessary for the successful individual and family life, but should add to that a preparation for the enlarged social efforts which our increasing democracy requires. The democratic ideal demands of the school that it shall give the child's own experience a social value; that it shall teach him to direct his own activities and adjust them to those of other people" (*Democracy* 81). Addams described education in her own era as preaching brotherhood but actually fostering ambitions for personal distinction and intellectual accumulation. In the schools where I have taught, I have found a similar focus. In my own experiences as a student and a teacher, I have found that schools serving middle-class students, so occupied with Advanced Placement curriculum and college-entrance statistics, sometimes neglect to prepare students for "enlarged social efforts." Emphasis on college admissions encourages students to overextend themselves academically and extracurricularly, with an eye toward building their résumé. My school has embraced the trend of encouraging as many students as possible to take Advanced Placement courses, implicitly endorsing a curriculum designed around a test, rather than around students. I currently teach sophomore students on an AP track, and while the students themselves are not necessarily test-focused, parents frequently suggest more work and test preparation to "get them ready" for later courses. My department also follows the trend of increased ACT preparation, even though the state does not require private-school students to take the test, sometimes at the expense of time spent in more student-centered activities.

Even social action is, for many students, not a personal undertaking but one either chosen or required because of its perceived value on the college admission application. The notion of "service hours," however, especially when not tied to any particular academic purpose, tends to endow the students at my school with a spirit of benevolence, or worse yet, a chore, but rarely with a sense of participation in society. True social action for Addams "is not philanthropy nor benevolence, but a thing fuller and wider than either of these" (*Twenty Years* 80). This "sense of humanity" seems to me more likely to grow in a classroom context as a habit of mind rather than of minimum recorded hours. Additionally, linking service and justice to topics outside of their religion classroom allows my students to interact with society with a wider perspective, not simply because the school or church tells them to, but also because they belong to their community and therefore are responsible for its upkeep.

So, what does this mean in my classroom? Working in private schools, I have found an unexpected freedom in determining the curriculum for each course I teach. I have had the opportunity to introduce new drama courses and to integrate new texts and teaching strategies into long-standing traditional English syllabi. In essence, I try to approach my classroom as Addams approached her settlement house. She is clear about this approach:

> [T]he one thing to be dreaded in the Settlement is that it lose its flexibility, its power of quick adaptation, its readiness to change its methods as its environment may demand. It must be open to conviction and have a deep and abiding sense of tolerance. It must be hospitable and ready for experiment. It should demand from its residents a scientific patience in the accumulation of facts and the steady holding of their sympathies as one of the best instruments for that accumulation. It must be grounded in a philosophy whose foundation is on the solidarity of the human race. (*Twenty Years* 85)

Although my high-school classroom differs from a settlement in many ways, I hope to emulate these crucial elements. I teach performance, literature, and composition and constantly strive to implement activities and assessments that illuminate the "solidarity of the human race" implicit in all three. I try to observe and listen to my students closely, asking for their input throughout each unit and at the end of each year. I have seen them respond to literature and activities that emphasize community in and out of the classroom. I take very seriously my students' questions about why we're studying a particular topic. I had a student once ask why I was "making her read *Frankenstein*." She was nearly halfway through it and conceded that she was learning some new vocabulary. When the unit was completed and the students had researched and written essays examining the relationship between science and social ethics, I asked Hannah if she saw the point. She said she did, and, in asking the question, she reminded me that I must always try to make the connections between literature and the world clearer in order to validate the work my students do as well as the work that I do as their teacher.

One decision I have made is to dispense with objective tests on literature. I believe that such tests contribute more to the individualistic drive for personal distinction and intellectual accumulation than any other tool in the classroom. I agree with Carol Jago, who argues in "No More Objective Tests Ever" that standard multiple-choice tests are not prudent because they privilege the teacher's reading of the text over the students,' when "[i]deally, every voice will have weight and substance, and every voice will add to the group's collective understanding of the text. For this to happen, however, students must respect one another's varied interpretations and regard one another as able thinkers" (5). Jago's philosophical opposition to objective literature tests sounds so much like Addams's explanation of a democracy that it seems a crucial theoretical ground rule in any classroom. I have seen "alternative forms of assessment" promoted for their value in breaking up the monotony for teachers and students alike. I am also convinced that students are more likely to engage in authentic learning through projects and inquiry. Through Jane Addams's lens, I am beginning to see how students' connections between literature and lived worlds encourage participation in the latter as well as the former. As my teaching philosophy has developed in this direction, I have integrated more speeches, debates, essays, and service learning into my courses. I have done this not only to encourage students' engagement with literature, but more importantly, to encourage their engagement with their own and others' lived worlds. This kind of engagement foregrounds the family and social claims as Addams describes them.

One example is a unit I am continuing to develop based around the idea of "making a difference." One part of the unit focuses on Markus Zusak's *I Am the Messenger*, a young-adult novel focused on a nineteen-year-old cab driver whose self-image improves because of his participation in the lives of others in his community. He is given "messages" by an unknown source and faces the challenge of determining and then meeting the unique needs of strangers, relatives, and friends. The novel proceeds to connect the family claim and social claim in a way that honors Addams's scholarship. In our classroom activity, we try to do the same. With each section of the book, students must look for ways to make a difference in the lives of others, including family members, classmates, individuals in the school community, and people in the students' own neighborhoods. The students' success is measured not only in their mastery of the literature we study but also through self-assessment of completed written assignments and personal projects, which give their actions a social value and encourage them to "direct [their] own activities and adjust them to those of other people."

While the individual missions remain essentially personal and "ungradeable," the students' written reflections on the value of the project are heartening. Patrick wrote about his mission to befriend a schoolmate whom he did not know; he was determined to find the person and figure out exactly what it was he or she needed. Kate discussed her charge to be a positive change in the life of a particular teacher; she wasn't in his class but went out of her way to meet him and show kindness to him every day. Devlin found a project sitting right next to him in health class; he asked a few questions and went home and burned several CDs of the kid's favorite band that night. Another memorable message detailed Karoline's commitment to be a positive change in the life of her father; she described spending time with him and sharing their unique and connected stories. These simple missions may pale compared to the grand idea of social action, but they allow the students to see how they can make a difference in their family and their world and perhaps encourage them to take on larger causes on their own.

We also look to past societies for examples of "making a difference." We read and discuss excerpts from Thomas Mallory's *Morte d'Arthur* and "Sir Gawain and the Green Knight" and generate working definitions of chivalry, analyzing the actions of the literary characters and real-life heroes. This year, in our preliminary "roundtable" discussion, some students argued that chivalry is simply a myth, while others asserted that the more accurate term would be that it is an "ideal." One insightful student, Samantha, convinced her peers that the ideal was useful in creating a social order at which to aim, rather than an unrealistic description of a dangerous and complex historical era. After studying and evaluating the actions of the knights, we have a "knighting ceremony" in which the students present their personal shields, filled with heraldic symbols of their personalities and values, and are charged with taking their beliefs out of the classroom into the world. The unit culminates in the "Knights of Marist" project, in which students research modern examples of chivalric causes and present examples of social service which they can complete with their classmates. This assignment synthesizes the literary study of the code of chivalry with responsible research methods and effective communication through a Power Point presentation.

My preliminary attempt to perform a whole-class action project was well-intentioned but ultimately failed as the students' proposed sites, while certainly well-researched and deserving, were unable to accommodate our numbers. As I'm sure I already knew, large-group, onetime projects are less authentic than a regular commitment from a smaller group or individual. I have hence revised the project for small groups in the hopes of making it more meaningful for both the students and the service sites with whom they work. I continue to have high expectations, along with my students, for empowerment, change, and, indeed, heroism. But I found, even without the class trip I originally envisioned, my students were totally committed to the research and ideas they were presenting and were taking up this "social claim" with the enthusiasm that Addams predicted. In this year's revised version, I was astounded by the students' creativity and participation in both school-sponsored and self-designed service projects. Some students worked within the frameworks of social organizations to which they already belong: Colin held a book drive with support from his Boy Scout troop; Sian and Julia led a book-club discussion for elementary-school students through their local library's teen group. Others participated in school and church service projects: Anna presented a weekly undertaking in which she served hot chili in an impoverished neighborhood; Sam, Tabitha, and Danielle worked at a soup kitchen with peers from their religion class. Still others created projects in their own neighborhoods and families: J.P., Kevin, and Jim shoveled snow on their block; Amanda and Hailey shopped and cooked for their grandmothers.

One student, Kelly, stated her goals thus: "To feed the hungry, to help those that are less fortunate than me, to gain a new perspective on life, to experience the serious issues in our world today, to make a difference, to inspire others." She worked with friends at St. Blasé soup kitchen and presented their mission "to work for justice by following the 'pray, study, act' model . . . [to] . . . pray for those in need, study issues that allow justice to grow, provide opportunities for people to make a difference." The research component of the assignment forced Kelly to look beneath the surface of service at the goals of the organization and see a larger picture. Her actual service involved wrapping silverware and packing boxes of donated food, but she was able to reflect on her actions through the lens of chivalry, seeing her project in relation to such ideals as justice and loyalty. She shared that she "did this to help those less fortunate than me because I felt that it was the right thing to do, even though there are some people who think that these people should help themselves . . . [and] . . . volunteering my time to this cause shows that I am committed to making a difference in the community." Her success in this project was evident in the enthusiasm of her presentation and the sincerity of her reflections.

Another example of students' positive experience with the social claim was a group of boys (Brian, Joe, Josh, and Matt) who set out to shovel snow in their neighborhood. Their research focused on who might need help with the task—the elderly, the handicapped—and they felt a sense of duty to use their youth and health to assist them. They presented their project as "shoveling snow and not accepting a reward but doing it because it's the right thing to do for others." They also reflected a very Hull-House attitude in their work, saying, "We had the courage to confront strangers and offer them our service." Their conclusion in the project was inspiring: "We truly and sincerely believe that we have helped contribute to our community. We discovered that shoveling snow can make a difference in peoples' lives, especially those that are handicapped and have difficulty doing common tasks such as shoveling snow. Most importantly, we discovered that doing service can be enjoyable." This last discovery seems most important to me as their teacher as well, because it illustrates Addams's theory that young people want to do something, that they are not always self-centered but sometimes even joy-centered, appreciating the intangible rewards of sharing with others in their community.

An additional outcome of the class presentations is that the students have the opportunity to share their experiences with each other and find out more about community issues and activities they may want to participate in. For example, everyone wanted to know more about the animal rescue center where Mike had spent a Saturday playing with puppies. As students reflect on their projects, many voice a hope to continue their commitment or find out more about the people with whom they have worked. On another level, the project gives meaning to an historical era that most of my students study in social studies as well as English. Examining chivalry as an ideal that helps to give order to a chaotic world allows them to make a connection between the distant past and the present and also to see that they can play an important role in their own community.

Besides these "alternatives to assessment," I also see the inestimable value in welcoming current events into my literature classroom as a way of encouraging my students to attend to the social claim. Although so often pressed for time to adequately cover the many demands of literacy education, I am finding more and more that ignoring current social debates in order to do so often means missing crucial opportunities to give students' experiences social value. As Addams writes, "[T]he [current] event suddenly transforms abstract social idealism into violent political demands, entangling itself with the widest human aspiration" (*On Education* 213). Addams discusses the impact of the Scopes trial on the discourse of her time, noting that "it seemed possible to educate the entire community by a wonderful unification of effort and if the community had been able to command open discussion and a full expression of honest opinion the educational opportunity would have been incomparable" (213). How much more opportune, then, is the use of current events in the classroom when students have immediate access to happenings around the world! Why bother to discuss literature of the Holocaust without considering current instances of genocide in Africa? Why analyze various ideas of leadership in *Julius Caesar* without comparing them to the leaders in the students' own communities? Again, I argue for this engagement in current events not only as a means for engagement in literature (although it certainly fosters that) but as a means for students' participation in the social life, which Addams insists we must recognize.

Additionally, current events may sometimes supplant the literature as students seek to tell their stories about what happens in their school and their world. For example, a class discussion of *Brave New World* found its way into a discussion of the tragic shootings at Virginia Tech, and I found myself abandoning my original lesson plan to allow students to explore their own and each other's varied reactions to the events. In fact, our study of *Brave New World* culminated in a debate that incorporated several topical issues. I divided the class into two teams to present the cases of John the Savage for freedom and Mustapha Mond for happiness and order. Students cited the war in Iraq, Hurricane Katrina, and the materialist media culture to support both sides of the ideological conflict. One of my proudest teaching moments came when an ordinarily shy student, Molly, refused to let the typically outspoken Andrew off the hook about the topic of the war. "We have to talk about it!" she asserted. "That's the whole point!" My students frequently illustrate Addams's theories about "the spirit of youth" as they struggle to understand current events and articulate their own developing interpretations of them. Jane's philosophy encourages me to honor these young people's desire to actively participate in community events rather than allowing standardized tests and College Board requirements to take precedent. I think this flexibility makes space for students' interaction with the social claim because the current event—and the students' interpretation of it—gains equal footing with the regular curriculum.

The curriculum in my drama classes is also based in a communal learning environment built on trust and creativity rather than competition and correctness. Through performance, writing, and group projects students practice, in Addams's words, "directing their own activities and adjusting them to those of others." We discuss the importance of arts education and the valuable link between drama and society, especially as young people are becoming ever more aware of the powerful influence of the media on their self-image and relationships. We also examine the ways various playwrights explore important social issues through personal relationships that student-actors can easily try on. For example, white students can explore African American perspectives in an August Wilson play, or black students can consider the experiences of Anton Chekhov's characters in Revolutionary Russia. Indeed, the character of Nora in Henrik Ibsen's *Doll House* has been, in many classes, the spark of the most valuable discussions as students not only study her transformation in dramatic terms but also argue over approaches to playing her onstage as either a selfish egotist who abandons her family (notably, Jane Addams's interpretation) or as an oppressed individual who seeks self-discovery instead of perpetuating a cycle of male dominance and female dependence. Family claims and social claims are often implicit in such discussions, and students' individual interpretations of a character's motives and morals allow them to see alternatives and perspectives they may otherwise overlook.

The Moral Life about Them: School Contexts

Working in a school that independently determines its own curriculum, I have been fortunate to be able to incorporate an Addams-like flexibility in choosing what plays and novels to study with my students. In both dramatic and fictional forms, I think it is crucial for students to go beyond mere aesthetic principles to the social issues at play in various texts, especially in a college-prep setting, where students often cling to the aesthetic principles because of a desire for questions and answers that are concrete and academic. Acting out characterizations and interpreting literature forces students to consider opposing viewpoints and articulate why they hold the values they do, thus encouraging their critical participation in "the moral life about them." I agree with Bob Fecho, who says that "those of us who muck with various forms of inquiry-based pedagogy have to resist the reflex to seek a too easily won comfort and instead . . . embrace that which feels threatening, open it to investigation, and learn from the process" (90). Fecho discusses his work in a mostly minority, urban setting, but his democratic ideals resonate in any classroom. Jean Bethke Elshtain points out that "class" was of little concern to Jane Addams, who believed that "Americans should think of one another as neighbors and fellow citizens who have had vastly different experiences" (124). Addams's framework reveals how true democracy can and should motivate all students and teachers, regardless of background or opportunity.

Working in a Catholic school, I often take for granted the opportunity to present students with a sense of "the moral life," but I also take seriously the necessity to allow each student to form his or her own conscience. I feel privileged to be allowed to openly discuss my own beliefs in my classroom; however, I feel that treating my job as one of indoctrination would be extremely harmful to my students. As stated earlier, one of the advantages of the social-claim theory that Addams purports is that it can be equally at home in a religious and secular context. It contributes to the mission of a Christian school and can foster a "wonderful unification of effort" in that, like most of Addams's work, it is, in Katherine Joslin's words, "pre-disciplinary." The philosophy of Marist High School states that "the educational program . . . is designed to provide a formation in faith by integrating the religious and secular aspects of learning . . . and to graduate young men and young women who are . . . aware of their civic and humanitarian responsibilities" (Marist High School Handbook). Likewise, the social claim is politically broad, allowing students to act in society on their own terms, rather than according to the agenda of the teacher, be she liberal or conservative, like or unlike her students.

Like other teachers, I'm sure I fail as often as I succeed. And I'm sure that sometimes my philosophy is too idealistic and that I've been spoiled by my experiences with kids whose futures are, for the most part, relatively secure. My job in many ways, however, is to enhance my students' present. Jane Addams serves as an excellent example for me as a teacher because of her ability to see the similarities among Americans of all ethnic and economic backgrounds. Her personal and professional experiences navigating the challenges of balancing the family and social claims illustrate a framework that applies to my classroom. The challenges that Addams faced in her time continue to persist, particularly among middle-class students who experience the desire to *do something* with the abundance of educational opportunities they receive. Today's young people confront the traditional pressures of duty to family, compounded by the powerful influence of a materialist culture. In the movies and television they view, as well as the books they read, students are constantly presented with characters whose choices, in different ways, dramatize these claims and complicate the relationship between them. Addams correctly asserts that educators have the vital responsibility of presenting the social claim as legitimate to young people and encouraging the "healing compromise" that allows for the growth of true social democracy.

Works Cited

Addams, Jane. *Democracy and Social Ethics.* Urbana: University of Illinois Press, 2002.
———. *The Spirit of Youth and the City Streets.* Urbana: University of Illinois Press, 1972.
———. "The Subjective Necessity of Social Settlements." In *The Jane Addams Reader.* Ed. Jean Bethke Elshtain. New York: Basic Books, 2002. 14–28.

———. *Twenty Years at Hull-House.* New York: Signet, 1961.

Brown, Wendy. *Edgework: Critical Essays on Knowledge and Politics.* Princeton, N.J.: Princeton University Press, 2005.

Dewey, John. *Democracy and Education.* Radford, Va.: Wilder Publications, 2009.

Elshtain, Jean Bethke. *Jane Addams and the Dream of American Democracy.* New York: Basic Books, 2002.

Fecho, Bob. (2004). *"Is this English?": Race, Language, and Culture in the Classroom.* New York: Teachers College Press, 2004.

Fleck, Ryan, dir. *Half Nelson.* Sony Pictures, 2007.

Harvey, David. *A Brief History of Neoliberalism.* Oxford: Oxford University Press, 2005.

Jago, Carol. "No More Objective Tests Ever." *English Leadership Quarterly* 14.1 (February 1992): 2–9.

Joslin, Katherine. Lecture. English 557. University of Illinois at Chicago. Hull-House, Spring 2007.

Knight, Louise W. *Citizen: Jane Addams and the Struggle for Democracy.* Chicago: University of Chicago Press, 2005.

Lagemann, Ellen Condliffe. Introduction to *On Education,* by Jane Addams. Ed. Ellen Condliffe Lagemann. New Brunswick, N.J.: Transaction, 1994. 1–42.

Marist High School Handbook. Chicago: 2007–8.

Muccino, Gabriele, dir. *The Pursuit of Happyness.* Sony Pictures, 2007.

9 Story and the Possibilities of Imagination

Addams's Legacy and the Jane Addams Children's Book Award

SUSAN C. GRIFFITH

Jane Addams respected imagination as a wellspring for creativity and compassion. She saw creativity and compassion as essential, active agents for democratic living in a world community. Her contemplation of the influence of imagination on private life and the social world begins early in her work and is a strong theme in much of her writing in succeeding years. So much so that, according to her biographer Katherine Joslin, "It is fair to say that Addams, over the twenty years between 1910 and 1930, came to see art and the possibilities of the imagination as hopefully as she had seen society and the possibilities of the intellect in her relative youth" (225).

Addams explored the possibilities of the imagination through the art of storytelling. She relied on stories to deepen, clarify, and expand her own ideas about social justice, peace, and world community. She trusted stories to open the hearts of her readers and listeners so that they could imagine the experiences of others with compassion.

Educators committed to social justice today continue to trust stories to nurture imagination and build compassion in their students. They seek stories focused on concepts of social justice that will deepen, clarify, and expand students' ideas of themselves, others, and society at large. Children's books honored by the Jane Addams Children's Book Award are just such stories.

In 1953, the Women's International League for Peace and Freedom (WILPF; an organization Addams herself cofounded) became the sponsoring agency for a children's book award brought to them by the WILPF member Marta

Teele who, in the aftermath of World War II, conceived an award for children's books that promote peace (Chalmers). The award, fittingly named the Jane Addams Children's Book Award, has been given annually since that time by a committee of WILPF members who are social-justice activists as well as educators, librarians, teachers, child advocates, and children's literature specialists. The award is now administered by WILPF's educational affiliate, the Jane Addams Peace Association.

The Addams Award recognizes excellence in rendering themes of social justice in children's books. Addams Award winners and honor books ask children to think about social justice and social responsibility in their own lives and the lives of others. They tell stories about people like those Addams encountered in Chicago and around the world. Like her stories, these stories touch hearts to create openings for the growth of imagination and compassion.

The 2006 Jane Addams Children's Book Award winners invite young readers to explore the past, link it to the present, and imagine a just and compassionate world now and in the future. Karen Blumenthal's *Let Me Play: The Story of Title IX, the Law that Changed the Future of Girls in America* chronicles the genesis and stormy history of the law best known for guaranteeing equal athletic opportunity to girls in the United States. The heart and meaning of *Let Me Play* comes through the stories Blumenthal peppers throughout this chronology. Through stories of missed opportunities for stellar athletes like the swimmer Donna deVarona and for struggling athletic girls who just wanted to play ball or run, Blumenthal magnifies individual losses and shows the cost to society at large.

The picture book *Delivering Justice: W. W. Law and the Fight for Civil Rights* (Haskins), illustrated by the late artist-activist Benny Andrews, profiles the life of the civil-rights activist and mail carrier Westley Wallace Law—a man who "delivered more than just the mail to the citizens of Savannah; he delivered justice, too" (6). Jim Haskins creates Law's story from a series of telling incidents. Each titled vignette adds information about actual circumstances of Law's life while revealing how each incident shaped his values and the nonviolent transformation of his beloved community.

Linked to Addams by name and theme, these and all of the other Addams Award winners and honor books have made her legacy present in the world for over five decades. A close examination of Addams's ideas about imagination shows that these strong connections can become stronger when framed with an approach that emulates her way of thinking through stories with imagination and compassion.

Addams's way of thinking through stories is a model for approaching Addams Award winners and honor books. Bringing Addams-inspired thinking to these award-winning books amplifies the power of their stories to nurture imagination and compassion. Linking present-day experiences with story to those of Addams invites young people to develop the imagination that she saw as the source of creativity and compassion.

Cultivating Moral Imagination

In *Democracy and Social Ethics,* Addams's first published collection of essays, she made a direct connection between imagination and building world community. In words that startle because they resonate so strongly with contemporary need, she attributed "much of the insensibility and hardness of the world . . . to the lack of imagination which prevents a realization of the experiences of other people" (8).

Because Addams linked lack of imagination to insensibility in the world, she thought deeply about cultivation of this powerful, humanizing force. She recognized imagination as natural in the lives of children (Lagemann 4). Children live in the actual world and in the world of the imagination. Play is no less than "the business of youth"—a business that reaffirms beauty and joy, bringing with it spontaneity that is a source of new vitality in the world (Addams, "Play Instinct and the Arts" 416–17).

While Addams recognized one of the benefits of imagination as relief from the limiting circumstances of the world (Addams, "House of Dreams"), she blanched in the face of arts and entertainment that provided only escape. Addams expected much more from the arts, imagination, and people. She sought "a limited transport, a brief journey that would double back and leave the reader with a heightened sense of moral responsibility to reform the flaws of the world" (Joslin 95)—a cultivated imagination that would encourage the transition from romantic conceptions built in "a house of dreams" to perceptions of the actual world grounded in compassionate, creative visions of human possibility (Addams, "House of Dreams" 161).

Addams advocated for "moral imagination" (Joslin), an imagination that fostered justice, as Grace Paley points out, by illuminating what is not known and by shedding light on what has been hidden (qtd. in Joslin 2). Moral imagination encourages the capacity to recognize the actual circumstances of the world while, simultaneously, seeing what lies beneath them and the possibilities that lie beyond them—a capacity that Addams demonstrated repeatedly in her own life and writings and that she saw as essential for democratic living in a world community.

Addams cultivated moral imagination by thinking and teaching through her own storytelling. She understood that ideas must be dramatized to reach masses of people (Joslin 15). She was "attuned to narrative structure, the requirements of drama, and the need to tether important ethical decisions to concrete and vivid events" (Elshtain, *Jane Addams and the Dream* 17). The stories she told reflect the fabric of her thinking.

Thinking through Stories

Addams linked individual and family life to larger social life through pointed, reflective, vivid stories. By thinking through stories, she drew on her own imagination to create stories that illuminated hidden dimensions of the lives of others. These stories engaged the imagination of her readers and listeners and encouraged them to reflect, to build upon their insights, to question the present, and to create an equitable future.

Two stories demonstrate Addams's thinking through story. In a discussion of "only a few of the problems connected with the lives of the poorest people with whom residents of a Settlement are constantly brought in contact" (Addams, *Twenty Years at Hull House* 175), Addams tells the story of an overworked mother. She reflected on a moment when her path crossed that of a woman whom she knew from her neighborhood. With unflinching detail, she described the situation and used her imagination to create a heart-rending image of what the overworked mother faced when she arrived home. With drama and passion, she demonstrated the effects of forcing women to leave their children untended to work for long hours at low pay:

> I cannot recall without indignation a recent experience. I was detained late one evening in an office building by a prolonged committee meeting of the Board of Education. As I came out at eleven o'clock, I met in the corridor of the fourteenth floor a woman whom I knew, on her knees scrubbing the marble tiling. As she straightened up to greet me, she seemed so wet from her feet up to her chin, that I hastily inquired the cause. Her reply was that she left home at five o'clock every night and had no opportunity for six hours to nurse her baby. Her mother's milk mingled with the very water with which she scrubbed the floors until she should return at midnight, heated and exhausted, to feed her screaming child with what remained within her breasts. (Addams, *Twenty Years at Hull-House* 174)

In a second story, told as Addams detailed the effects of Hull-House residents' public-health investigations, she pondered the efforts of another mother to protect her daughters. As she traced the mother's misguided efforts, she uncovered the dimensions of community that tie us to each other whether we recognize them or not, revealing that pain results when individuals isolate themselves from the communities that surround them:

> In the summer of 1902 during an epidemic of typhoid fever . . . two of the Hull-House residents made an investigation of the methods of plumbing in the houses adjacent to conspicuous groups of fever cases. They discovered among the people who had been exposed to the infection, a widow who had lived in the ward for a number of years, in a comfortable little house of her own. Although the Italian immigrants were closing in all round her, she was not willing to sell her property and to move away until she had finished the education of her children. In the meantime she held herself quite aloof from her Italian neighbors and could never be drawn into any of the public efforts to secure a better code of tenement-house sanitation. Her two daughters were sent to an eastern college. One June when one of them had graduated and the other still had two years before she took her degree, they came home to the spotless little house and to their self-sacrificing mother for the summer holiday. They both fell ill with typhoid fever and one daughter died because the mother's utmost efforts could not keep the infection out of her own house. The entire disaster affords, perhaps, a fair illustration of the futility of the individual conscience which would isolate a family from the rest of the community and its interests. (Addams, *Twenty Years at Hull-House* 297)

In these stories and others she wove into her writing, Addams makes her points plainly and powerfully through literary craft. First, she establishes the actual circumstances of her and her neighbors' experiences. She makes these circumstances clear and reveals what hides behind them through careful plotting and choice of detail. Building dramatic pull through vivid images, she then melds the emotional punch of the stories to searing political insight through metaphor, symbolism, and irony.

The account of Addams's meeting with the overworked mother moves from a casual encounter between acquaintances to an indictment of unjust labor practices through the series of images she chose to tell the story: first, Addams herself standing formally dressed near a woman scrubbing the floor on her knees; then, the woman standing drenched from neck to toe; next, a conversation revealing the true source of the woman's wet clothes; and finally, a tableau of an exhausted mother with a screaming child at her breast. The irony of the drama crests in Addams's metaphor of "mother's milk mingled with the very water with which she scrubbed the floor." The image of this forlorn mixture is arresting—in a flash, Addams leaps from the literal truth to the symbolic, leaving no doubt of the sickening costs of such injustice to this woman and to society at large.

In her story of the 1902 typhoid epidemic, Addams sets the stage through contrasting images. The image of Italian immigrants in tenements "closing in all around" contrasts with the "quite aloof" widow in a "comfortable little house of her own." The image of Hull-House residents investigating plumbing on behalf of the community stands in relief to that of the widow working diligently to keep only her own hearth, home, and family clean and safe. With the backdrop in place, Addams unfolds the chronology of the "entire disaster" and implies a final comparison. Her story of a widow's fear of literal contagion symbolizes the "fear of contagion" that underlies prejudice and injustice in the world; the futility of her isolated efforts symbolizes the futility of isolation from "the rest of the community and its interests" in any attempt to address fear of contagion and the injustice it engenders.

Detail and image create the dramatic pull of Addams's stories. Metaphor, symbol, and irony evoke their compelling images. It is their reflective, compassionate tone, however, that sheds love as well as light on their subjects. She is not a narrator standing above her story. She is on the same plane, in the thick of it. Her tellings affirm the truth as she saw it: "[U]nless all . . . contribute to a good, we cannot even be sure it is worth having" (Addams, *Democracy and Social Ethics* 9). The way out of injustice lies in the hearts, heads, and hands of us all.

Working alongside Others

By thinking through stories, Addams positioned herself as a learner, working alongside people in her neighborhood. She practiced sympathetic understanding (Elshtain, *Jane Addams and the Dream of Democracy* 122), recognizing differences and the power inequities that surround those differences. The philosopher Charlene Haddock Seigfried describes Addams's stance: "Addams self-consciously acknowledges her limited perspective as an upper-class, wealthy, educated, white woman and as such does not claim to be exploited. Nor does she pretend that she can take the place of the other, no matter how closely she works with them. She recognizes that she can never identify with the frustration, poverty and suffering of her neighbors to such an extent that she loses the privilege of her position" (Seigfried, Introduction xxxii). Addams's ability to imagine the perspective of others while bound by her own limited perspective stands out in her essay "Charitable Effort." In this extended exploration of cross-class encounters, she drew from the experiences of charity workers and the residents of surrounding neighborhoods. Through story and with sympathetic understanding, she articulates the dimensions of thinking that guided the working-class and poor people in her neighborhood as well as those that shaped young female charity workers, college-educated and white like herself. Seeing from two perspectives, she uses moral imagination to clarify actual circumstances while bringing to light the underlying values and hidden assumptions of each group. Thus, she enables her readers to imagine and, thus, to understand the complexity of the situation.

In what is in essence an argument to convince readers to work alongside, rather than for, immigrant and poor people, she examines the influence of what she calls the two groups' "diversity in experience" (Addams, "Charitable Effort" 18). She reveals the effects of the invisible differences in their thinking through vignettes about building savings accounts, early marriage, children's responsibility in caring for their parents, the importance of clothes, and the nature of charity itself. Addams zeroes in on telling details and expands their meaning to show the perspectives of both parties:

> Because of this diversity in experience, the visitor [charity worker] is continually surprised to find that the safest platitude may be challenged. She refers quite naturally to the "horrors of the saloon," and discovers that the head of her visited family does not connect them with "horrors" at all. He remembers all the kindnesses he has received from there, the free lunch and treating which goes on, even when a man is out of work and not able to pay up; the loan of five dollars he got there when the charity visitor was miles away and he was threatened with eviction. He may listen politely to her reference to "horrors," but considers it only "temperance talk." (19)

The value of sympathetic understanding—seeing another's story compassionately while understanding the limits of your own understanding—shines through in these commonplace events. The ramifications of such a stance in building an imagined future with others is starkly captured in the words of a young trade-union woman invited to dine at Hull-House: The woman "reported that Jane Addams had risen to greet her just as if she were any other lady and on seating her said: 'I have asked you to come here to see what we could do with each other for the girls in your trade.' . . . If Miss Addams had said 'for you' . . . I would have said proudly, 'I want to do for myself,' but when she said 'with,' that made it different. I have been with her ever since" (qtd. in Seigfried, *Pragmatism and Feminism* 263).

Addams saw democracy as a complex, dynamic way of life grounded in the capacity to imagine the lives of others while understanding the limits of one's own perspective. Democracy is always a work in progress, forged from reflections on, and results of, the experiences of all. She believed that the good must be extended to all of society before it can be held secure by any one person or any one class.

Because democracy requires people who are "widely at home in the world" (Addams, *Democracy and Social Ethics* 96), Addams sought to enlarge consciousness so that individuals and families saw themselves as part of the larger social order. She challenged educators to give children's own experiences a social value, to show them how to direct their own activities, and to teach them to adjust their activities to those of other people (Addams, *Democracy and Social Ethics* 81).

Sharing a Vision

Today, elementary and middle-school educators committed to social justice look to the possibilities of the imagination and empathy in much the same spirit as Addams did. Like Addams, they respect the imagination of children as a vital source for renewal and community in the world. They see imagination as a wellspring for compassion that can transform insensibility and hardness in the world, and they understand the power of stories to foster the capacity for seeing what lies beneath present circumstances and the possibilities that lie beyond them.

What Addams conveyed through her reflective stance and rhetorical approach, educators affirm in their essays and research: Stories offer starting points for critical thinking about morality and ethics (Noddings 163). The passion and feeling that stories evoke spark self-examination and reflection, which encourage imagination, or, as Maxine Greene says, the ability to look at things as though they might be otherwise. Stirring stories of individual lives arouse feelings that create openings for imagining our own lives and the lives of others (Noddings; Greene; Bomer and Bomer; Dressel). However, the passion and feeling evoked by stories, while necessary, are not enough to nurture moral imagination in young people (Greene; Bomer and Bomer; Noddings; Dressel). Randy Bomer and Katherine Bomer note that concepts critical to social justice "though . . . revered in our culture, are not dominant, and . . . do not come naturally to people" (21). These two educators therefore call for emphatic and purposeful emphasis on social-justice concepts with young people through the arts, specifically the form of art most readily available and acceptable in schools—literature.

An emphatic focus on social-justice concepts connects literature to the wider world. It offers opportunities to build shared communities that support living democratically. It thereby also addresses the challenge Addams made to educators just over a century ago: "The democratic ideal demands of the school that it shall give the child's own experience a social value; that it shall teach him to direct his own activities and adjust them to those of other people" (Addams, *Democracy and Social Ethics* 81).

A recent study of young people's experiences with multicultural literature reinforces the need for clear and direct focus on principles of social justice. Janice Hartwick Dressel conducted a study of written responses to multicultural literature introduced to primarily white middle schoolers with a literary focus typical of classroom literature study. She found that readers from the dominant culture like reading multicultural literature and are quite capable of responding to the passion and feeling it evokes. They do not, however, naturally recognize differences between their own social power, class, or culture and those of characters unlike themselves. These readers base their understandings on presumed similarities between themselves and characters and on the assumption that their own experience is the norm by which all experience is measured (Dressel 83).

Rather than seeing the world through the eyes of characters from nondominant cultures, dominant-culture readers appear to re-create the characters in their own image. For example, drawing from commentary on *Journey of the Sparrows,* a story about a young illegal immigrant named Maria, Dressel says: "Students assumed that characters from nondominant cultures were free to act without the constraints imposed by systems favoring the dominant culture. . . . The . . . assumption enabled Beth to recognize Maria's illegal immigrant status in *Journey of the Sparrows* yet to assume, without recognizing the dire consequences, that Maria could simply quit her job if she chose" (63).

In addition to making this fundamental point, Dressel found that "readers who had strong aesthetic responses to their books also learned the most about the cultures [the stories presented]" (83). Her research confirms what other educators concerned with teaching for social justice (Rosenblatt; Greene; Noddings; Bomer and Bomer) put forward: sparking deep, personal, passionate reader response through stories "is primary, and this is where teachers must begin" (Dressel 84). If teachers are to create "episodes for critical thinking . . . liberally sprinkled with turning points—points at which the thinker reaches toward the living other with feeling that responds to the other's condition" (Noddings 161–63), they need to reach young readers through the aesthetic power of stories first.

Young readers need guidance to see another's story compassionately while understanding the power and limits of their own empathy. They need teachers committed to social justice who regularly reinforce episodes for critical thinking. They need models like Addams to emulate. And they and their teachers need vivid, compelling stories of resistance, injustice, and social action to share and ponder together.

Linking Literary Experiences to Addams

Children's books commended by the Jane Addams Children's Book Award offer such vivid, compelling stories to teachers and young readers. They invite young readers to think creatively and humanely about injustice and conflict. For example, Beverly Naidoo's short story collection *Out of Bounds: Seven Stories of Hope and Conflict* (2003), recognized by the Addams Award in 2005, powerfully and poignantly portrays life under apartheid in South Africa. Naidoo traces the pain caused by such blatant injustice in seven chronologically sequential stories, the first set in 1948, the last in 2000, when children and naïve readers might think that apartheid's deadly ramifications would be over. Each story reveals its message through vivid details and telling incidents, just as Addams's stories and vignettes make their points. Each is a short, purposeful story of ordinary life constricted by larger social conditions, just as Addams's stories are. And each, like Addams's stories, invites discussion and interpretation to understand the way in and the way out of the tangle of competing claims it convincingly represents.

Like *Out of Bounds,* other Addams Award winners and honor books revolve around questions and problems related to gender, culture, class, compassion, resistance, justice, and social responsibility in the world of the past and present. They encourage young readers to stretch their imaginations beyond the concerns of their individual and family lives so that they can grapple with the world's problems courageously and nonviolently.

Addams Award winners and honor books tell stories—about children's struggles in society past and present, about people who devote their lives to fighting injustice, and about the importance of working together. These are stories of people like those Addams encountered in Chicago and around the world. Like the stories Addams herself told, they ground the discussion of critical, moral, and ethical issues in concrete and vivid events. While crafted in a variety of literary forms, Addams Award winners and honor books are first and foremost compelling stories. Like the compelling stories Addams told, they invite deep thinking about the effects of injustice and repression on society and about the power of resilience and imagination in building community.

Addams Award–winning children's books spark feelings that create openings for imagining our own lives and the lives of others. As a body of literature, they offer opportunities to frame discussion of social-justice issues in ways that educators like Dressel, Bomer and Bomer, and Noddings tell us are critical in moving readers beyond enriched personal response. Using Addams's accomplishments and ways of thinking as a frame, teachers can shape literary experiences with Addams Award Books so that young people have both the spark and the framework needed to think critically about social justice and social action in the wider world.

Addams explored the complexity of differences among people in society, particularly differences based in class, culture, and power. She did so through pointed, reflective, vivid stories that recognized her own power and position and how they differed from the power and position of others.

Presenting Addams as a model, we can link our efforts to hers. By offering Addams's way of using reflection and imagination to build understanding, we can strengthen and stretch young readers' capacities to imagine the perspectives of others while remaining cognizant of their own. Based in the guiding questions and themes of the Addams Book Award (see the appendix), we can offer substantive points of reflection for young readers' reading, discussion, and writing about the Addams Award books.

For example, Addams's story of the overprotective mother resonates strongly with Chris Crowe's *Getting Away with Murder: The True Story of the Emmett Till Case* (2004), a 2004 Addams Award Honor Book. Crowe's thorough documentary unflinchingly chronicles the 1955 lynching of the fifteen-year-old Chicagoan Emmet Till in rural Mississippi. Crowe grounds this explosive, heart-rending tragedy historically and contemporarily. Through careful, respectful attention to the courage, resolve, actions, and words of Emmet's mother, Mamie Till Bradley, Crowe reveals Mrs. Bradley's own story. He shows us a woman who, in insisting upon an open casket for her son's funeral, demanded that the world pay attention to his short life and his appalling death. He shows us a woman who, six months after Emmet's murder, said, "The murder of my son has shown me that what happens to any of us, anywhere in the world, had better be the business of us all" (Crowe 121).

Both stories, Emmet's and his mother's, lead to the same questions that Addams asks in her story: How can we transcend apparent differences and boundaries to see the deep connections between individuals and families, and to society at large? How can we build on these connections to create a world where racism, fear, and prejudice no longer cause personal and societal tragedy? Using the story of the overprotective mother as scaffold, young readers can identify the themes and questions raised in Addams's story. They can use these themes and questions to focus their reading of Emmet Till's more complex, shocking, and disturbing story. Like Addams, they can then reflect on tragedy, understand its circumstances, and raise questions about community, isolation, and connection in a democratic society.

Another of Addams's stories is closely linked to a children's picture book honored by the Addams Award. In this vignette found in *Twenty Years at Hull-House* (1925), Addams composed a story that highlights the disparity in power between herself and her neighbors:

> Our very first Christmas at Hull-House, when we as yet knew nothing of child labor, a number of little girls refused the candy which was offered them as part of the Christmas good cheer, saying simply that they "worked in a candy factory

and could not bear the sight of it." We discovered that for six weeks they had worked from seven in the morning until nine at night, and they were exhausted as well as satiated. The sharp consciousness of stern economics was thus thrust upon us in the midst of the season of good will. (198)

Here, Addams recognizes the need to move outside her own experience to understand the children in front of her. Spurred by the disconnection between her own idea of the holiday season and the children's response, she gathers more information about the children's lives. With this in hand, she exercises her own imagination to make sense of what she's learned through story—a story that brings to light the hidden factual, emotional, and political dimensions of the children's lives for herself and her readers.

Compare this to the 2005 Addams Award Honor Book *Henry and the Kite Dragon* (2004), by Bruce Edward Hall, with pictures by William Low. It is 1920 in New York City, on the border between Chinatown and Little Italy. When Henry Chu's grandfather's kite clashes with Tony Guglione's homing pigeons, it is what the groups don't know about each other that hardens feeling and causes conflict. As in Addams's story, these characters need more information about each other before their conflict can be solved. With Addams's story in hand, young readers can focus on how the conflict between two immigrant groups is resolved. They can make meaning of the story by using Addams's process as a model: recognize difference, use imagination to ask questions, gather information, and forge interpretation that incorporates fact, emotion, and politics.

The literature commended by the Jane Addams Children's Book Award waits to be tapped using reflection and imagination as Addams did. Novels written by the Canadian activist Deborah Ellis (2004), the Palestinian-American Naomi Shihab Nye (1997), and the South African expatriate Beverley Naidoo (2000, 2003) offer stories of ordinary present-day children whose lives are constricted by injustice in Afghanistan, Malawi, Nigeria, Palestine, England, and the United States. Historical studies, such as the 2004 honor book *Shutting out the Sky* by Deborah Hopkinson (2003), bring children's stories to life with telling detail and a sense of drama. And picture books offer a range of literature for readers of all ages; they tell the life stories of activists like Cesar Chavez (Kathleen Krull, 2003), illuminate the need to work for peace (Betsy Hearne, 1997), question the concept of "enemy" (Walter Dean Myers, 2002), and portray conflict among children in everyday life (Karen English, 2004). Rich in variety and import, the Addams Award stories offer opportunities to move young readers beyond enriched personal response to critical thinking about social justice in the world at large.

Conclusion

Recognized for their literary excellence in rendering themes of peace and social justice, books commended by the Jane Addams Children's Book Award offer compelling, vivid stories especially suited to purposeful, emphatic study of social justice with young readers. Because each is expressly linked to Addams's spirit, accomplishments, and philosophy through the Addams Award, they comprise a body of work that offers multiple opportunities, singly and in combination, to stimulate critical thinking inspired and directed by Addams's way of thinking critically and compassionately through story.

Jane Addams, members of the Women's International League for Peace and Freedom, and contemporary educators all see imagination as critical for social justice and democratic living. They advocate nurturing this imagination through experiences with stories that "tether important ethical decisions to concrete and vivid events" (Elshtain, *Jane Addams and the Dream of Democracy* 17). Like the Uruguayan essayist Eduardo Galeano, they also understand that while to "claim that literature on its own is going to change reality would be an act of madness or arrogance . . . [it would be] no less foolish to deny that it can aid in making this change" (192). Given this understanding, they see that nurturing the ability to see the world as though it might be otherwise, especially in young people, requires compelling stories and the guidance of teachers who place concepts of social justice front and center in their classrooms and who create frameworks that give these stories depth and resonance.

Bringing an Addams-inspired stance of sympathetic understanding to children's books honored by the Jane Addams Children's Book Award amplifies the power of these stories to nurture imagination by constructing a framework that calls forth critical reflection on concepts of social justice. Linking young people's present-day experiences with story to the experiences of Addams herself invites them to cultivate compassionate, creative visions of human possibility grounded in perceptions of the actual world—that is, to develop the moral imagination that Addams saw as a dynamic source of compassion, creativity, and justice in the world.

Appendix

Official Guidelines for the Jane Addams
Book Awards

1. Books considered for the Awards should invite answers to one or more of the following questions:
   - How can people peaceably settle disputes but with a special emphasis on diverse make-up and outlook?
   - How can we begin to think more creatively and humanely about injustice and conflict, past or present, real or fictionalized?
   - How can young people participate in creative solutions to the problems of war, social injustice, racism, sexism, homophobia, ageism, and the concerns of the physically challenged?
   - How can people of all races, cultures, nations, and economic systems live peacefully together?
   - Does the book promote an understanding of the role of women in society, gender roles, the need to overcome gender stereotypes, e.g. role models of both genders?
2. Book themes may include:
   - Solving problems courageously and nonviolently
   - Overcoming prejudice
   - Breaking cycles of fear
   - Approaching life with self-confidence and strength
   - Understanding human needs with compassion
   - Broadening outlook to appreciate a variety of cultures
   - Accepting responsibility for the future of all peoples.
3. Books eligible for this award may be fiction, poetry, or nonfiction.
4. Entries should be suitable for ages two through twelve.
5. Entries may be books of any length.
6. Entries should be well-written and well-illustrated (however, illustrations are not required).

—Adopted by the Jane Addams Peace Association, January 1994

Works Cited

Addams, Jane. "Charitable Effort." In *Democracy and Social Ethics*. Urbana: University of Illinois Press, 2002. 11–34.

———. *Democracy and Social Ethics*. Urbana: University of Illinois Press, 2002.

———. "House of Dreams." In *On Education*. Ed. Ellen Condliffe Lagemann. New York: Teachers College Press, 1994. 143–61.

———. "The Play Instinct and the Arts." In *The Jane Addams Reader*. Ed. Jean Bethke Elshtain. New York: Basic Books, 2002. 416–31.

———. *The Spirit of Youth and the City Streets*. Urbana: University of Illinois Press, 1972.

———. *Twenty Years at Hull-House, with Autobiographical Notes*. New York: Macmillan, 1925.

Blumenthal, Karen. (2005). *Let Me Play: The Story of Title IX, the Law that Changed the Future of Girls in America*. New York: Atheneum, 2005.

Bomer, Randy, and Katherine Bomer. *For a Better World: Reading and Writing for Social Action*. Portsmouth, N.H.: Heinemann, 2001.

Chalmers, Ruth. Interview with the author. New York, July 25, 2005.

Crowe, Chris. *Getting Away with Murder: The True Story of the Emmet Till Case*. New York: Dial Books for Young Readers, 2003.

Dressel, Janice Hartwick. *Teaching and Learning about Multicultural Literature: Students Reading outside Their Culture in a Middle School Classroom*. Newark, Del.: International Reading Association, 2003.

Ellis, Deborah. *The Heaven Shop*. Allston, Mass.: Fitzhenry and Whiteside, 2004.

———. *Parvana's Journey*. Toronto: Groundwood, 2002.

Elshtain, Jean Bethke. *Jane Addams and the Dream of American Democracy*. New York: Basic Books, 2002.

———, ed. *The Jane Addams Reader*. New York: Basic Books, 2002.

English, Karen. *Hot Day on Abbott Avenue*. Illus. Javaka Steptoe. New York: Clarion, 2004.

Galeano, Eduardo. *Days and Nights of Love and War*. New York: Monthly Review Press, 1983.

Greene, Maxine. *Releasing the Imagination: Essays on Education, the Arts, and Social Change*. San Francisco: Jossey-Bass, 1995.

Hall, Bruce Edward. *Henry and the Kite Dragon*. Illus. William Low. New York: Philomel, 2004.

Haskins, Jim. *Delivering Justice: W. W. Law and the Fight for Civil Rights*. Illus. Benny Andrews. Cambridge, Mass.: Candlewick Press, 2005.

Hearne, Betsy. *Seven Brave Women*. Illus. Bethanne Anderson. New York: Greenwillow, 1997.

Hopkinson, Deborah. *Shutting out the Sky: Life in the Tenements of New York, 1880–1924*. New York: Orchard/Scholastic Inc., 2003.

Jane Addams Peace Association. "Jane Addams Children's Book Award." Accessed March 31, 2008. http://wwwjaneaddamspeace.org.

Joslin, Katherine. *Jane Addams: A Writer's Life*. Urbana: University of Illinois Press, 2004.

Krull, Kathleen. *Harvesting Hope: The Story of Cesar Chavez*. Illus. Yuyi Morales. New York: Harcourt, 2003.

Lagemann, Ellen Condliffe. Introduction to *On Education,* by Jane Addams. New Brunswick, N.J.: Transaction Publishers, 1994. 1–42.

Myers, Walter Dean. *Patrol: An American Soldier in Viet Nam.* Illus. Ann Grifalconi. New York: HarperCollins, 2002.

Naidoo, Beverley. *The Other Side of Truth.* New York: HarperCollins, 2000.

———. *Out of Bounds: Seven Stories of Conflict and Hope.* New York: HarperCollins, 2003.

Noddings, Nel. "Ethics and Imagination." In *A Light in Dark Times: Maxine Greene and the Unfinished Conversation.* Ed. William Ayers and Janet L. Miller. New York: Teachers College Press, 1998. 159–69.

Nye, Naomi Shihab. *Habibi.* New York: Simon and Schuster, 1997.

Rosenblatt, Louise M. *Literature as Exploration.* New York: Appleton-Century Co., 1938.

Seigfried, Charlene Haddock. Introduction to *Democracy and Social Ethics,* by Jane Addams. Urbana: University of Illinois Press, 2002. ix–xxxviii.

———. *Pragmatism and Feminism: Reweaving the Social Fabric.* Chicago: University of Chicago Press, 1996.

10 Participating in History

The Museum as a Site for Radical Empathy, Hull-House

LISA LEE AND LISA JUNKIN LOPEZ

At the turn of the twentieth century, museums around the country awoke and responded to the conditions and spirit of the Progressive era. Shedding the Gilded Age tendency toward spiritual uplift removed from the experiences of daily life, cultural institutions including the Metropolitan Museum of Art and the Art Institute of Chicago began to reach out to audiences including immigrants and the working class. These museums sought to shape the cultural and civic life of these populations, with the varied goals of promoting citizenship, democratizing education, addressing rapid industrialization, and expanding the public sphere (Trask). By developing educational programming for new audiences and expanding and reframing collections, forward-thinking museums enacted progressive education values within an informal learning environment. As a leader of progressive education and social reform, Jane Addams would have been aware of these shifts in cultural institutions. This knowledge was applied to her work at the Labor Museum at Hull-House, which is exemplary of the Progressive-era inclination for museums to become democratic sites.

Jane Addams could not have anticipated that the Hull-House Association, the social-service institution that continued to operate after her death, would close its doors after 122 years, and what would remain vibrant and active would be a museum operating from within the two remaining settlement-house buildings.[1] In this essay, we delve into the history of the Labor Museum, one of the less-explored endeavors at the Hull-House Settlement, and one of Addams's own favorite projects. We also describe how her educational philosophies continue to resonate and inform our current efforts to preserve and interpret the two remaining settlement-house buildings and the artifacts within the collection at the Jane Addams Hull-House Museum (JAHHM), now a part of the College of Architecture and the Arts at the University of Illinois at Chicago.

Founded in 1889, Hull-House acted as a large and multifaceted community center in Chicago's most diverse neighborhood. It offered programs, classes, and social opportunities related to the English language, woodworking, theater, gardening, child care, social sciences, union building, literature, modern dance, and more. The hope was to create a social center that not only alleviated the conditions of modern urban life for immigrant residents of the Near West Side but also birthed an expansive form of democracy that prioritized social, cultural, and economic rights in addition to political and civil rights. Julia Lathrop, a resident of Hull-House who went on to direct the U.S. Children's Bureau, describes the higher aims of the settlement: "I would venture to say that, considered upon American soil, the settlement may be regarded as a humble but sincere effort toward a realization of that ideal of social democracy in whose image this country was founded, but adapted and translated into the life of to-day" (Lathrop 110). These goals mirror the broader goals of progressive education at the turn of the twentieth century, as Lawrence Cremin identifies: "Progressive education began as part of a vast humanitarian effort to apply the promise of American life—the ideal of government by, of, and for the people—to the puzzling new urban-industrial civilization that came into being during the latter half of the nineteenth century. The word *progressive* provides a clue to what it really was: the educational phase of American Progressivism writ large. In effect, progressive education began as Progressivism in education: a many-sided effort to use the schools to improve the lives of individuals" (Cremin viii). This description of progressive education rings especially true in regard to the Hull-House Labor Museum, which sought to teach immigrants about the history of industry and was Addams's pet project in her early years at Hull-House.

The Hull-House Labor Museum

Founded in 1900, the Labor Museum offered exhibitions that presented immigrants with an historical context for factory work that included references to ethnic craft traditions. Through its pedagogy and aesthetics, the museum served to frame the industrialized world in a way that made sense to new immigrants to America, who often emigrated from rural communities and found employment, and bewilderment, within Chicago's urban factories.

Early exhibits included mapped routes of the silk trade, histories of textile crafts, modern techniques, and topics of interest, including the cultivation of

Figure 1. Women in the Labor Museum spinning wool. Jessie Luther, "The Labor Museum at Hull House," *The Commons* 70.7 (May 1902): 8. Courtesy of Jane Addams Hull-House Photograph Collection, JAMC-0000-0177-0475, University of Illinois at Chicago Library, Special Collections.

materials such as flax and cotton. After the first year, the museum expanded to include six departments, including book-binding, textiles, pottery, wood, metal, and grain, with the last three departments highlighting industries central to Chicago's industrial development. On Saturday nights the museum exhibits came to life when immigrant neighbors demonstrated craft traditions while wearing clothing from their countries of origin. Occasional lectures buttressed these presentations; for example, one presenter spoke on the conditions of weaving districts in the north of England and the rise of trade unionism among textile workers (Addams, *First Report* 11). Immigrant workers from the Nineteenth Ward, which at that time served as the city's garment district, visited the Labor Museum after long shifts in factories to digest this information about industry within a broad and interdisciplinary context.

Addams and Jessie Luther, the first appointed director of the Labor Museum, understood the museum as a unique and valuable space for teaching, believing that it could address some of the limitations of formal education. Early on, Addams recognized that adults wouldn't want to attend the museum if it was titled a "school," and that the word "museum" connoted a sense of spectacle that appealed to her ideal audience (*First Report* 3). In her first report on the

Labor Museum, Addams writes: "From the very first month it was evident that a number of people were attracted to the museum who had never cared to attend the other educational advantages offered by Hull-House, and also that some of the most intelligent students from the various Hull-House classes and clubs cared a great deal for this new attempt at actual demonstration. During the winter, numbers school children and classes of teachers visited the museum, and on several occasions the museum itself became peripatetic (sic), and carried its demonstrations to normal schools (3). As the performance-studies scholar Shannon Jackson has written, the Labor Museum, like the settlement as a whole, functioned as an "alternative pedagogical space" (Jackson 257). Addams's writing on the Labor Museum reveals that it epitomized several progressive education values that were particularly well-served in museums, including shared authority and an educational focus on the issues of daily life.

Sharing Authority within the Museum

"Shared authority" is a term used within museums and historic sites to open the interpretation of history to the public. Within progressive education circles, the term echoes in Paolo Freire's democratic classroom and, in the Progressive era, John Dewey's equal exchange of ideas. Dewey advocated for schools and museums that radically redefined the structures of learning by democratizing the relationship between traditionally defined learners and teachers. He found such a space at Hull-House, which he describes as "not merely a place where ideas and beliefs may be exchanged . . . but in ways where ideas are incarnated in human form and clothed with winning grace of personal life. Classes for study may be numerous, but all are regarded as modes of bringing people together, doing away with barriers of caste, or class, or race, or type of experiences that keep people from real communion with each other" (Dewey, *The School and Society* 107). As Hull-House residents upended traditional class divisions to form meaningful relationships with their immigrant neighbors, the Hull-House Labor Museum became a space for immigrants to share their knowledge and cultural capital for the benefit of the broader community. On Saturday nights, Addams's curated exhibitions dropped to the background, and neighbors from the community took the stage, performing craft traditions mostly from their countries of origin. This reversal of the museum's core audience constituted a major shift in museum practice. Suddenly, Labor Museum performers were positioned as the experts in their trades, and their cultural domain and reformers like Addams had everything to learn from them. Visitors from across Chicago came to view these performances, instilling a sense of pride among the participants and creating a diverse cultural center.

Figure 2. Women and girls at the Labor Museum. Wallace Kirkland. Courtesy of
Jane Addams Memorial Collection, Department of Special Collections, University
Library, University of Illinois at Chicago, JAMC 1148

These weekend performances assisted in fulfilling the one goal of the Labor
Museum: to make industrial processes "more picturesque and given a content
and charm which is usually laid upon the more barren life of business, or solely
upon recreation" (Addams, *First Report* 1). Why was this sense of "charm" important to Addams? In part, her intent was to raise the status of both the labor
and the laborer. Addams and her Hull-House cofounder Ellen Gates Starr were
devotees of John Ruskin and the Arts and Crafts movement, a response to the
rise of industrialization that valued art and objects skillfully made by hand. In
all aspects of settlement life, Addams and Starr worked to create an aesthetic
vision that reflected the social goals of Hull-House, dignifying immigrants and
their work.

The Labor Museum's use of performance and shared authority is a powerful
example of Addams's belief that cultural difference must be maintained and valued within a democratic society. The Labor Museum can be distinguished from
cultural-assimilation programs that encouraged Americanization or Anglo-
conformity for immigrant groups. Such programs were based in "melting pot"

theories of assimilation and dictated behavioral, cultural, and language rules for new Americans. By contrast, the Hull-House Labor Museum highlighted the skills and talents that immigrants brought from their countries of origin—skills that were otherwise undervalued within Chicago's urban industrial landscape. Addams worked to extend the promise of democracy, and its attendant social, cultural, and economic rights, to all people. The Labor Museum contributed to this broad goal by serving as a platform for a plurality of artistic practices and skills to be viewed and appreciated.

Additionally, Addams saw that some Americans did not recognize the intelligence and talents of immigrants and hoped that the Labor Museum would change their minds: "The older people, who are habitually at such a disadvantage because they lack certain superficial qualities which are too highly prized, would have an opportunity, at least for the moment, to assert a position in the community to which their previous life and training entitles them, and would be judged with something of an historic background" (*First Report* 1). It wasn't only American-born citizens who regarded immigrants as backward; often the children of immigrants carried this impression as well. As remains common among immigrant families today, children at the turn of the century often adapted American culture more quickly than their parents, learning to speak English, eat American foods, and play American games. These children sometimes came to resent their parents, who appeared old-fashioned or un-American by contrast. Addams hoped that the museum would reveal immigrant parents in a new light. Hilda Satt Polacheck, a participant in the Labor Museum, felt that the effort was successful: "For such children the Labor Museum was an eye-opener. When they saw crowds of well-dressed Americans standing around admiring what Italian, Irish, German, and Scandinavian mothers could do, their disdain for their mothers often vanished" (Polacheck and Epstein 66). The Labor Museum therefore not only instilled pride in the immigrants who performed their crafts but allowed the value of their work and expertise to be acknowledged by an outside audience.

Praxis and the Education of Daily Life

Throughout the settlement, but particularly at the Labor Museum, praxis, the fluidity of moving between theory and practice, informed and inspired the residents' work. As Addams explains: "Two sound educational principles we may perhaps claim for the labor museum even in this early state of experiment—first, that it concentrates and dramatizes the inherited resources of a man's occupation, and, secondly, that it conceives of education as 'a continuing reconstruction of experience.' More than that the best 'education' cannot do for

any of us" (*First Report* 15). John Dewey frequently wrote about the importance
of education as a site of praxis and considered that museums might be ideal
spaces for this kind of learning (Dillon, Hein). These ideas in part come from
his close observations of the Labor Museum. Exhibitions and performances
at the museum responded practically and theoretically to an especially sticky
issue at the dawn of the twentieth century: the rise of industrialism and the
alienation that immigrant workers often felt upon being thrust into a working
environment that was unfamiliar and rife with exploitation.

Hilda Satt Polacheck, a Jewish teenager from Poland who volunteered and
performed at the Labor Museum, exemplified the challenges with industrialization faced by immigrant laborers and the solution that the Labor Museum
offered. Employed at a sewing factory by day, Polacheck describes her work
not only as grueling and exploitative but also as tedious and exceedingly dull.
In her autobiography, the only known first-person account of Hull-House
written by an immigrant woman, she writes: "The deadly monotony of this
work was worse than the actual work" (Polacheck and Epstein 63). Polacheck
filled her evening hours with exhibits and performances at the Labor Museum,
a transformative experience: "Miss Hill started out by taking me on a tour

Figure 3. Hilda Satt
Polacheck demonstrates
Russian spinning. Courtesy
of Jane Addams Memorial
Collection, Department
of Special Collections,
University Library,
University of Illinois at
Chicago, JAMC 247.

of the museum. Our first stop was in front of four cases that had been set up against a wall. These cases showed the evolution of cotton, wool, silk, and linen. I recall how surprised I was when I discovered that cotton grew out of the ground. I had never thought just how the cotton cloth that I worked with every day was made. I could not tear myself away from the case" (64). Addams must have been pleased; she hoped that the Labor Museum would resonate with young people working in shops and factories, changing the way they understood their work and its broader context (Addams, *First Report* 1).

The relevance of the Labor Museum to its core audience of garment-district workers cannot be overstated. At this moment, the crisis of industrialism was a significant and ongoing conversation at Hull-House, within progressive education circles, and in the international Arts and Crafts movement. To fully understand the Labor Museum's costumed interpretation and exhibits on industrial processes, which may seem strange or even patronizing by today's standards, modern readers must remember how current it must have felt for immigrants to study murals depicting how ancient forests become lumber, to learn about weaving techniques from their neighbors' traditions, and, in visiting other areas of the settlement, to hear songs of the injustices of sweat-shops and learn of new union organizing. The value of the Labor Museum extended beyond the immigrants of the Near West Side, too; American-born Chicagoans journeyed to the settlement for a first look at the cultural prac-tices of the city's newest residents.

Museums and Social Change?

Some readers may feel that the Labor Museum was complicit with factories in not doing enough to change their exploitative practices, and for encouraging immigrants to view art as constructive leisure time rather than explore its radical potential to foment change. The scholar Mary Ann Stankiewicz has written that for Addams, "art at Hull House was to be nonthreatening but socially valuable. . . . While art in Addams's view was politically impotent, it made life in the city more tolerable" (38). At the Hull-House Museum, our staff has come to a different interpretation of art at Hull-House. Drawing on the work of scholars including Shannon Jackson and Cheryl Ganz, we assert within our exhibits and tours that the settlement as a whole was a site for significant labor reform and one that privileged cultural rights for all, itself a radical act.

It should be noted that settlement efforts beyond the Labor Museum met the goal of improving working conditions for immigrants. Hull-House was a place where labor organizers met to imagine and advocate for a future with an eight-hour workday, a basic minimum wage, safety standards, and child-labor

laws. Hull-House also helped to form unions for women workers in the garment trades that surrounded Hull-House. True, the Labor Museum in itself
did not improve labor conditions within the factories—this was best left to
unionizing and legislation—but it did have the power to influence the cultural
landscape of the Near West Side. Addams always understood cultural rights to
be as important as political and civil rights in a healthy democracy. Through
the Labor Museum and art classes, Hull-House encouraged all people to see
themselves as creative and emotive beings and to claim their right to such
notions as beauty and truth. Far from a politically impotent act, through
the creation of culture at Hull-House, community members demanded to
be seen and heard as contributing members of society, to be fully American
even as they maintained their ethnic cultures, and to imagine and perform
a pluralistic democracy where their contributions were integral and desired.

The Permanently Impermanent

At the JAHHM today, we infuse our work with Addams's playful and experi-
mental attitudes and continue the commitment to cultural exchange, shared
authority, participatory democracy, and the insistent blurring of boundaries between art and life that were characteristics of the historic Hull-House
Settlement projects like the Labor Museum. In addition, we have committed
ourselves to the most defining characteristic of Addams's pragmatist philosophy by developing public programs and exhibits that intertwine theory
and practice, with an emphasis on the experiential dimensions of learning
and the creation of knowledge. We believe that thinking and learning take
place through activity. Reflection is inseparable from practice, and action
produces theory.

It is not, of course, an entirely seamless historic legacy that we inherit.
We passionately embrace Addams's belief that the making and creating of
culture should be valued in a world where there is so much unmaking and
destruction. Like Addams, we insist that a just and peaceful society includes
more than the achievement of political and economic rights; it also includes
creative, cultural, and social rights, and through cultural practice there is a
basic acknowledgment of an individual's agency. However, the critical activities and services that the Hull-House Settlement once offered its neighbors
within the diverse immigrant neighborhoods it served, including the organizing of labor, child care, medical care, counseling services, and programs that
addressed food security, are no longer the focus of the work of the JAHHM.
And we are also self-reflexive about the fact that museums, like other educational institutions, are highly contested sites within civil society. They have

played a socially critical role as appendages of power and privilege used to legitimize state power, enforce national identities, and maintain the status quo, while also at other times serving as catalysts for positive social change, for revolutionary struggle, and for challenging hegemony and dominant narratives (Duncan). In other words, there is nothing inherent in the structure of a museum that guarantees a progressive agenda that might carry on the legacy of Addams and the other reformers from that era.

With this knowledge, we embrace the idea of institutions as *permanently impermanent*. The museum cultivates the ability to nimbly adapt to changing contexts, rather than calcifying into a static monument. This idea resonates with Addams's fundamental principles for her own work at Hull-House that she articulates in a lovely section in one of her most important essays, "On the Subjective Necessity for Social Settlements": "The only thing to be dreaded in the Settlement is that it loses its flexibility, its power of quick adaptation, its readiness to change its methods as its environment may demand. It must be open to conviction and must have a deep and abiding sense of tolerance. It must be hospitable and ready for experiment" (17). Addams's understanding of institutional malleability reflects a particularly keen insight into the relationship between social change and institutional transformation. "The good we secure for ourselves is precarious and uncertain, is floating in mid air," she passionately insists in this same essay, "until it is secured for all of us and incorporated into our common life" (19). Addams was not committed to a particular vision of an institution but rather to the institutionalization—the creation of structures of feeling, built environments, attitudes, and habitats—of the common good. This is one reason why so many different institutional frameworks flourished within the settlement complex—classrooms, kitchens, gymnasiums, libraries, a coffee house, a theater, a dancehall, music rooms, and museums and exhibition spaces—and all were considered and deployed as potential sites for social transformation and contributed to the establishment of a sense of common purpose.[2]

Within the museum context, we strive to create experiential spaces and exhibitions for this same purpose, and just as Addams did in the Labor Museum, we do this by fostering opportunities for learning through doing and by nurturing new ways of recognizing and forging community. In addition to the core exhibition in the Hull home, for example, we host a weekly communal food program called "Re-Thinking Soup." This dynamic gathering takes place in the historic Residents' Dining Hall and brings diverse members of the community together for a free bowl of soup made from local ingredients and organic conversation about a topic related to food justice. We link food to women's rights, labor, poverty, and other local and global issues. We feed

Figure 4. Advertisement for Hull-House soup-delivery program, Courtesy of the University of Illinois at Chicago Library, Special Collections, Hull-House Collection, Series 9, Folder H.

people's minds, their bellies, and their hunger for community. This project was inspired by a previously overlooked artifact we found in our collection while scouring for evidence of programs related to food security in the archives.

Contemporary public programming provides a new lens to see and magnify artifacts and to amplify historical narratives that have been marginalized or forgotten, and the historic programs of Hull-House have provided unique ways of addressing critical modern-day issues with progressive solutions. The intimate gesture of breaking bread with strangers lays the foundation for extending our sense of whom and what we know and believe. It is part of the humanistic process of recognizing *commonalities* without erasing *differences*.

Collateral Learning

JAHHM also defiantly challenges many standard institutional museum practices, introducing alternative ways for enacting the work of preserving and interpreting artifacts and finding new ways for different publics to come to our space to perform and bring the common good into being. One of the fundamental ways we do this is through our curatorial practices that rely on interactive and participatory collaboration rather than solitary creation. Unlike many institutions that assign the jobs of curator—caring for, conducting research on objects, and developing exhibitions and publications—to an individual who is a specialist, we actively engage in a collective curatorial practice that includes the entire staff working with and challenging one another, and also inviting community members to join us in this sometimes messy process. In this way, the museum is a space for not only teaching about democracy but also practicing it. This reflects our embrace of one of Addams's most famous quotations: "Social advance depends as much upon the process through which it is secured as upon the result itself" (Addams, *Peace and Bread* 133). Often times, our collaborative ideals are not necessarily explicitly visible to visitors coming to the museum, but they contribute to the egalitarian constellation of relationships, the style of the institution, and the openness to discourse and discovery that make up the institution. In *Experience and Education,* John Dewey refers to the impact of these attitudes as the "collateral learning" that occurs in schools, which may well be of more long-range importance than the explicit school curriculum: "Perhaps the greatest of all pedagogical fallacies is the notion that a person learns only the particular things he is studying at the time. Collateral learning in the way of formation of enduring attitudes, of likes and dislikes, may be and often is much more important than the spelling lesson or lesson in geography or history that is learned. . . . [T]he most important attitude that can be formed is that of desire to go on learning" (48). In our practices in the museum, we focus less on the concrete transmissible information about Addams, the settlement, or the Progressive era than on the creation of an experience that fosters an affective emotional attitude and inspires curiosity and the desire to learn even more about the history of our site.

One emphatic example of this is the museum's collaboration with the artist, health activist, and scholar Terri Kapsalis, who created a new label for Jane Addams's travel medicine kit, which we borrowed from the Rockford Historical Society.

Kapsalis asked many questions about Addams's health, about which we knew so little because it had never been discussed at length in scholarly works. We knew scattered details, such as the fact that she had been born with Potts disease, which left Addams with a curvature of the spine, and that her appendix had been taken out mistakenly in an emergency procedure performed while on her bed at Hull-House. We knew about her anxiety

Figure 5. Jane Addams's travel medicine kit. Photo credit: Dr. Adam Negrusz.

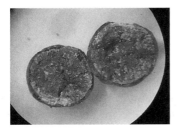

Figure 6. Round pill cut in half. Photo credit: Amy Turrenne.

Figure 7. Close-up of pills. Photo credit: Amy Turrenne.

about her weight and a surgery she had to remove a breast while she was on a speaking tour in Japan because of cancer. Although she never wrote about her experience, we also learned that Addams, like many women of her generation, had been treated by Silas Weir Mitchell—the doctor who popularized the so-called rest-cure in the Victorian period. This treatment for women deemed "hysterical" included enforced seclusion and bed rest with no forms of stimulation, including books, papers, or pens, and required a nearly constant feeding of a fatty, milk-based diet. Addams invited Charlotte Perkins Gilman to come stay at the Hull-House shortly after the publication of her short story "The Yellow Wallpaper," which depicts a woman gradually becoming insane on the rest cure. Kapsalis partnered with pharmacists and forensic experts at University of Illinois at Chicago to test the pills in the kit, and forensic photos, lab notes, and other scientific documentation became key material for the label.

The final label, which is a sixty-page essay in book form, is the most complete health history of Jane Addams and pairs observations about this scientific investigation with a meditation on rest and restlessness, antagonism and peace, domesticity and social justice, and medicine and poison. To facilitate the reading of this label, visitors are invited to take a seat in a Windsor chair nestled in a corner of Jane Addams's bedroom in the Hull home, decorated with the original William Morris wallpaper, and amongst Addams's personal artifacts, including her Nobel Peace Prize, articles of clothing, and the strikingly beautiful painting of her partner Mary Rozet Smith by the acclaimed artist Alice Kellog Taylor. The museum staff brings the visitor a cup of freshly brewed herbal tea to enjoy as he or she settles in to read the label. In this project we challenged ourselves to reimagine the common museum label—so often the omniscient voice that provides factual evidence that simply identifies and transmits information about artifacts and objects in a museum's collection—as a catalyst to sensually engage the visitor, to inspire passion, desire, and curiosity, and to provide an experience of pleasure and comfort.

A short series of excerpts from Kapsalis's essay label provides a tantalizing example of our efforts:

> Since ancient Greece, physicians believed domestic life to be a woman's ultimate remedy. Mitchell was no different. He put marriage in one vial. Motherhood in another. Moral reeducation in the third.
>
> Why did Addams refrain from writing about Mitchell's treatment? She knew that even the little antagonism that lives in the corner of the mind, if given too much attention, can someday find itself bearing arms. And war is not acceptable.
>
> In her 1902 book *Democracy and Social Ethics,* Addams does not discuss her own health history. She does write, *To be put to bed and fed on milk is not what [a young woman] requires. What she needs is simple, health-giving activity which involves the use of all faculties.*
>
> Mitchell believed inactivity to be a cure for inactivity. Mitchell: *Wise women choose their doctors and trust them. The wisest ask the fewest questions.*
>
> Addams's medicine kit does not contain any of Mitchell's remedies.
>
> Do we need to identify the medicines in order to understand Addams's travel medicine kit? Would this knowledge change our minds? The University's College of Pharmacy is down the street from the Museum. (Kapsalis 19–21)

Unfinished Business

One final example serves to underscore the JAHHM's commitment to Addams's most fundamental educational beliefs about the impact of culture in the practice of democracy and furthering social change. The museum includes a rotating exhibition space called "Unfinished Business," which is devoted to making connections between Hull-House history and contemporary issues while also seeking to unleash our radical imaginations about our collective futures. The exhibitions in this space acknowledge that while much progress has been made on the issues that Jane Addams and the reformers cared about, there is still more to accomplish, and that the work of creating a more just society continues.

A past exhibit, from September 2011 to September 2012, linked the history of the first Juvenile Court founded by Hull-House reformers with current progressive actions to imagine alternatives to incarceration. Working with contemporary grassroots social-justice organizations, "Unfinished Business" conveyed the pressing issues of juvenile justice and prison reform in the United States and propelled the museum visitor from passive spectator to active participant.

The museum collaborated with the Tamms Year Ten group of attorneys, artists, and ex-prisoners of Tamms, a "super-maximum" prison in Illinois where prisoners are held in solitary confinement for long periods of time in a way that has been declared a human-rights violation by groups such as Human Rights Watch. This group came together after asking inmates what people on the outside can do to alleviate the stress of prolonged isolation. "Send poems!" was one of the answers. We worked with Tamms Year Ten to create a writing station in the exhibition that included poetry books, pencils, and address labels of the current prison population at Tamms. Visitors were asked to take a moment to complete the postcard with a poem in solidarity with and in recognition of the humanity of those incarcerated. The museum mails the postcards to the prisoners, but they are also read by guards who are charged with censoring mail, and both groups have expressed immense gratitude for the generosity of spirit that the project evokes.

Figures 8 and 9. Postcard by museum visitor to an inmate at Tamms maximum-security prison as part of the Unfinished Business exhibition, Jane Addams Hull-House Museum, 2010. Photo credit: Lisa Yun Lee

An important thing that we learned from this collaboration and project was that it doesn't take all that much to open up a world of possibilities and to create the conditions for people to participate in acts of creativity, kindness, and humanity. We know that between September 2011 and September 2012, over five thousand members of the general public took the initiative at the end of their visit to the museum to learn about the history of the founding of the juvenile justice court by Hull-House reformers, which emphasized compassion and nurturing rather than discipline and punishment. Visitors developed empathy for incarcerated human beings who are suffering under inhumane circumstances. Addams recognized the immense power of empathy and compassion to affect relationships, culture, and the course of history. Cultivating the capacity for compassion and sharing others' feelings—whether from another period of time or another walk of life—is a fundamental aspect of the museum's work, and it is also a powerful emotion in developing a sense of common purpose.

"Unfinished Business" is also a reference to the work of Paulo Freire, who was passionately resolute about developing a "pedagogy of the unfinished": "Hope coincides with an increasingly critical perception of the concrete conditions of reality. Society now reveals itself as something unfinished, not inexorably given; it has become a challenge rather than a hopeless limitation. This new critical optimism requires a strong sense of social responsibility and of engagement in the task of transforming society; it cannot mean simply letting things run on" (Freire 13). In this way, the museum seeks to extend a horizon of hope to a visitor's experience. Through observation, empathy, critical thinking, and participation, the exhibition affords the possibility to participate in history, rather than simply be subject to it, and to embrace the process of our own becoming as part of the making of a better world.

One of Addams's most provocative beliefs, too often ignored in light of all of her other contributions, is her insistence that artistic, cultural, intellectual, and manual labor form the foundation of a democratic nation. In these times, arts and cultural institutions are too often regarded as supplemental learning sites and relegated peripheral roles in organizing efforts and movements for social change and social justice. However, just as Addams recognized in her work with the Labor Museum at the settlement, museums can promote social connectedness as well as valuable experiences of difference. As we evolve through the practice of making our exhibitions and programs in the legacy of Addams and the Hull-House Settlement, we continue to provide civic spaces for critical reflection and creativity and offer the possibility for transformation.

178   LISA LEE AND LISA JUNKIN LOPEZ

Notes

1. The Hull-House Association, the direct legacy organization of Addams's settlement that on average provided assistance to over sixty thousand people a year in Chicago, closed its doors on January 27, 2012, due to rising costs and dwindling fundraising.

2. See Deegan (249–56) for a particularly useful discussion of Addams's intellectual ties to the Chicago school of pragmatists and sociologists and the marked difference between her attitude toward institutions with those of the others.

Works Cited

Addams, Jane. *First Report of the Labor Museum at Hull House, Chicago, 1901–1902.* Chicago: Hull-House, 1902. 1–16.

———. "On the Subjective Necessity of Social Settlements." In *The Jane Addams Reader.* Ed. Jean Bethke Elshtain. New York: Basic Books, 2002. 14–28.

———. *Peace and Bread in Time of War.* Urbana: University of Illinois Press, 2002.

Cremin, Lawrence A. *The Transformation of the School.* New York: Alfred A. Knopf, 1961.

Deegan, Mary Jo. *Jane Addams and the Men of the Chicago School, 1892–1918.* New Brunswick, N.J.: Transaction Publishers, 1990.

Dewey, John. *The School and Society.* Chicago: University of Chicago Press, 1899.

———. *Experience and Education.* Boston: Free Press, 1997.

Dillon, Diane. "The Hull-House Labor Museum: An Innovative Model in Education." *Urban Experience.* Jane Addams Hull-House Museum, April 25, 2006. Accessed March 12, 2014. http://tigger.uic.edu/htbin/cgiwrap/bin/urbanexp/main.cgi?file=new/show_doc_search.ptt&doc=344.

Duncan, Carol. "Art Museums and the Ritual of Citizenship." In *Exhibiting Culture.* Ed. Ivan Karp and Stephen Levine. Washington, D.C.: Smithsonian Institute, 1991. 88–103.

Freire, Paulo. *Education for Critical Consciousness.* New York: Continuum, 2005.

Ganz, Cheryl, and Margaret Strobel. *Pots of Promise: Mexicans and Pottery at Hull-House, 1920–40.* Urbana: University of Illinois Press, 2004.

Hein, George E. *Progressive Museum Practice: John Dewey and Democracy.* Walnut Creek, CA: Left Coast, 2012.

Jackson, Shannon. *Lines of Activity: Performance, Historiography, Hull-House Domesticity.* Ann Arbor: University of Michigan Press, 2000.

Kapsalis, Terri. *Jane Addams' Travel Medicine Kit.* Jane Addams Hull-House Museum, University of Illinois Chicago, 2011.

Lathrop, Julia C. "What the Settlement Work Stands For." In *National Conference of Charities and Correction Proceedings.* Ed. Isabel C. Barrows. Boston: N.p., 1896. 106–10.

Museum Education at the Art Institute of Chicago. Chicago: Art Institute of Chicago, 2003.

Polacheck, Hilda Satt, and Dena J. Polacheck Epstein. *I Came a Stranger: The Story of a Hull-House Girl.* Urbana: University of Illinois Press, 1989.

Stankiewicz, Mary. "Art at Hull House, 1889–1901: Jane Addams and Ellen Gates Starr." *Woman's Art Journal* 10.1 (1989): 35–39.

Trask, Jeffrey. *Things American: Art Museums and Civic Culture in the Progressive Era.* Philadelphia: University of Pennsylvania Press, 2012.

11 Manifestations of Altruism

*Sympathetic Understanding, Narrative,
and Democracy*

DAVID SCHAAFSMA

Jane Addams was, among many other things, a gifted storyteller, as some
have pointed out (Elshtain 2002; Joslin 2004; Deegan 1988), including several
of us in the present collection of essays, though some of us here speak of
her work in this area in somewhat different terms. Petra Munro Hendry (in
this volume), for example, speaks of the importance of memory and history
in considering neglected aspects of Addams's work, and Bridget O'Rourke
and Todd DeStigter (in this volume) speak of experience as central to understanding Addams's contributions to our thinking. My related point is that
story is the principal genre Addams employed as she worked from memory,
history, and experience to make sense of social and political realities in her
world; she wrote various kinds of stories—her own and the stories of others
she appropriated—and she shared them in numerous speeches and essays,
for various ameliorative purposes. As Katherine Joslin (2004) helps us see,
Addams was, from the time she was a student at Rockford College, a *writer,*
inscribing her understandings in several books, speeches, and essays and
drawing on the reading of theoretical and imaginative literature in her explorations. As a writer, Addams often acted through what she saw as her role
and responsibility as *citizen,* as Louise Knight (2005) makes clear, as part
of her commitment to forging a way to improve the world. But it was Ellen
Condliffe Lagemann (1994) who helped us see that in writing her stories
as a citizen, Addams was also functioning as an *educator*—not, primarily,
by vocation but by sensibility—as part of the very process of working with
various communities.

The welfare of children was central to Addams's work at Hull-House
(Hamington 2009, 28), and child-welfare policies were regularly debated

in her tenure there. Addams helped develop playgrounds for children and early-childhood classes, sometimes in the context of day care. Addams was a particular kind of educator, influenced by—and influencing—the work of her friend, the University of Chicago sociologist George Mead, who thought that play and improvisation were keys to learning and society, and these ideas shaped her vision of Hull-House and democracy more generally. Addams, in whatever work she did with others, was foremost a listener (Robinson 1990), willing to listen to and attempt to negotiate the competing needs of a variety of people and perspectives in the process of doing the work she and the community in which she elected to live determined it needed to do. This work, which she in one place identifies as "manifestations of altruism" (Addams 2007), is the work of citizenship, civic engagement, and learning how to live productively with others across the racial, class, and gender lines that she saw as ever-present in late nineteenth-century Chicago. Addams may appear from a contemporary perspective to have initially approached her work at the Hull-House with various groups in what might seem to us somewhat elitist or naïve ways; for instance, she held classes with new, often deeply impoverished and overworked Italian immigrants on such topics as the novels of George Eliot, perhaps hoping they might through their reading spiritually "rise above" their daily circumstances in some way, or glean some ideas from Eliot's social philosophy. Such an approach, wherein all curricular and pedagogical decisions emanate from a teacher who decides "what's best" for her students, is what James Berlin (1987) might label "current-traditional" (x). Over time, however, Addams came to adopt an approach that required a focus on listening to the neighbors who were sometimes also her students, an approach she named "sympathetic understanding," one more aligned with a social-constructivist tradition wherein teachers and students in effect co-create the curriculum (Stock 1995), or one focused on a commitment to contributing to community needs and specifically focused on acts of equity. Thinking of her activist work as a kind of "curriculum" focused on and informed by an exchange of stories between and among various constituents may be helpful for those of us struggling to understand the nature of knowing and learning.

As a listener who came to eventually work not from the hierarchical perspective of charitable giving that Paolo Freire might have called "malefic generosity" but from more democratic intentions, Addams saw the exchange of stories as a pragmatic approach to the various dilemmas she faced in trying to work with members of the community to improve their lives. Out of this notion of sympathetic understanding she created relationships with her neighbors, and this relationship-building was grounded in listening to the stories—told from a range of perspectives—she was hearing from her neighbors on a daily basis, and retelling those stories in speech and writing in order to make sense for herself and others of the issues she felt compelled to explore. Story, as Paul Ricouer (1990) sees it, may be a "model for the re-description of the world" (19) in that one may explore various possibilities through it in a way that traditionally categorical, winner-take-all arguments do not. The novel, M. M. Bakhtin (1982) said, is like a "cultural forum" (132) in that it invites a consideration of issues through multiple voices and per-spectives as a way of helping us understand particular issues. As with any cultural forum, we can't expect a perfect enactment of democracy through an exchange of stories, but the attempt to listen and tell was nevertheless an admirable process Addams set in place, with some occasionally remarkable effects.

Addams could be seen as occasionally didactic in her storytelling, perhaps less exploratory than sermonizing, since as someone who was committed to social justice she seemed at times to be impatient about helping effect solutions to what seemed like intractable social problems, but her central approach was to *explore* rather than argue about issues through the medium of story as she conducted meetings and discussions on socially relevant topics at the Hull-House. She usually distrusted simple or single causal explana-tions for social problems, explanations grounded in Grand Theories that seemed to her to be insufficiently subtle and complex in their approach to social understanding, which was the case with her distrust of Marxism, for instance. In contrast, to practice sympathetic understanding was for her to listen to and engage in an exchange of stories across differences of opinion. Storytelling in the way she engaged in it was for her the practice of citizen-ship and democracy, especially on behalf of those in greater need than she, which is one model for classroom learning that any teacher might attempt to enact with his or her students.

The way that Addams often practiced storytelling, the way that seems to me to have the most useful implications for classroom practice today, is exemplified in an essay, "Women's Memories—Transmuting the Past, as Il-lustrated by the Story of the Devil Baby," that embeds a series of stories and versions of stories within a larger story. The principles she seems to embrace in this essay are present in many other essays and stories she tells, but here we see most clearly the way she refuses to dismiss viewpoints others quickly dismissed in an effort to understand the storytellers and in the process gain a better understanding of the issues involved in working across differences within her particular community. In a sense, the essay might be seen as a story about the importance and uses of storytelling for her, her neighbors, and her readers. If we can think of Addams's project as the enactment of one kind of model for radical democracy—one analogous to John Dewey's notion of conversation (Dewey 2005), where many people are to have voices in decisions affecting their daily lives—the analog for this process is storytelling.

The "Devil Baby" story, retold in greater detail elsewhere in this volume (Hendry, O'Rourke), is an often-analyzed narrative in the Addams canon. Briefly, it's a story of Addams coming to grips with an emerging conviction in her community that an actual "devil baby" was at the Hull-House for safekeeping during a six-week period in 1916. Similar stories of a Devil Baby existed in various cultural and ethnic myths of the time and had been handed down over generations, told in the various home countries of the immigrants with whom she lived, so this "sighting" could have been dismissed and ridiculed by her as a "mere" myth embraced largely by the ignorant and uneducated, as it was by most academic and community leaders of the time, including her close friend John Dewey.

Through listening "sympathetically," Addams begins to understand the power of this narrative in women's lives. She writes: "It stirred their minds and memories as with a magic touch, it loosened their tongues and revealed the inner life and thoughts of those who are so often inarticulate. They were accustomed to sit at home and to hear the younger members of the family speak of affairs quite outside their own experiences, sometimes in a language they did not understand. . . . The Devil Baby story evidently put into their hands the sort of material with which they were accustomed to deal. They had long used such tales in their unremitting efforts at family discipline, ever since they had first frightened their children into awed silence by tales of bugaboo men" (Addams 2007, 10). By seeing beyond what others viewed as the "ignorance and gullibility" of these women, Addams pays attention to some of the most marginalized members of society, taking seriously their lived experience. In a decidedly patriarchal culture, in which women's experiences were often distorted or denied, Addams extended pragmatic and democratic thought to the most disenfranchised by valuing their stories, by incorporating them into the decision-making process. For Addams, telling various versions of her neighbors' Devil Baby story is not sheer reminiscence but enacting an active process of reflection on her and their experiences in an attempt to learn from them. As Seigfried says, "She emphasizes the ways in which memory is not merely passive recall but a dynamic factor in making sense of often painful experiences and radically changing one's core beliefs in the process" (Seigfried 2007, xiv). Addams says, "Sometimes we need folktales and myths and memory to transmute daily pain" (2001, 17). The process of "transmutation" of memory through the strategic functions of metaphor, analogy, and story is part of what Joslin (2004) refers to as the "associative structure of memory and art" (171): "A good storyteller knows how to use the ghostly fingers of memory to shape events, however random, to create convincing and entertaining narratives. A well-told story has the power to give beauty and significance to rough reality and transform resentment, unhappiness, and horror into art" (174).

I would contend that Addams demonstrates that this is as true for her own storying process as it is for the women whose stories she tells. As she says, "While I may receive valuable suggestions from classic literature, when I really want to learn about life, I must depend upon my neighbors" (Addams 2001, 4). She's drawn to these stories, and these women in particular: "Whenever I heard the high eager voices of old women, I was irresistibly interested and left anything I was doing in order to listen to them" (10), but in the process of listening, "Something in the story or in its mysterious sequences had aroused one of those active forces in human nature which does not take orders, but insists only upon giving them" (9–10). As Addams sees it, "[T]he vivid interest of so many old women in the story of the Devil Baby may have been an unconscious, although powerful, testimony that tragic experiences gradually become dressed in such trappings in order that their spent agony may prove of some use to a world which learns at the hardest; and that the strivings and sufferings of men and women long since dead, their emotions no longer connected with flesh and blood, are thus transmuted into legendary wisdom" (4).

But if tales such as the Devil Baby story have for some of their tellers didactic purposes, as a form of domestic instruction, Addams's story of the various tellings of the story has different moral purposes—to explore and understand the nature and purposes of such stories for the tellers. As she points out, "[T]he story seemed to condense that mystical wisdom which becomes deposited in the hearts of man by unnoticed innumerable experiences" (Addams 2001, 11). She listens to her neighbors and treats their views with respect, even positing "mystical wisdom" developed over time as a possible reason we might pay attention to their stories.

Are we right to be skeptical about the process she claims takes place in this or any exchange of stories? Of course, and we might be skeptical, too, in a postmodern age, about their and her interpretation of the text and the process, but that she takes each of the interpretations or versions seriously and treats their tellers with respect has important pedagogical implications, ones that carry over into Addams's approach to social process and policy. Does Addams sometimes lose what academics might refer to as "critical distance" through this process of listening and sympathy? Might she seem at times naïve or overly optimistic about the power of story to transform social life? Perhaps, but Addams "knows" that the Devil Baby does not literally exist and has not been housed at the Hull-House, as many were said to believe. What ground she may seem to lose on the field of "objectivity" in the realm of argument and some rational notion of "truth" by not pronouncing this claim she gains in what I call critical engagement with the women she talks with and listens to, and in developing trusting relationships with and respect for the women with whom she works and lives. So much gets accomplished in the process, as Hendry points out in her essay in this volume: a renewed appreciation for the knowledge of elderly, immigrant women and of story as a mechanism of social control. Legends, folktales, myths, and superstitions are not reflections of a "primitive" past that we might denounce as merely "made-up" stories but are themselves *experience*. Addams makes it clear that story is an important aspect of relationship, of community, of extending a reach across classes and cultures, and it has to be taken seriously as such. She helps us as educators to begin to imagine a curriculum based on an exchange of stories, an examination of myth and the nature and uses of narrative in everyday life. What would it mean to take our students' stories and beliefs seriously?

Story for Addams has an important function in social processes: "Our social state is a like a countryside—of a complex geological structure, with outcrops of strata of very diverse ages" (Addams 2001, 65). She understands that story may function structurally on various levels in social life, and it is her and our job as readers to look at the various levels at which story may function for each teller. What purposes do these stories serve for their tellers? What does that story mean for an understanding of their personal and social needs? "At moments, however, baffled desires, sharp cries of pain, echoes of justices unfulfilled, the original material from which such tales are fashioned, would defy Memory's appeasing power and break through the rigid restraints imposed by all Art, even that unconscious of itself" (Addams 2001, 35). Her desire is to define and illustrate interpretive art, "one of those free, unconscious attempts to satisfy, outside of life, those cravings which life itself leaves unsatisfied" (34), and in the process of telling a woman's story, "her voice merges with the woman's voice, speaking with them and for them" (Joslin 2004, 175).

What are the educational implications of such an approach, of speaking *with* students instead of merely *for* them? Addams advocates, with Dewey, for what was seen then as a new educational process, learning conceived pragmatically as a "continuing reconstruction of experience." Though neither Dewey nor Addams identified the process of "reconstructing experience" as "narrative," and it certainly wasn't limited to storytelling, the phrase is consistent with Bakhtin's notion of the novel as "cultural forum," or the myriad "turns of the screw" that the pragmatist William James's brother Henry saw as an important novelistic strategy, seeing and telling the world from myriad perspectives. This process is one of bringing to consciousness an idea through storying from multiple angles, using each story as a means of reevaluating an experience and assessing it as a way of viewing the world. Another way to put it is that following Dewey, Addams draws on experience—shaped in the form of a story—to reach theoretical conclusions (Seigfried 2002, xxx). "What made her voice sound like a novel," Joslin says, "was the interweaving of voices" (Joslin 2010, 33). In drawing on many voices in the work she did with people at the settlement house, she was hoping to accomplish "in exchange for the music of isolated voices the volume and strength of a chorus" (Addams 2007, 21). In the writing she did out of that settlement work, she was "moving away from the monologic prose of science and toward the dialogic or polyvocal possibilities of fiction, from objective, rational, linear expression toward subjective, imaginative, associative prose" (Joslin 2010, 36).

What kind of stories influenced Addams in her development as a more "literary" storyteller? Joslin, in *Jane Addams: A Writer's Life* (2004), explores Addams's writing as work in part influenced by the American literary realism of the time, and particularly by the novels she loved. Knight (2005) similarly catalogs the books—many of them novels—that Addams read, especially those she read while growing up and through her twenties. While she read widely and often deeply into theory as she considered the problems of the Hull-House community, she seems to never be far from the literary narratives of her day. In her writing, there's the presence of biblical story, myth, and fable, as well as novelistic reflections on social issues. As Joslin (2004) suggests, *The Long Road of Women's Memory* draws in part on "the living accumulated folklore with its magic power to transfigure and eclipse the sordid and unsatisfactory surroundings in which life is actually spent" (18). Some of that accumulated folklore she gathers from the various people she meets and whose stories she hears, and some of the folklore includes the stories she reads in novels and stories, whose ideas influence her and whose form shapes her own ways of telling. She reveals her mode of storytelling when she admits that "tragic circumstances come dressed in . . . trappings" (Addams 2001, 21). A good storyteller knows how to use "the ghostly fingers of memory" to create convincing and entertaining narratives (Joslin 2004, 174). Addam's craft, Joslin says, is "interpretative art" (174).

In the second volume of her memoirs, *The Second Twenty Years at Hull-House* (1930), Addams makes a statement of method, too: "A writer ought to think of herself free to record seemingly disconnected impressions, images, and narratives that flow through her mind, confident that what emerges will be an accurate account of experience" (208). Although this sounds suspiciously like what literary analysts might call "free association," an approach many readers might see as inaccessible as it may be admittedly psychologically "realistic," Joslin (2004) reminds us, "Hers is a conversational style, accessible to many readers, filled with associative logic and relaxed musings" (209). Referring to Addams's biography of Julia Lathrop, Joslin notes, "In this book, as in others, she casts herself as a listener, an honest transmitter of other voices. . . . [W]hat sets the book apart is Addams's willingness to let the voices speak for themselves" (253). Listening, fundamental to the process of sympathetic understanding, is also important to Addams's research method, and reciting what she hears is key to her analysis of experience.

Addams's primary data, the basis for the storied analyses we find embedded in her texts, include many forms of letters, anecdotes, friends' recollections, and her own memories. Her reflection on social issues is much in the mode of autobiography or memoir, which might have been seen as "soft" from the perspective of the emerging standards of the discipline of sociology, which was hoping to gain credence in the world where "hard" science was setting the bar. The attempt for her is realism, snapshots of life "as it is," and particularly psychological or emotional realism, capturing a "character's" perceptions and motivations. The realists and naturalists of the time focused on the fringes of society, the criminals, the fallen, the down and out, earning as one characterization of their work the phrase "sordid realism" (Frye 2007). There's also a subjectivity of vision akin to romanticism in such an approach, which is not to say that it "takes liberties" with a representation of reality any more than in any supposedly "objective" depiction. If the nineteenth-century naturalist novelist Emile Zola saw himself as a "scientist" of society, testing hypotheses through his novels, or if Dewey saw his pragmatism as a kind of "scientific" approach to the world (which is to say, closely observing experience without the use of a theoretical lens), so does Addams intend to use narrative, influenced by the American literary and philosophical naturalism of her time, to pose as a literary scientist of urban Chicago, grounded as literary realism was in its commitment to the world and its problems, and as "romantic" as some of the great nineteenth-century novels were in their commitments to feeling and intuition.

When we think of Addams as a storyteller, we have to see her as part of a tradition to which Frank Norris, Theodore Dreiser, Upton Sinclair, and James Farrell belonged—a tradition of narrative serving purposes of social investigation. We should also see her art as akin to, though more "balanced" than, the muckraking journalistic novels of her day. The first decade of the twentieth century saw several novels, and particularly ones based in Chicago, that exposed corruption in big business and government. Upton Sinclair's *The Jungle* (1906) led to reforms in federal laws for food inspection as it related to the Chicago stockyards. Truths are evident in the faithful representation of life in the world Sinclair depicts; the work carries the conviction of actual accounts of trials of the day, of phenomena observable by others, truths evident in the physical details of the here and now. Diction and sentence structure tend toward a plain style, highlighting the characters and story versus the teller, but they also reveal passionate commitments to social justice for those who are clearly suffering. Surely Addams must be seen in the tradition of Sinclair, as she participated in garbage strikes and helped pass food-quality legislation. And perhaps in the tradition, too, of Anton Chekhov, as John Berger (2011) describes it: "The role of the writer is to describe a situation so truthfully, that the reader can no longer evade it" (66). Possibly Addams found narrative fiction to be a greater tool for the confrontation of reality than other genres.

Guests at the Hull-House included philosophers, politicians, and theorists from a variety of emerging disciplines across an astonishing political range, but Addams also invited and befriended numerous storytellers such as Charlotte Perkins Gilman ("The Yellow Wallpaper") and somewhat later, Willard Motley, who published the "sociological" novel about juvenile delinquency, *Knock on Any Door*. As a graduate student in urban sociology at the University of Chicago, Motley lived for a time at the Hull-House, but after working through what he saw as a reductive approach to the problems of youth in the Hull-House settlement area, couched as they had been largely in the newly minted language of social science, he decided to enact his observations of the young people he worked with in the more complicated and complicating venue of story: fiction. Perhaps Motley was familiar with and even influenced by his fellow University of Chicago scholar John Dewey, who, while no novelist, said, "The aesthetic [. . .] in alliance with its chief instrument, the imagination, provides the motive force for all those symbolic stratagems by which a culture's wisdom or ignorance is refracted and transmitted" (2005, 149). Perhaps Dewey's friend Jane Addams also read and understood—or maybe even influenced through her storytelling—Dewey's ideas on the nature of art. As the pragmatist scholar Giles Gunn (2001) also suggests, the "aesthetic text," an example of which is story, allows one to address aspects of "human subjectivity that in other forms and genres might otherwise tend to be glossed, ignored, discounted, shunned, or mystified; aesthetic texts cast these aspects in forms that allow the feelings as well as the intellect to interrogate them" (152).

In some ways, we can see how Addams took the pragmatist vision of William James (1907/2006) and welded it to the fictional impulses of Henry James, because her interests were almost as literary as they were pragmatist or feminist. Dewey was a philosopher and wrote like one. He crafted the pragmatic vision that he and his colleagues Charles Sanders Peirce and James in many ways shared, as one would expect any philosopher to do. Addams, a pragmatist storyteller and not a professionally credentialed philosopher, carefully read and thought through this approach and enacted aspects of it through everyday experience (Hocks 1974).

Literature was useful as one way of reading the world for Addams, but as an influence on her writing, it may have been limited compared to the stories of real life told by those who lived in the settlement neighborhood. Of her training in the humanities, she speaks in her memoir of the reading and writing she did in school as "the snare of preparation": "This is what we were all doing, loading our minds with literature that only seemed to cloud the really vital situation spread before our eyes" (1981, 45). In spite of what we can say about her writing style and how we might document her lifelong commitment to reading literature, she also claimed that learning through literature amounted for her to "merely receiving impressions versus the active emotional life led by our grandmothers and great-grandmothers" (1981, 46). This privileging of experience over literature in the development of ideas was made clear to her in her post–college graduation European trips that underscored for her the difference between the high culture of museums with art seen as a collection of artifacts versus "the conditions of life experienced by humble, hard-working folk" (1981, 48). These trips, including her visit to the settlement house in London, seemed to cement in Addams certain ideals of democracy she had first found in literary texts, but these ideals became tested and refined in her work in the Hull-House community.

Indeed, we might view Hull-House and its various programs as a kind of democratic learning institution, an "applied university" of developing ideas and solutions to various real social problems. As Maurice Hamington puts it, "In many ways, Hull House was an epistemological experiment and Jane Addams was its resident philosopher. Knowledge was generated through communal experience situated in the neighborhood" (2009, 34). She envisioned settlements as like an institution of higher learning: "The ideal and developed settlement would be an attempt to test the value of human knowledge in action" (Addams 2007, 187). This pragmatist idea that shaped Addams's view of learning is consistent with the progressive spirit of the times and her own pragmatist impulses. The settlement, immersed in actual human problems, was unlike the insular university, typically separated from knowledge. The settlement instead is grounded in what Maurice Merleau-Ponty called "the things themselves," as classroom teachers find themselves immersed every day. New teachers often remark, as they embark on their first years of teaching, how abstract and distant university teacher education was; as they near the end of their college education, they too see "the snare of preparation" as somewhat limiting compared to the actual work in classrooms.

As may be the case with most teachers (see Stock 1995 on the function of the anecdote), Addams thinks contextually and narratively rather than abstractly. She increasingly argues for and illustrates an approach to social life and ethics and an approach to social action grounded not in higher principles but in democracy, reciprocity, and improvisation. Adaptation to circumstances and the needs of the moment trump abstract commitments. As her biographer and grandson James W. Linn (2007) claimed, "Everything she said proceeded from her daily experience" (117); this was Addams, playing "the outdoor game of neighborliness" versus "the indoor game of scholarship" (194).

For Addams the social relation was a reciprocal one, meaning that in spite of the power differential—her wealth, her education—that separated her from her neighbors, she made an attempt to speak *with* and not only *to* her less academically educated neighbors. But her focus on reciprocal social relations was also true in her relationship with the residents of Hull-House, her most consistent colleagues in the shaping of settlement policy and practice. Residents were typically educated, middle-class women, many of whom, like her, had little initial experience with impoverished urban environments. One such woman who shaped Addams as a thinker was the Marxist Florence Kelley, of whom Hamington says, "More than anyone else Florence Kelley turned Jane Addams from a philanthropist to a reformer" (2009, 27). Views on a variety of social problems evolved on a daily basis as the intellectually and emotionally committed group of residents talked through issues with each other and their neighbors. Addams listened to Kelley's arguments in favor of activism, for instance, regarding worker's rights and child labor. Addams, drawing from her vision of social democracy in attempt to remain open to all views, and Kelley, from her understanding of Marxist socialism, insistent on taking a stand against all perpetrators, shaped each other's thinking and learned from each other how to best face social problems the community faced, creating *in-the-moment* strategies for how to approach them. Addams grew from Kelley's thinking and came to adopt a position to the left of charity and to the right of anarchism. As a pragmatist, she was ultimately resistant to ideology of any kind, including Marxism and Christianity. She was a realist seeking tangible solutions.

But it would be a mistake for those in academia to view Addams as a "mere" practitioner. As Mary Jo Deegan (1988) sees it, Addams was the greatest sociologist of her day, but she disagreed with the emergent field's emphasis on academic or theoretical issues—its elitism, patriarchy, and intellectualism. The issue, familiar to academics in most disciplines, is the tension or opposition between "applied" and "theoretical" work. Addams at times resisted Hull-House as a site for the Chicago school of sociology's "laboratory" approach. Though Deegan says that Addams's views were deemed too "radical" for the trustees of the University of Chicago, her storytelling was consistent with Mead's symbolic interactionism supporting education and community action tailored to the needs, interests, and social worlds of the community. Though Addams was an invited lecturer there on numerous occasions, and she in turn invited many scholars from the University of Chicago to visit Hull-House throughout the years, her work was generally viewed by academics there and elsewhere, according to Deegan, as "nonscientific" and "sentimental" social work (1988, 218). Having participated in quantitative research such as the Hull-House Maps and Papers project (Residents of Hull-House 2007), she saw the usefulness of such approaches for understanding some aspects of poverty in the Hull-House area, but she came quickly to add the stories of individuals to the process to aid in readers' understanding of her neighbors' plight. She felt that all researchers needed to deliberately put themselves "in a vital relationship with the distressing aspects of industrial life" (Addams 2007, 148). As opposed to the emotional detachment and "objectivity" privileged as "rigorous" by the academy, Addams's stories privileged the stories of women and children seen in sympathetic and respectful relationship. Addams wanted to go "deeper" than the numbers, and for that she turned to the actual voices of those who were poor and her own storied observations of poverty.

From an academic—and, as Deegan sees it, patriarchal—standpoint, such an approach to the accumulation of knowledge may be seen as "soft" or even "weak," but Addams's research goal was contiguous with her goal as a person in the neighborhood: to inculcate and foster sympathetic understanding in her readers. She urged scholars to understand and interpret the immigrant's experience so that others might appreciate it and understand it from an etic, or "experience near," as opposed to an emic, or "experience distant," perspective. She wanted readers and listeners to feel and not only to think about these experiences and perspectives. As Deegan sees it, the place of the literary, which was also the place of empathy and of relationship, gets lost in the standardized, all-is-argument world that separates thinking into "academic" and "nonacademic," privileging certain ways of thinking as better or worse.

And what "good" did this "soft" narrative approach accomplish? As her biographer Allen Davis (1973) suggests, while Addams was not a radical in religion, economics, or politics, she nevertheless became a remarkable social reformer; a defender of organized labor; one who saw that it was her duty to eradicate poverty and not only comfort the poor; and a progressive who helped pass child-labor laws and improve housing and sanitation, making the city a better place to live in for everyone's advantage. Her goal, as Davis saw it, was creating a "community of cooperative differences" (102). To that end, her key personality trait was "conciliation" (110). She saw different perspectives in a conflict as potentially partly right and tried to work with as many competing views as possible.

She probed her own experience as she examined and shared the experiences of others; in other words, as Davis says, "she thought autobiographically" (1973, 158). She shared her story in her memoirs because she thought it might be useful for others, because she knew from her own experience that telling, reading, and hearing stories can potentially make sense of the world for her and others.

As Jean Bethke Elshtain (2002) sees it, there is a narrative method in which Addams engages: its purposes include acts of citizenship, a way of exploring and modeling democracy and social change, and a way of enacting sympathetic understanding, which among other things might be described as "compassion without condescension" (121) and might be seen as a model of moral development affirming the dignity of persons, of lived lives, of history: "Addams was never much interested in grand, apocalyptic theories that did violence to lived life, belying the concreteness of particular places and ways of being. Grand theories wiped out stories and reduced human beings to faceless anonymity" (124). In the present volume, most authors align themselves with Addams in choosing story over grand theory.

Teacher scholars in various essays in this book share their stories of practice to help us see how Addams might still be relevant in the present century. The college composition professor Lanette Grate, in her essay "Jane Addams: Citizen Writers and a 'Wider Justice'" in this volume, reimagines the rhetorical situation of the first-year college writing classroom as active civic participation by drawing on Jane Addams's theories of transactional education applied to the issue of wrongful conviction. In "Efforts to Humanize Justice," a chapter in *The Second Twenty Years at Hull-House,* Addams analyzes wrongful conviction, which she considers to be the "epitome of injustice," and calls for a "wider justice." Inspired by Addams's charge that each generation must purify and increase justice, Grate provides an opportunity for first-year college writing students to become involved in a wrongful-conviction case in their home state of Arkansas known as the West Memphis Three. Besides researching and writing about the case, students organized and participated in campus-wide presentations, statewide rallies, and petition-signing and letter-writing campaigns. After completing the course, students had the opportunity to continue their involvement by joining the UCA Demand Justice Student Panel, created and sponsored by the author, which raises awareness about wrongful conviction. Grate tells a story of how a classroom can help students realize possible relations between learning and life, with possible contributions to real human needs.

Drawing from Hamington's conception of Addams's social philosophy as rooted in democracy, the Madison, Wisconsin, high-school teacher Beth Steffen shares classroom stories, as Addams shared neighborhood stories, in her essay "Student Stories and Jane Addams: Unfolding Reciprocity in an English Classroom" in this volume. Steffen tells of her experiences that help us see how Addams's ideas are alive today. Influenced by her use of narrative to illuminate rather than to objectify the complex lives and urban issues of her neighbors, Steffen's essay tells tales that draw from the stories of her students. Not unlike Addams in turn-of-the-century Chicago, Steffen works with individuals from divergent backgrounds, clamorous to be valued. As Addams at Hull-House created a space for multiple perspectives and incrementally developing respect between ethnicities, generations, and religions, Steffen depicts her and her students' collaborations to create communities of mutual learning.

Addams's project was radical democracy, where all people were intended to have a voice in decisions affecting their daily lives. She once described the work as "manifestations of altruism" (2007, 17) or selflessness, which means that the work came out of an "unselfish" concern for the welfare of others. Is it even possible to negate the self in the process of doing work in a community where needs are great? Probably not, and yet this impulse to help others in need is at the heart of many teachers' work and life. Addams's project, as one model of an attempt toward democratic practice informed by such impulses, is one from which teachers and teacher educators interested in similar practices can learn.

Works Cited

Addams, Jane (1930). *The Second Twenty Years at Hull-House, September 1909 to September 1929, with a Record of a Growing World Consciousness*. New York: MacMillan.

——— (1981). *Twenty Years at Hull-House*. New York: Penguin.

——— (2001). "Women's Memories—Transmuting the Past, as Illustrated by the Story of the Devil Baby." In *The Long Road of Women's Memory*. Urbana: University of Illinois Press. 7–16.

———(2007). *Newer Ideals of Peace.* Intro. Bernice A. Carroll and Clinton F. Fink. Urbana: University of Illinois Press.

Bakhtin, M. M. (1982). *The Dialogic Imagination: Four Essays.* Ed. Michael Holquist. Trans. Caryl Emerson and Michael Holquist. Austin: University of Texas Press.

Berger, John (2011). *Bento's Sketchbook.* New York: Pantheon Books.

Berlin, James (1987). *Rhetoric and Reality: Writing Instruction in American Colleges, 1900–1985.* Carbondale: Southern Illinois University Press.

Davis, Allen F. (1973). *American Heroine: The Life and Legend of Jane Addams.* New York: Oxford University Press.

Deegan, Mary Jo (1988). *Jane Addams and the Men of the Chicago School, 1892–1918.* New Brunswick, N.J.: Transaction Books.

Dewey, John (1927/1988). *The Public and Its Problems.* In *The Later Works, 1925–1953, Vol. 2.* Ed. Jo Ann Boydston. Carbondale: Southern Illinois University Press. 238–372.

———(2005). *Art as Experience.* New York: Perigee Press.

Elshtain, Jean Bethke (2002). *Jane Addams and the Dream of American Democracy.* New York: Basic Books.

Fleischer, Cathy, and David Schaafsma, eds. (1998). *Literacy and Democracy: Teacher Research and Composition Studies in Pursuit of Habitable Spaces; Further Conversations from the Students of Jay Robinson.* Urbana, Ill.: National Council of Teachers of English.

Frye, Northrop (2007). *Anatomy of Criticism: Four Essays.* Toronto: University of Toronto Press.

Gunn, Giles (2001). *Beyond Solidarity: Beyond Differences in a Globalized World.* Chicago: University of Chicago Press.

Hamington, Maurice (2009). *The Social Philosophy of Jane Addams.* Urbana: University of Illinois Press.

———(2010). *Feminist Interpretations of Jane Addams.* University Park: Pennsylvania State University Press.

Hocks, Richard A. (1974). *Henry James and Pragmatic Thought: A Study in the Relationship between the Philosophy of William James and the Art of Henry James.* Chapel Hill: University of North Carolina Press.

James, William (1907/2006). *Pragmatism.* New York: CreateSpace.

Joslin, Katherine (2004). *Jane Addams: A Writer's Life.* Urbana: University of Illinois Press.

———(2010). "Re-reading Jane Addams in the Twenty-First Century." In *Feminist Interpretations of Jane Addams.* Ed. Maurice Hamington. University Park: Pennsylvania State University Press, 2010. 31–53.

Knight, Louise W. (2005). *Citizen: Jane Addams and the Struggle for Democracy.* Chicago: University of Chicago Press.

Lagemann, Ellen Condliffe (1994). Introduction to *On Education,* by Jane Addams. Ed. Ellen Condliffe Lagemann. New Brunswick, N.J.: Transaction, 1994, 1–42.

Linn, James W. (2007). *Jane Addams: A Biography.* Cambridge, Mass.: Swinburne Press.

Residents of Hull-House (2007). *Hull-House Maps and Papers: A Presentation of Nationalities and Wages in a Congested District of Chicago, Together with Comments and Essays on Problems Growing out of the Social conditions.* Intro. Rima Lunin Schultz. Urbana: University of Illinois Press.

Ricouer, Paul (1990). *Time and Narrative.* Vol. 1. Chicago: University of Chicago Press.

Robinson, Jay L. (1990). *Conversations on the Written Word: Essays on Language and Literacy.* Portsmouth, N.H.: Boynton-Cook.

Seigfried, Charlene Haddock (1996). *Pragmatism and Feminism: Reweaving the Social Fabric.* Chicago: University of Chicago Press.

———. (2002). Introduction to *The Long Road of Women's Memory,* by Jane Addams. Urbana: University of Illinois Press. ix–xxxiv.

Sinclair, Upton (1906/2001). *The Jungle.* London: Dover Publications.

Stock, Patricia L. (1995). *The Dialogic Curriculum: Teaching and Learning in a Multicultural Society.* Portsmouth, N.H.: Heinemann.

Afterword

The Fire Within: Evocations toward a Committed Life

RUTH VINZ

The globe is less a pastiche of continents than a network of experiences and destinations she treats as if all these places *could be* a huge Hull-House, tangles of arteries carrying her social and ethical questioning from one house, one part of town, one community, down narrow streets and alleyways into cities and countrysides and moving across continents as far as Tolstoy's Russia. Hull-House itself is a small point within a neighborhood constellation of ten thousand Italians (Sicilians, Calabrians, Lombardians, Venetians, Neapolitans) between Halsted Street and the river. Nearly the same number of Germans have settled to the south, and on the side streets the Polish and Russian Jews carve out a community. Extending further south are the Jewish colonies. Canadian-French settle to the northwest and Irish more northward.

Jane laments the movement of the wealthy Irish and Germans away from this "huge Bohemian colony, so vast that Chicago ranks as the third Bohemian city in the world."[1] Such a move, she is convinced, will result in fewer social interactions and experiences among diverse people who have much to learn from one another. In a moment like this, darkness fills her, spreads from the back of her head into her eyes. She gulps and swallows as if this will put things in order. She walks down the long corridor and into her room. The house is quiet. When Jane lies down, she closes her eyes and murmurs this conviction: "Nothing so deadens the sympathies and shrivels the power of enjoyment as the persistent keeping away from the great opportunities for helpfulness and a continual ignoring of the starvation struggle which makes up the life of at least half the race."[2]

Often, she is in pain. Early in life a curvature and spinal tuberculosis kept her from standing upright. Was she conscious of a little tilt of her head to one side that may have pressed her view of the world toward something aslant? She remembers the surgery and a long recuperation that involved her strapped into a back harness until she was near to bursting while convalescing at her sister Alice's house. She is only twenty-two and has already given up her dreams of attending Smith College or the Woman's Medical College in Pennsylvania. She wavers with feelings of despair, depression, and inadequacy. "How can I make anything of my life?" She asks this question often. Later it will be sciatica, her stepmother's health issues, bouts of mental illness for her brother and stepbrother, one sister's fragile health, and the births and deaths of nieces and nephews that delay Jane from more than contemplating the next steps toward her future. Physical and mental discomfort—her constant companions since childhood. And, there is a continual longing for purpose and a search for where and how to commit her energies and beliefs.

She travels to postpone or perhaps to prepare for what is to come. First, it is to entertain and educate herself. By the second trip, her sight sharpens and focuses on the poor. How many miles of streets, pathways, alleyways, and tenements must she inhabit to understand poverty and oppression? How do the thousands of miles lead her to see that there are actions to be taken? When does she start to imagine a place that will fill the corridors she is traveling in her mind? A plan of action is brewing in the glimpses of life's difficulties. She carries with her the images of child laborers, lines of immigrants standing long hours in search of a job—the sounds, the smells, the talk of the streets. She is on the move constantly. She talks with and listens to everyone: school children, street vendors, strangers on trains and buses, mothers whose children cry with hunger. There is a very personal fire smoldering within Jane Addams—a commitment, vast in its promise and purpose and simple in its call to action.

*   *   *

I have this vision of Jane Addams that I carry in my mind's eye, the angle commonly portrayed of her in side-view across her years from childhood to within a few months of her death. Jane at nine with those beyond-the-camera-lens eyes. Jane at eighteen—taciturn, a glazed-stare out into a world yet to be known. Shortly before her death, her eyes are cast on a book, but her gaze is elsewhere—some longing, something yet to be done. In the straight-on shots over the years, serious, still, quiet—as if always looking outward for some glimpse of something more to come, a search to understand what she *will become* in life. She appears less than tethered to the moment or to the imagined photographer standing with raised hand. "Look at my hand. Ready now. Right here. At me!" Not Jane, she is elsewhere—her attention on the shadows of a little band of sparrows hovering further out. This tiny flock reminds her that everything is in motion. The present and the past moving toward a future. Much later, William James will say of her: "You are not like the rest of us, who see the truth and try to express it. You *inhabit* reality; and when you open your mouth truth can't help being uttered."[3] The easy claims in the words "truth" and "reality" take a new turn of meaning in our poststructural moment, juxtaposed with her timeline of life, but I understand his meaning to be in the *doing* rather than the *talking about*. "To inhabit" carries with it the connotation of *being present*. And, in the photographs particularly, Jane Addams seems lost from present moment, inhabiting, instead, some *what if* world beyond the immediate.

I found myself not only looking closely but also listening to and breathing in the photographs. No sounds of children playing in the streets, or of noisy factories. No smell of street markets, sewer ditches. Jane will write: "Insanitary housing, poisonous sewage, contaminated water, infant mortality, the spread of contagion, adulterated food, impure milk, smoke-laden air, ill-ventilated factories, dangerous occupations, juvenile crime, unwholesome crowding, prostitutions, and drunkenness are the enemies which the modern city must face and overcome would it survive."[4] In the stillness of photographs, she casts her gaze into a *beyond-ness*. The click of the shutter links two moments in time: a moment in which Jane is caught between what *is* and what *might be*, eyes cast outward, her vision extending toward *a horizon of possibility*.

*　*　*

"Papa . . . Well, when I grow up, I shall live in a big house. But it will not be built among the other large houses, but right in the midst of horrid little houses like these."[5] It is 1867, and Jane is six, visiting her Papa's mill in Freeport. She slumps back into her seat with that faraway look in her eyes. The two of them pass the homes that bank the mill as the buggy pitches and rolls her forward and a light rain starts to fall. Years later, as Jane Addams searches out the right house for her settlement, it might seem almost unbelievable to her that she ever called the houses "horrid." It will embarrass her sensibilities, and she will wonder why that moment with Papa doesn't dissolve into bits and pieces like so many of the memories she just can't seem to bring back. Gradually she moves on to other things, but the memory of this moment carries her to the smell of Papa next to her, the sway of the buggy, and the word "horrid" left hanging in the air.

Nearly fourteen years later, a soft rain reminds her of Freeport. Jane gets up slowly from her writing desk, glances at the handwritten pages scattered before her. She leaves words hanging and pauses in midsentence: *The words*

I need aren't here yet. After hours of writing and thinking, Jane takes a walk through the fields surrounding Rockford Seminary and wishes for the sound of the grist mill and the creek at home in Cedarville. She almost sees flocks of wrens, white-throated sparrows, and mourning doves. They take flight from burrows of earth as if she is behind her father's mill. A gust of wind hunts her down. Caught off guard, she turns her head to the sky, spinning around and around until the imagined flocks swirl above her. *How can I express the need to dig into all that life has to offer? It's in the doing.*

When her junior oratory for her Rockford classmates is finally written, she has the center of her commitment articulated: "That in labor alone is happiness, and that the only true and honorable life is one filled with good works and honest toil."[6] She articulates a fine line of distinction between bread-givers who "give good, sweet, wholesome bread unto our loved ones" and a bread-giver who also performs "good works and honest toil on behalf of others."[7] Watching her classmates' reactions, the room awashed in filtered light, her heart pounds in her ears, and she believes she has taken her class slogan of "bread-givers" and made it a call to action. Maybe she senses the importance of what she has said. And, yet, saying it *is* a long and well-traveled road from the less frequented path of knowing how to act those feelings and beliefs into meaning.

In these undergraduate years, the story of Cassandra also serves as metaphor for Jane to develop her understanding of the relationship between prophecy/intuition and action. Apollo gives Cassandra the gift of prophecy, but when she resists his attempted seduction, Apollo curses her by making her prophecies unbelievable to others. As a result, when Cassandra foretells the destruction of Troy, no one believes her. Hers is a narrative of how intuition is not to be trusted. Jane reasons that intuition must be accompanied by *authoritas*—the power to convince and gain confidence. Authority, she is starting to believe, results from taking "the active, busy world as a test for the genuineness of her [women's] intuition."[8] Insight comes by the interplay of intuition and action until "sympathies are so enlarged that she can weep as easily over a famine in India as a pale child at her door, then she can face social ills and social problems as tenderly and as intuitively as she can now care for and understand a crippled factory child."[9] Jane uses the opportunity in her valedictory speech at Rockford in 1881, given a year after her junior oratory on bread-givers, to puzzle toward a belief that *taking action* in the world is a *way of being* in the world that is all part of her developing articulations of sympathetic understanding. To "feel" isn't enough, she is thinking. Much later in life, she will express these ideas that fed the fire of her passion even in youth: "When I really want to learn about life, I must depend upon my neighbors, for, as William James insists, the most instructive human documents lie along the beaten path."[10]

Jane does not fully recognize at this moment that she will forge that beaten path in her own unique ways. Passion and empathy/sympathy turn conviction into action. Hers is not social work but social action built on the steadfast belief that moral and ethical action *is* citizenship. "Make the world more decent" is a motto etched in her mind. She thinks of her father often and wonders if his commitments are hers—his purported sheltering of runaway slaves, successes in business that he takes into helping others succeed—and it might not ultimately matter if his good works forge the fire in her. For both of the double-d Addamses (a term of endearment from Abraham Lincoln to her father), action is the central way to engage one's sympathetic understanding. Search for direction plagues Jane's ability to move ahead, particularly in these years after Rockford Seminary, when the what-to-do-next doubts creep in. At times, she despairs. Imagine her up early in the morning, at her writing table, sipping tea, thinking all this through. Travel is a way of moving forward, but she wonders if she is running away from or toward a future.

But the future arrives, as it always does, in an ordinary series of todays. By September 1889, Hull-House opens its doors. Hull-House—imagine Jane putting her hands on the cool brick, feeling the anticipation of what is to come. Hull-House—a call to action. Yes, forging a commitment through action, a concrete mortar-and-front-stoop understanding of how democracy might be manifest in a move from a political to a social concept. And yet, her mind is restless. What is the measure of humanness? What does it mean to lead a sympathetic life? So, next, of course, in the grand scheme is to put Hull-House to *good use*. It is not only the fixing up but also what will happen within, after all, that shapes much of what Jane hopes to accomplish and to understand about leading a committed life.

*   *   *

When I awake, the room fills with the pink light of a pending snowfall. Jane Addams is next to me. That is, *Twenty Years at Hull-House* sits spine-up beside me somewhere into chapter 7, "Some Early Undertakings At Hull-House." I am falling in love with the idea of her life and the fullness of imagination it awakens—how a person, this Jane, can translate an abstract idea like "helping others" into a way of life. Hers is not a vision of social heroism, although it may have begun with that inclination. It is the trample of the daily steps toward justice and social advancement *with* others. In the *doing,* she creates a living example of how people look out for one another because each has a stake in the other's well-being. I read again:

In spite of poignant experiences or, perhaps, because of them, the memory of the first years at Hull-House is more or less blurred with fatigue, for we could of course become accustomed only gradually to the unending activity and to the confusion of a house constantly filling and refilling with groups of people. The little children who came to the kindergarten in the morning were followed by the afternoon clubs of older children, and those in turn made way for the educational and social organizations of adults, occupying every room in the house every evening. All one's habits of living had to be readjusted, and any student's tendency to sit with a book by the fire was of necessity definitely abandoned.[11]

Her new life on Halsted Street brings her into contact with people in deep ways, and she learns much by living *with, in,* and *through* others. She does not close the door of Hull-House and take the long trip home each night, away from the settlement, satisfied that she has done good works. Her firm belief that "the idealism fitted to our industrial democracy will be evolved in crowded sewer ditches and in noisy factories"[12] is what she lives out in her writing and her life in action.

*   *   *

Narrating moments to evoke Jane Addams's life in the present tense is my intended way of trying to represent her as both *present* and a *presence within* me as I read, experience, interpret, and *step into* some experiential and affective/aesthetic understandings of her. My co-constructing work is not meant to capture a truth or a reality (she is *present* through her writing, the legacies of her good works through the concrete and the conceptual manifestations of them, and through others who knew her and rendered her into meaning in so many ways). As a (re)searcher on Addams, my intended purpose is to *experience* and to *be* in her presence and to find a way to represent what I am learning through evocations that render her/me into meaning in an attempt to understand one of her most poignant legacies: her ever-growing understanding of how one comes to live a committed life of service *with* others.

That legacy is founded on the ways in which Jane Addams opens *participatory spaces,* both in her writing and through the mortar-and-brick version of Hull-House—to live with and in relation to other people across varied landscapes of difference. From each person she gains knowledge of human conditions, of the world around her, of the social issues she will take up and fight for and against. And she hopes the spaces opened will allow them to do this for each other as well. Her narratives are storied moments, with detailed episodes and vignettes that move her/us *into* the details of others' lives to embody their feelings and experiences, creating intersectional locations and spaces, much again like she does concretely with Hull-House. The legacy, then, is in the examples of participatory and intersectional spaces that obviously helped her and can help us imagine how to act ourselves into more democratic ways of becoming.

I am reminded that Paul Ricoeur's term *solicitude* might be fitting here. While aiming for a good life *with* and *for* others is central to the concept of ethical aims, *solicitude* directs attention to the *mutual exchange of self-esteem.*[13] Mutual reciprocal esteem requires focusing on the capacities of others and not only on their actions. Ricouer defines ethical intentions as "aiming for the 'good life,' with and for others, in just institutions."[14] Put in terms of Jane Addams's life, she determines ways to act her life into meaning. She learns along the way that she must engage with other voices, other selves, and other ways of being in order to "educate" herself. She extends her associations by reaching out as far afield from her own experiences as possible, and, as she does so, she works to "inhabit" the experiences of others. By living out narrative possibilities of *Who are we?* in relation to each other, she answers the question *Who am I?*

For Jane, the physical manifestation of this idea resides in a place, a space— Hull-House as part of an ongoing creative attempt to act herself and others into a more democratic space of *being* together to create, nurture, protect, and enrich lives. She leads me to believe in the possibility of a concept that I describe through the phrase *transmigration of empathy.*[15] Commerce of empathy, such as that Addams creates through Hull-House's events and experiences, circulates in ways that offer possible spaces to feel *with* and *through* others. The fruit of empathetic response is empathy itself. In empathy, one can learn to move with others toward, across, and within a give-and-take (not with an ultimate goal of consensus but with a "felt sense" of others' experiences) that has the potential to ensure how we work in relation with others. I have come to think of empathy as something akin to hospitable imagination— mingling the experiences of our lives with those of others in ways that have reciprocal benefits in (re)informing each of our lives. Empathy's commerce leaves in its wake a series of interconnected relationships, and a kind of decentralized cohesiveness emerges. Empathy perceived in this way is a social, and not only a psychological, phenomenon. Empathy is not a thing nor a commodity; it cannot be used up or consumed, which makes it even more troubling how parsimonious we are with empathy in daily interactions. Jane Addams used the term *sympathetic understanding,* which may be an attempt to name something beyond sympathy. Most often *sympathy* is defined as a heightened awareness of another's plight in ways that we feel for another's circumstances or pain. Addams's ways of working seem more in keeping with empathy, which is most often defined as an attempt *to understand* the subjective experiences of another. To the degree that we desire empathy and can learn to be empathetic, I think Jane Addams is one keeper of a story of empathy dependent on action *with* others.

*   *   *

From her window, the neighborhood roofs are white in the moonlight. She hears the evening sounds of Hull-House: voices of children, the clink of dishes accompanying the late-night talk in the dining room, a concert just ending, and boys shouting in the gym as late evening blankets the busier hours. She watches Ella reading at her desk and feels the urge to say something like this: "We must carry each other. If we don't, who will we and our place become?" A shadow-past creeps in, and she motions Ella to climb with her through the haunted attic[16] and out a small square of window to sit on the roof. The direction of the wind, perhaps, brings the smell of smoke from their fireplace, and an image comes to mind of a few of the old settlers talking or napping, faces glowing with the fire's warmth. She pauses. Takes Ella's hand. All around, voices echo through the creak of tree trunks swaying in the night sky.

The idea of this place is as intimate as love.

From the rooftop, Jane cannot escape the smell of garbage-filled streets. Tonight she commits herself to action. The solution: A few weeks from this moment, she will become an inspector, the only paid position she will ever hold. At 5:00 A.M. three times a week, she and a deputy inspector will follow the nine garbage wagons on their rounds to make certain they pick up garbage and take it to the city dump. But, on the roof, this night, she simply makes the promise to do something.

What must she be thinking as she gazes out across Polk Street filled with darkness, the moon cresting on one side while the other is filled in darkness? She turns toward Ella. What is the future? The sounds of laughter and bustle fade below. With a sigh, Jane motions the two of them back in to the end of the day's work. There is always more bread-giving to do, but, in this moment, she is thinking of the people she meets who so often "prove that those who are handicapped in the race for life's goods, sometimes play a magnificent trick upon the jade, life herself, by ceasing to know whether or not they possess any of her tawdry goods and chattels."[17]

*   *   *

December 1889. An obvious question: So what exactly might we buy the children for an extra special treat this first Christmas at Hull-House? One obvious answer: *candy.* And, as Jane describes the obvious made contextual:

"When we as yet knew nothing of child labor, a number of little girls refused the candy which was offered them as part of the Christmas good cheer, saying simply that they 'worked in a candy factory and could not bear the sight of it.' We discovered that for six weeks they had worked from seven in the morning until nine at night, and they were exhausted as well as satiated. The sharp consciousness of stern economic conditions was thus thrust upon us in the midst of the season of good will."[18]

This narrative jewel stands as example of how the intersectional spaces of Hull-House contribute to Addams's understanding that meaning is determined through association and reassociation. Imagine Jane saying, her voice echoing through the room, "I must set aside what I think I know and let others' stories flow through me." Provisional meanings are disrupted and constantly reworked as fragments of experience, ruptured spaces between being and knowing, and multiple and partial voices of experience circulate. Hull-House becomes a space of stitched-together actions, experiences, and understandings—a community basted together by living in intersectional spaces of *multi*—people, cultures, discourses, and practices. What better than a theater, a library, a dining room, or a nursery school to construct a living space to learn with and about others? Place matters. The shared and public spaces of Hull-House embody a working democracy.

Take the metaphor of Hull-House further. The connection between temporal experience and transmigration of empathy relies on experiential ruptures similar to the candy incident. If I can, however partially, "experience" something within a life I am not living, if I *can* coauthor meaning with another's experiences, if I can dislocate or rupture some aspect of my perspectives for even a moment, is it possible to enter into intersectional spaces with others? Hull-House becomes a provocateur—a palimpsest of identities, constantly constituted and reconstituted and circulating through everyday performances of reciprocal engagements with kinship, care, learning, performing, and experiencing. Service work at Hull-House, with multidirectional aspects of beneficiary/benefactor and giver/recipient, unsettles versions of others.

* * *

"It is impossible that you should live in a neighborhood and constantly meet people with certain ideas and notions without modifying your own."[19] The fruits of memory, ripe and palatable, guide you to this understanding, Jane. The tone and texture of these words offer an incomplete version of the companions who accompany you through everyday tasks and events and life dramas. In the company of writers and literary characters, you are honing sensibilities and fashioning your dreams, too, and hoping that literature has some power to develop a caring imagination. And, yet, you wonder if imagined experience can substitute for confronting others' experiences.

You question your own understandings as you remember the young boy named Jacob, the youngest of seven children, his swollen arm in a makeshift sling. You hesitate. His mother leans into him. You see the depth of agony in her eyes and the dark bruise on her cheek from the blow by a father she tried to stop from wringing the child's arm. You say to them, "We have a great surprise. Another adventure of Prince Roland for you to hear!" It is Tuesday, and the boy's club is meeting in the dining room. "Follow me." And you lead them through the door. "Today, you should be Roland." You turn to the mother and see Medea in her face as you do often in the faces of too many mothers.[20] But there is a shimmering hope *as if* she is waiting for something more.

Jacob turns to his mother. "Go on," she tells him and gives him a little nudge into the already crowded room. You do not smile but simply watch Jacob, who shifts on his feet. And here you are caught in the irony of your own words. You question your own beliefs in this moment, and you wonder now if "lumbering our minds with literature that only served to cloud the really vital situation spread before our eyes" is too hasty a judgment.[21] Here you are, offering up the salve of literature, *Song of Roland,* to ease this boy's immediate pain. Your own attempts to feel the mother's pain are recast into the face of Medea. Maybe literature does serve as a medium beyond experience to feel the lives of others—opportunities to pause and face the irreducible. In this moment, you almost believe your own words: "[T]he settlement makes a constant effort through books, through the drama, and through exhibits, to connect passing experience with those expressions of permanent values which lie at the basis of world culture. . . . If this is well done, it should heighten the sense of companionship in the neighborhood itself."[22]

But, you, Jane, let these thoughts fall away, and your attention focuses on Jacob as he takes a first step into the room filled with other boys. You nod and turn to the mother and brush bits of longing from your fingers.

*   *   *

The last slivers of light cast shadows onto the drawing room walls. Earlier in the day, the kindergarteners made quite a ruckus on the corner designated as stage. It would be several years before Jane would build an actual stage in the gymnasium, and longer still before her dream of a Hull-House theater becomes reality. Here, now, in this moment she thinks of the joy of play, of imagining, and images of the young people's clubs flash through her mind, and she sees them rehearsing for all types of dramatic occasions. She feels the electricity in the air. And the excitement of discovery as she comes to realize that people of all ages never tire of staging dramatic performances of one type or another. Today is particularly poignant with the playing and romping about of the little ones. Jane thinks back to the early successes of the kindergarten. Within a month of moving in, she and Ellen, with former students Jennie Dow and Mary Rozet Smith, had an active kindergarten with twenty-four children and another seventy or more on the waiting list. *There is still so much more to do,* she is thinking now, as she looks at the phantom stage and remembers the kindergarteners, all smiles today, and Mary Rozet Smith playful with them. Her thoughts turn to Mary, and a puzzling commotion arises in her heart. Little does she know in this moment that for much of the rest of her life Mary will be a constant companion and bring solace to the ever-beating need to keep doing more.

Her thoughts turn toward a conviction. Theater improves life conditions: "One of the conspicuous features of our neighborhood . . . is the persistency with which the entire population attends the theater. . . . [T]he theater, such as it was, appeared to be the one agency which freed the boys and girls from that destructive isolation . . . and gave them a glimpse of that order and beauty which even the poorest drama endeavors to restore the bewildering facts of life."[23]

Here and now she notices her mixed sense of satisfaction and relentless fatigue. As early as 1890, Addams mentions Shakespeare readings in her diary, and by 1896, she develops separate, distinct drama programs within Hull-House and establishes the Hull-House Dramatic Association. Full-blown productions in her "little theater" are added as early as 1899 and serve as a spark to ignite little theaters and community theaters that will enrich the lives of neighborhoods throughout the country in ways that Jane Addams could never imagine. At this moment, however, Jane is contemplating a role for the talented Laura Dainty Pelham, who will serve as the group's first director. And, in another few years, John Galsworthy will be pleased to see one of his plays performed.

In the spring of 1891, she realizes that approximately nine hundred women, men, and children have participated in the clubs and classes offered. Seventy or more volunteers have led activities or taught classes that included Shakespeare, mathematics, drawing, Roman history, and German language. She intends the nursery, kindergarten, social clubs, public lectures, classes, and concerts to nurture the capacity for wonder and joy. Rock solid in her conviction that drama has great educational value and creates a magic space in which to explore life and reveal the "larger world which surrounds and completes our own," Jane keeps expanding the potential spaces for learning.[24]

All these projects, from public playgrounds to dance clubs, drawing classes, reading groups, pottery studios, and athletic fields, are essentials of a democratic society. Her approach is problem-centered and encourages rethinking education in a more holistic way that concentrates on the needs of adults and children, families, community, towns, and cities. Her vision is an extension of what she once called "the dream of transcendentalists that each New England village would be a university," where active engagement in community life would encourage mutual respect and sympathy toward a more democratic life.[25]

On the other hand, there is this: "Among the many disappointments which the settlement experiment has brought to its promoters, perhaps none is keener than the fact that they have as yet failed to work out methods of education, specialized and adapted to the needs of adult working people in contra-distinction to those employed in schools and colleges, or those used in teaching children."[26]

She continuously puzzles over the "how to" in educating people. "We are impatient with the schools which lay all stress on reading and writing, suspecting them to rest upon the assumption that the ordinary experience of life is worth little, and that all knowledge and interest must be brought to the children through the medium of books. Such an assumption fails to give the child any clew [sic] to the life about him, or any power to usefully or intelligently connect himself with it."[27]

She nurses the nagging feeling that she is not doing enough. If not to promote culture and politics as central to life experiences, then what might education be for?

As she had said recently to Ellen, school is not an end in itself but a means to enhance life and community and democracy. Much of this was realized in her relationship and regard for John Dewey. Dewey visited Hull-House frequently. Jane describes what she learned from him: "In those years when we were told by scientists, or at least by the so-called scientists, that the world was in the grasp of sub-human forces against which it was absurd to oppose the human will, John Dewey calmly stated that the proper home of intelligence was the world itself and that the true function of intelligence was to act as critic and regulator of the forces which move the world."[28]

This is the Jane who had been reading Eliot, Hawthorne, Tolstoy, and Ruskin during the eight years after her father's death, who had two extended tours in Europe, who studied art and architecture. She read Walter Besant's novels and visited Toynbee Hall. "Let us realize before it is too late that in this age of iron, of machine-tending, and of sub-divided labor, that we need, as never before, the untrammeled and inspired activity of youth."[29]

But it is at Hull-House where she has the most profound insights into education. From here she understands that abstract concepts like *justice, equality,* and *freedom* can only be achieved through daily, lived experiences. Recognizing that literature and play and imagination and books and theater are crucial, Jane acknowledges that daily lived experiences trump all these as a driving force for learning. And with this realization, she knows that there is more to do.

Each house added to the first "house" of Hull-House is an artifact and metaphor, if not testament, to Jane's belief in the mediating power of multiple forums for engagement with others. The first addition was an art gallery, and the second a public kitchen. Then, a coffee house, a gymnasium, a swimming pool, a cooperative boarding club for girls, a book bindery, an art studio, a music school, a circulating library, and a labor museum. Little did she know when she looked at the makeshift stage that by 1907 there would be thirteen buildings surrounding the original Hull-House. The creation of this vibrant public sphere, accessible to all in the community, offers a mechanism for a plurality of interests, differences, and sites of learning that works to enact participatory features of democracy.

*   *   *

I first read about Jane Addams and Hull-House in coursework taken in the early 1970s, where the professor discussed the two very different trajectories taken by Dewey and Addams in how they enacted their visions of democratic education. I had been teaching high-school English for six or seven years by then and felt that my classroom was an assemblage of literary texts and writing and reading practices that I had learned as a student, and a series of research and writing activities that often felt disconnected from the world in which my students were living. An inner logic was missing—a connecting thread between the classroom and the larger world. Reading Jane Addams at that point in my career gave me an image and a way to articulate how and why educational spaces might be more participatory and collaborative with an end goal of creating spaces for student-citizens to learn with and from others.

As is often the case, a confluence of events—the coursework on democratic education, the end of the Vietnam War, Whan Ho Lei, and my increasing dis-ease with the *why* of my teaching—created an opportunity to think of a version of Hull-House, or more accurately, Jane Addams's concept of the participatory in my teaching.

The story begins with Whan Ho Lei. I remember his earnest face. I can see him using his hands and working hard to communicate with all of us in the class. In halting English and with much imagining on his part and ours, he helped us understand that the rest of his family had been killed on a small boat as they attempted an escape from South Vietnam. I don't remember the exact year, but this was at some point in the mid-1970s. I will never forget the web of scars that creased the right side of his face. I remember that his right eye was glass. Whan Ho was eighteen and placed in my tenth-grade English classroom. He was the first in a series of war refugees that came to our high school over a three-year period. We didn't have ESL classes or any knowledge base for educating the stream of young people from Vietnam and Cambodia. Nor did I have the knowledge to understand why Whan Ho and Sing Lee, a young Cambodian refugee, didn't have immediate and easy alliances.

Determining ways to make certain that Whan Ho and other refugees were central participants in the class pushed me to recognize that the bulky literature anthology would not be a suitable text for this group of students, or probably any other group of adolescents. What I had learned from Jane Addams led me to recognize that the students were the first "texts to be read" in any classroom. If we could start in a common place, I reasoned, all students would have expertise on some level. The Vietnam War seemed the obvious choice, since in very different ways all of us had been experiencing the effects of this war, and the presence of our new classmates from Vietnam and Cambodia made this focus even more poignant.

By this time, the short stories written about Vietnam were published, so we read those together—aloud. We found stories of Vietnam in the community. Our group of Vietnamese students told their stories, and the Cambodians, impacted by the war in ways I had not understood, shared their experiences. We made audiotapes of everything. Vets had come home and gone back to work or hidden themselves away—a couple of them were in the local college, using benefits from the G.I. Bill, and others were teaching in our school or living next door.

The interviews with Whan Ho and all the students in our classroom from Vietnam and Cambodia were transcribed, and we published an anthology of their work for ourselves and for our community. I found as much literature as was available, and we stacked it up and grazed through it all. We did mini-studies with the sources available in the library, and since this was before the Internet, I spent winter break in New York City on microfiche and other arcane equipment putting together as extensive a news-reporting library as I could. We read war poets and literature from different times and places. The classroom turned into a production studio.

Through interviews, transcriptions, and writing versions of our own and others' experiences related to the Vietnam War, we began to learn about each other in ways not nearly as sophisticated as those Jane Addams facilitated in Hull-House. But it was a start. We decided to share what we were learning with a wider audience and took seriously the charge to disseminate in as many ways as possible everything we were learning about the people in our community whose lives were touched by the Vietnam War. From the refugees' stories, we moved to interview as many Veterans as we could. We continued to monitor news stories of the aftermath of the war along with any stories and poems that were published.

We interviewed host families and the families, unlike Whan Ho's, who had survived the ordeal. A few of these young people had been educated in Catholic Mission schools. Their impeccable English and fluent first language worked in stark contrast to the hard work of communication that characterized the rest of us. They were the experts, the conduits of communication and collaboration. I was a learner with the group, making my way by listening and learning. We wrote all these stories down, and before we were through, we published a 150-page collection of people's remembrances of Vietnam.

We decided to perform what we were learning as well. Students selected one of their interviewees and used the interview and narrative as the basis for a monologue that they wrote (fashioned after Edgar Lee Masters's *Spoon River Anthology*). We collected pictures and artifacts and pieced together an installation that served as backdrop for the performances of the monologues. After the performances (all done in the school cafeteria one evening, one lunch hour, and one afternoon), the audiences perused the artifacts. We read these monologues aloud on the school radio station, a station I had started with a group of students a couple of years earlier when we managed to convince the principal to give us an unused closet to broadcast before school and at lunch time through the school's decrepit P.A. system. Whan Ho Lei and Jane Addams conspired to help me think of ways to facilitate learning beyond the classroom walls. I began to see a concept I couldn't give name to then, but I started to understand that civic literacy might be the outcome of what I was hoping to engage students in. They were working with a set of overarching literacies where they could use their reading, writing, and researching skills and strategies for community awareness and involvement.

From all this, I'd like to suggest that the Vietnam project and the particular students who involved themselves in it taught me as I taught them—through our very different and unique ways of perceiving and experiencing this moment in history. There were new projects in subsequent years—the Safer

Places Project, the Teen Pregnancy Initiative, Small Schools/Big Questions, Body Images Teen Action Group, Muslim Youth Speak Out. Each project is a landscape for learning that is rich enough to make action and literacy-in-action and civic action the main goals of the work in the English classroom.

Each of these projects went through many revisions, but in each case, alterations and improvements were dictated not by orthodoxy and mandate but by growth in knowledge and determination. And what did the adolescents learn? Not an abstract notion of community, of war, of literacy completed as template arguments but as an actual point on the map, the tiny cluster of lights we can see from thirty thousand feet—that is, places where people walk their dogs, hang their hats, put out the garbage, bicker, make love, and buy cemetery plots. Getting to know a knowable landscape—that's what naming the inspiration might look like. Jane Addams spent her lifetime trying to find the means to connect what is deeply personal with what can be made public in order to reshape public spaces for continuing dialogue and possibility. She reminds me that this could be the ultimate goal of education and that we have much to do to achieve such a goal.

*   *   *

Often still, Jane whispers to me when I teach: *Promote action research and public-service writing.* Encourage cooperative groups to inform themselves about healthy behaviors and vital issues. Remember, Jane says, Dewey taught us that experience is always somebody's, but individual experiences are always in dialogue with others' experiences, always challenging singular versions and generalization. It is a communal responsibility to create occasions and spaces to make visible these differences that constitute the subjects of ourselves, our communities, our desire for a more democratic way of being. Jane might say: *Gather and investigate instances that demonstrate how we look to immediate human experience for knowledge, understanding, questions, and answers.* To exercise democracy is to be *in learning* with others.

And I might say to her: *We need to build on your story, Jane. We might need to rewrite your stories and perhaps write new ones altogether.* There is much work to be done to challenge the growing orthodoxies in education with new visions for rethinking and reimagining what it means to educate our children to be citizens of the world they will live in and experience. Writing ourselves toward an understanding of our own lives and others' lives might be a start. Making others present and giving them presence through writing could potentially lead us to experience transmigratory empathy. You, Jane, present a challenge not yet met in our time: how might we continue to find ways to invent a different vision for educating our children/citizens that speaks to their full participation in yearning for and creating human purpose and meaning in the world?

Notes

1. Addams, Twenty Years at Hull-House, 97–98.
2. Ibid., 116.
3. William James to Jane Addams, December 13, 1909.
4. Addams, *Newer Ideals of Peace,* 182.
5. Addams qtd. in Shepler, "Jane Addams."
6. Addams, "Bread Givers," 110–11.
7. Ibid.
8. Addams, "Cassandra," 36.
9. Ibid.
10. Addams, *Long Road of Woman's Memory,* xi.
11. Addams, *Twenty Years at Hull-House,* 147–48.
12. Addams, *Newer Ideals of Peace,* 95.
13. Ricouer, *Oneself as Another,* 21.
14. Ibid., 25.
15. Vinz, "Reading (Other)wise." In using the term *transmigratory empathy,* I am trying to distinguish a sense of feeling for others (sympathy) with a sense of living across, with, and through the perceived experiences of others. "Transmigratory" is intended to capture the idea that while we can never be another person, we can create *space for others within us* in a fluid and potentially elastic reciprocity. I first used this term in discussions of literary imagination as a way of describing how literature offers participatory spaces through which we experience empathy. "Transmigratory" is intended to suggest a response that is not a "reaction" to another's circumstances but a "living with and in" someone else's experience, suggesting a dynamic state of "felt" experiencing with and through another.
16. Addams, *Twenty Years at Hull-House,* 5. Before moving into Hull-House, Addams learned that the building was purported to have a haunted attic. Various versions of such hauntings continued through many years, and various tours of Chicago included the ghost hauntings of Hull-House as part of their regular lore of the area. Charles Hull's wife had died in the house in 1860, which gave rise to several stories of hauntings, as did all of the deaths in the 1870s of many residents when the house was used as a home for Little Sisters of the Poor. Jane Addams moved into Hull-House several years after Mrs. Hull's death and occupied the second-floor bedroom where Hull had died. Addams confided in Ellen that she awakened to sounds of loud footsteps at times. Jane moved into another room, but many overnight guests expressed concern about hearing sounds and seeing apparitions. A bucket of water was kept on the stairway, as there was a common belief that ghosts could not pass over water. Overnight guests began having their sleep disturbed by footsteps and what were described as strange and unearthly noises. In 1913, the Devil's Baby story took precedent over other ghost stories at Hull-House. In this story, a child born in the neighborhood was taken by his mother to Hull-House, where Addams attempted baptism but recognized the "devil" in the child and ended up locking it in the attic. Later, Addams wrote about the stories of the elderly women in the neighborhood and their use of memory and remembrance in constructing this and similar stories for particular purposes. Addams evidently shared some belief in the haunting of Hull-House. She told a friend that she saw a woman in white in several locations throughout the house, although she expressed no fear of the apparition.

17. Ibid., 105.
18. Ibid., 121.
19. Addams, "Social Settlements," 343.
20. Addams, *Long Road of Woman's Memory,* 10–19.
21. Addams, *Twenty Years at Hull-House,* 63.
22. Addams, *Second Twenty Years at Hull-House,* 4.
23. Addams, *Twenty Years at Hull House,* 385–86.
24. Addams, *Spirit of Youth and the City Streets,* 103.
25. Addams, "Subjective Necessity for Social Settlements," 3.
26. Addams, *Democracy and Social Ethics,* 199.
27. Ibid., 180.
28. Addams, "Toast to John Dewey," 203–4.
29. Addams, "National Child Labor Committee," 128–30.

Works Cited

Addams, Jane. "A Toast to John Dewey." *Survey* 63 (November 15, 1929): 203–4.
———. "Bread Givers" (Junior Class Oration). *Rockford Seminary Magazine* 8 (April 21, 1880): 110–11.
———. "Cassandra" (Valedictory). *Essays of Class of '81, Rockford Seminary* (June 22, 1881): 36–39.
———. *Democracy and Social Ethics* (1902). Urbana: University of Illinois Press, 2002.
———. *The Long Road of Woman's Memory* (1916). Urbana: University of Illinois Press, 2002.
———. "National Child Labor Committee." In *Proceedings of the First Annual Conference* (February 14–16, 1905): 128–36.
———. *Newer Ideals of Peace* (1907). Urbana: University of Illinois Press, 2007.
———. *Second Twenty Years at Hull-House.* New York: MacMillan, 1930.
———. "Social Settlements." In *Proceedings of the National Conference of Charities and Corrections, Twenty-Fourth Conference,* July 7–14, 1897. Boston: n.p., 1898. 338–46.
———. *The Spirit of Youth and the City Streets* (1909). Urbana: University of Illinois Press, 1972.
———. "The Subjective Necessity for Social Settlements" (1893). In *Philanthropy and Social Progress.* Ed. Henry C. Adams. Whitefish, Mont.: Kessinger Publishing, 2008.
———. *Twenty Years at Hull-House* (1910). Urbana: University of Illinois Press, 1990.
James, William. Letter to Jane Addams, December 13, 1909. Jane Addams Papers Project. Microfilm, 5-963.
Ricouer, Paul. *Oneself as Another.* Trans. Kathleen Blamey. Chicago: University of Chicago Press, 1992.
Shepler, John. "Jane Addams, Mother of Social Work." *A Positive Light,* May 7, 2001. http://www.execpc.com/~shepler/janeaddams.html.
Vinz, Ruth. "Reading (Other)wise: (Re)Readings and Missed Readings in Literature and Its Teaching." *Distinguished Lecture Series.* November 2008. National Council Teaching of English and National Literature Project.

Contributors

DAVID SCHAAFSMA, professor of English and director of the Program in English Education at the University of Illinois at Chicago, is author of *Eating on the Street: Teaching Literacy in a Multicultural Society,* coeditor (with Cathy Fleischer) of *Literacy and Democracy: Literacy and Composition Studies in Search of Habitable Spaces,* and coauthor (with Ruth Vinz) of *On Narrative Inquiry: Approaches to Language and Literacy Research.* His primary research interests include teacher education, literacy, democracy, and narrative inquiry.

TODD DESTIGTER, associate professor of English education at the University of Illinois at Chicago, is the author of *Reflections of a Citizen Teacher: Literacy, Democracy, and the Forgotten Students of Addison High,* which was selected for the NCTE Richard A. Meade Award. Todd's articles have appeared in *English Education* and *Research in the Teaching of English.* His primary research interests are literacy, democracy, and the ethnography of education.

BRIDGET K. O'ROURKE is an associate professor of English at Elmhurst College, where she teaches first-year composition and advanced writing. Her research investigates literacy in historical, political, and technological contexts.

BETH STEFFEN, the literacy coach at La Follette High School in Madison, Wisconsin, has published several pieces about her students' literate lives, including an NCTE Paul and Kate Farmer Award–winning article.

DARREN TUGGLE, an English teacher at Kelvyn Park High School in Chicago, completed his M.A. in English education at the University of Illinois at Chicago, and his essay in this volume is a revised draft of his thesis.

PETRA MUNRO HENDRY is the St. Bernard Chapter of the LSU Alumni Association Endowed Professor in the College of Human Sciences and Education at Louisiana State University. She is codirector of the Curriculum Theory Project, an interdisciplinary research initiative that endeavors to understand education within a broad social and cultural framework. Her scholarship examines the role of narrative in the construction of curriculum history, educational research, and teachers' life histories. Her most recent book is *Engendering Curriculum History,* which has a chapter devoted to the work of Jane Addams that focuses on the ways in which the settlement-house movement provides an alternative vision of education that is often marginalized in traditional curriculum histories of the Progressive era.

LANETTE GRATE is a full-time writing instructor at the University of Central Arkansas and sponsor of the UCA Demand Justice Student Panel, which raises awareness about the issue of wrongful conviction. In 2008 she cofounded Arkansas Demands Justice, a nonprofit organization created to promote criminal-justice reform in the state. She is the 2008 winner of the Rachel Corrie Award for Courage in the Teaching of Writing.

SUSAN C. GRIFFITH, associate professor of English language and literature at Central Michigan University, served on the Jane Addams Children's Book Award Committee for nine years, four of them as chair (2007–2010). She is a member of the Women's International League for Peace and Freedom and author of the book *The Jane Addams Children's Book Award: Honoring Peace and Social Justice in Children's Literature since 1953.*

JENNIFER KRIKAVA is an English teacher at Argo Community High School in Summit, Illinois. She studied Jane Addams as part of her master's degree program at the University of Illinois at Chicago in the teaching of English.

ERIN VAIL teaches English and drama at Marist High School in southwest Chicago. She published an article for the New England Association of Teachers of English on the use of film to teach novels. Her essay for this collection is based in part on her M.A. thesis at the University of Illinois at Chicago relating the work of Jane Addams to her own teaching.

LISA JUNKIN LOPEZ is a public historian, educator and organizer. She is the Associate Director of the Jane Addams Hull-House Museum, where she has worked for six years. She earned an M.A. in art education at the School of the Art Institute of Chicago and a B.A. from the College of William and Mary. She has worked in museums and art organizations since 2004. Lisa was awarded the 2011 Association of Midwest Museum's Promising Leadership award and the 2014 Outstanding Public History Project award by the National Council on Public History.

LISA LEE is a cultural activist, the director of the School of Art and Art History, associate professor in the Department of Art History, and visiting curator at the Jane Addams Hull-House Museum. Previously, she served as the director of the Jane Addams Hull-House Museum, where she reinvigorated public programs and created a new core exhibition that integrates contemporary art and radical museum strategies to link history with relevant contemporary social-justice issues. Lisa is also the cofounder of the Public Square at the Illinois Humanities Council, an organization dedicated to creating spaces for dialogue and dissent and for reinvigorating civil society. She has published a book about Theodor Adorno and articles about feminism, museums and diversity and sustainability, and strategies for creating democratic public spaces.

RUTH VINZ is a professor in English education at Teachers College, Columbia University, and holds the Enid and Lester Morse Endowed Chair in Teacher Education. She is the author of numerous articles and thirteen books on English/Language Arts curriculum, assessment, and instruction, including *Composing a Teaching Life,* which received the NCTE Conference on English Education Richard Meade Award for outstanding research in English education. Her scholarship and teaching focus on understanding how, when, or why learning happens and how multiple literacies shape those engagements.

Index

The University of Illinois Press
is a founding member of the
Association of American University Presses.

Composed in 10.5/13 Adobe Minion Pro
at the University of Illinois Press
Manufactured by Sheridan Books, Inc.

University of Illinois Press
1325 South Oak Street
Champaign, IL 61820-6903
www.press.uillinois.edu